The Deer Rifle

The Deer Rifle

L. R. Wallack

Winchester Press

Copyright © 1978 by L. R. Wallack
All rights reserved

Library of Congress Cataloging in Publication Data

Wallack, Louis Robert, 1919-
  The deer rifle.
  Includes index.
  1. Hunting rifles. 2. Deer hunting. I. Title.
SK274.2.W34   799.2'02832   78-5391
ISBN 0-87691-269-2

Published by Winchester Press
205 East 42nd Street
New York, N.Y. 10017

WINCHESTER is a Trademark of Olin Corporation used by Winchester Press, Inc. under authority and control of the Trademark Proprietor.

Printed in the United States of America

Contents

Foreword:
   A Tribute to the .30/30 Winchester   vii
1. The Deep-Woods Deer Rifle   1
2. The Mountains Deer Rifle   8
3. The Plains Deer Rifle   14
4. The Farm-Country Deer Rifle   17
5. The Lever-Action and Single-Shot   20
6. The Bolt-Action   35
7. The Pump-Action   53
8. The Autoloader   57
9. Custom Deer Rifles   63
10. Calibers up to .25   75
11. Calibers from .25 to .30   84
12. Calibers .30 and Over   103
13. Bores, Bullets, and Ballistics   132
14. Sights, Scopes, and Mounts   170
15. Selecting *Your* Deer Rifle and Setting It Up   197
16. Shotgun Slugs and Slug Guns   210
17. Whitetail Deer and Mule Deer   223
18. Favorite Deer Rifles   227

Appendix: Equivalent Cartridges   235
Index   239

Foreword

A Tribute to the .30/30 Winchester

If there is any rifle that better deserves to be called *the* deer rifle it would be hard to say what it might be. There have been more than 4,500,000 Winchester Model 94 rifles made as this is written in 1977. That's a hell of a lot of rifles. Why is the Model 94 so popular?

The Model 94 was introduced in the Winchester catalog issued in November 1894. It had been invented by John Browning, and U.S. patent #524702 was granted in August 1894. First available in two black-powder chamberings, .32/40 and .38/55 (both cartridges were Marlin-developed for the Ballard rifle), it was chambered for two new Winchester-developed smokeless-powder cartridges in 1895. These were the .25/35 and .30/30.

Smokeless powder developed higher pressures than black powder. The Model 94 was adequate to handle them, but special barrels were needed because smokeless burned hotter and eroded the soft-steel barrels suitable for black powder. Winchester introduced a special nickel-steel barrel with the new cartridges. Thus was born a whole new kind of sport shooting. (Smokeless powder had been in use in certain military cartridges a few years earlier).

The Winchester .30/30 cartridge was a triumph. It was loaded with 30 grains of smokeless powder and carried the usual black-

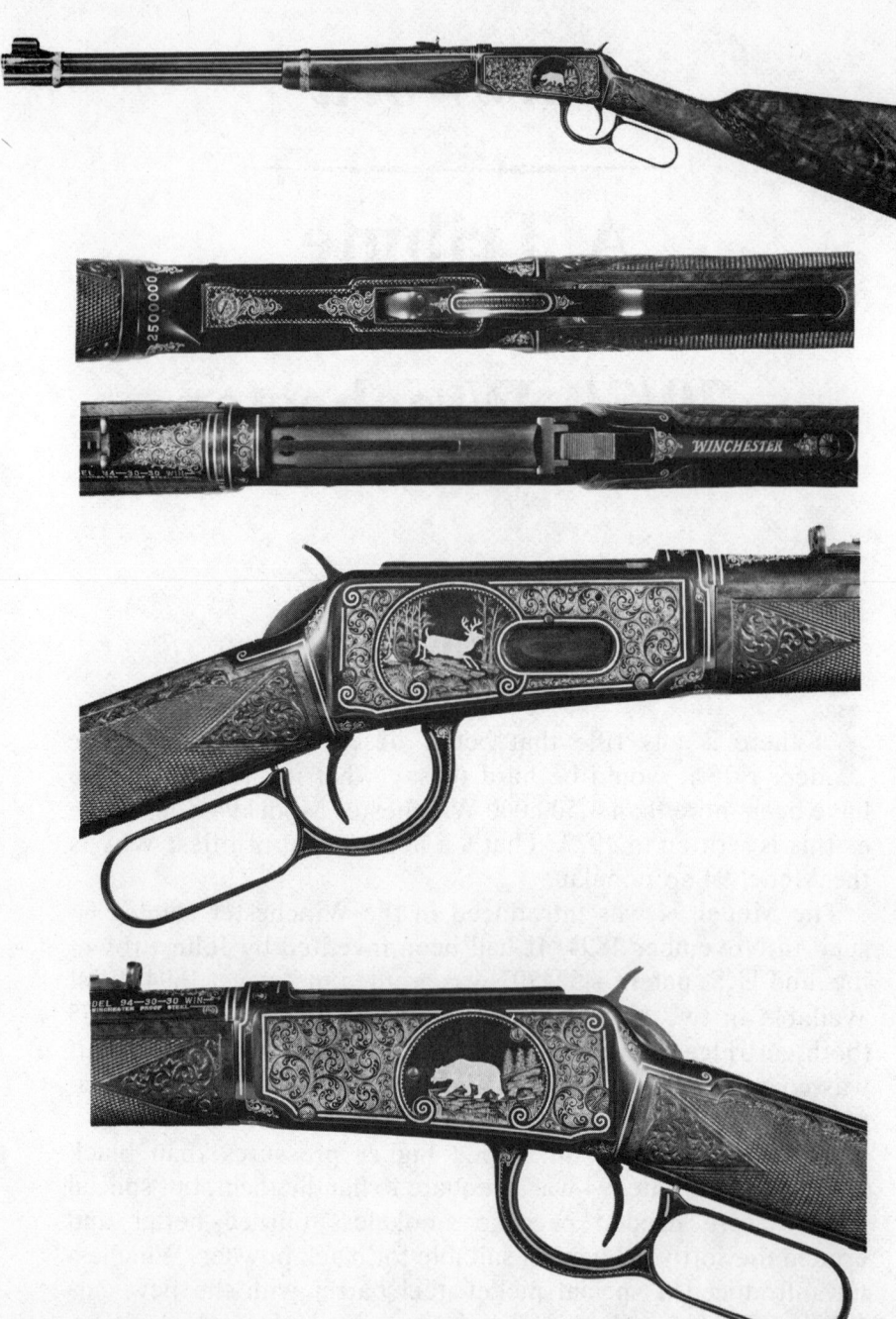

When Winchester production reaches a "milestone," the custom shop won't let the rifle out the door without working its wonders on it. This is Model 94 rifle, serial number 2,500,000, and you can see what they did to it. Over 4,500,000 Model 94 rifles had been made by 1977.

powder cartridge nomenclature; the first figure represents the bore diameter, and the second the powder charge. It was first loaded with a 170-grain bullet and virtually revolutionized sporting rifle shooting. The Model 94 in .30/30 was quickly seen as everyone's idea of what a sporting rifle ought to be. Its smokeless-powder power delivered all of the striking energy of larger black-powder rifles. Its flatter trajectory made longer-range hitting more certain. Its lighter weight and light recoil were much more pleasant. Its flat contour fitted a saddle scabbard neatly.

And the 94 rifle became popular in the American West, a fact which has never been lost on Winchester's promotional people, who still call the 94 "the gun that won the West." That's stretching it a little, but the motto helps sell guns.

Model 94 is a microcosm of the hunting rifle (for .30/30 Winchesters have been used for years to hunt much larger game than deer). Nothing so much says "hunting rifle" as the Model 94. It is the largest-selling sporting rifle in history.

In the near-century of the Model 94's existence it has been widely condemned in comparison with more modern, and admittedly superior, rifles and cartridges. Still, the old 94 keeps right on selling. It was only recently that another cartridge, the .30/06, began to outsell the .30/30, and the latter is still one of the top choices. It should be; the .30/30 is all one needs for a deer rifle. And more people hunt deer than any other big-game animal.

No matter what your choice of rifle or cartridge, you have to tip your hat to the .30/30 Winchester, because it made deer hunting what it is today. I have a rackful of better rifles—rifles that shoot closer and that have much more power, rifles that are more handsome and in which I take more pride. But no gun rack can ever be complete unless it has at least one Model 94—and, let me tell you this loud and clear, you need no more rifle for 90 percent of the deer hunting in North America today than a Model 94 .30/30 Winchester.

1

The Deep-Woods Deer Rifle

The terrain you hunt determines the type of hunting you will do and what caliber and type of rifle you use. You have no need of a long-range rifle with high-power scope if you plan to hunt in the deep woods. Moreover, the terrain may also dictate the type of hunting you will do; certain methods of hunting are effective in some types of terrain but are seldom employed in others.

For example, deep-woods hunting often calls for driving. The type of driving depends on the number in your party, the method preferred by others in the party, and the terrain. The area may include patches of swamp which can be easily driven while watchers man the points where deer are likely to exit the swamp. Deep woods also often call for still-hunting, a method favored by many hunters and almost a must for the lone hunter. A method often used by small parties is to wait on a likely spot for deer flushed out by the "weekend hunters." This is a method I used to use in the Adirondacks of New York when a couple of companions and I camped in the woods. We would still-hunt all week, then, when more hunters would come into the woods on Saturday and Sunday, we'd find a likely place before dawn and sit quietly. Often the increased activity would begin to move more deer.

To put this in gun terms, you will have little use in the deep woods for a .300 Winchester Magnum rifle with a high-power

Typical of a deep-woods rifle is the Marlin Model 336, shown here in carbine style with pistol grip. This model is available in .30/30 and .35 Remington and is a favored type for the brushy puckerbrush country found in many parts of the nation.

scope. Conversely, a rifle ideal for the deep woods, like a .30/30 lever-action carbine, would not be suitable for a 300-yard shot in open country. This example vividly illustrates how the terrain dictates the choice of a rifle.

It also is basic that you should choose a rifle which is capable of handling any game you are likely to encounter. Thus if you are hunting both mule deer and elk (the seasons overlap in many areas), you should choose a rifle that's capable of killing an elk. If you hunt down South in an area where Russian boar are plentiful, your rifle should be able to stop a boar. A boar takes a lot more stopping than any deer, and also can inflict considerable damage on a hunter who gets in its way. On occasion, you may have need of a rifle that will stop a grizzly when you're hunting deer. (The grizzly is close to nonexistent in the lower forty-eight states but plentiful in many areas of the Rockies in Canada).

A vast amount of the United States is covered by what we call "deep woods." It is by no means confined to the Southeast and Northeast. Puckerbrush is found throughout the country, and many Western deer are bagged in country that can be compared to the wooded country of Maine or Vermont, or the swamps of Mississippi and Louisiana.

Shots in deep-woods country are rarely more than 50 yards and almost never more than 100 yards. This means you may choose any rifle that will deliver "hunting accuracy" at 100 yards. This is usually defined as groups of 3 to 4 inches at a distance of 100 yards.

You determine the accuracy of a rifle by shooting it from a bench rest on a rifle range at a distance of 100 yards. Often this can be shortened to 50 yards if desirable. This shooting ought to be done from a shooting bench if possible; most gun clubs have at least one shooting bench available.

The reason for shooting from a bench, or a good steady rest position if no bench is available, is that you are simply checking the inherent accuracy of the rifle/ammunition combination. You try to eliminate the human element as far as possible. This is sometimes branded a "sissy" way to shoot. And there are many who say, "I can't shoot at a target, but just put a little hair on the target and I'll hit it." This is pure nonsense. The man who can't hit a target can't hit a deer either. Another fallacy is that you don't need to shoot from a rest because you won't shoot at a deer from a rest. And, some say, you should shoot from your hind legs "like a man."

This is all well and good, except you must not lose sight of the objective, which is to find out what accuracy your rifle can deliver. The notion that every rifle will hit where it is aimed is wrong, and to subscribe to it is stupid. It is also accepted by many that all rifles are sighted to hit the point of aim when you open the box, but this is asking for trouble. Most rifles are sighted at the factory, it's true, but this doesn't mean that all shooters are alike, see the same sight picture, or will be able to duplicate what factory shooters have done.

You must sight your own rifle, and you must know what your own rifle will do in your hands. To do this you must have a steady rest on which you place the forend—never the barrel. The best rest is a sandbag, although a rolled-up jacket will serve. You should never use a hard object like a rock or a log unless you place something soft, such as a folded jacket, on top. A hard object will scratch the forend and it will make the rifle recoil away from it, causing inaccuracy. Moreover, the use of a soft object will permit sighting that will duplicate hand-held accuracy. Never set the rifle barrel itself on a rest. Recoil will upset the natural barrel vibrations, and your shot will go way off the target.

Then you should place another, smaller sandbag under the butt, which you will regulate with your left hand to control elevation (by squeezing the bag) and windage (by moving it from side to side). You also must do your utmost to do everything exactly the same for each shot fired—the same pressure against the stock, the same grip, the same cheek contact, and so forth. You must strive for absolute consistency, because the rifle will begin to recoil before the bullet leaves the barrel (true of every rifle), and the way the rifle is handled in recoil has an effect upon the bullet's flight.

Excellent inexpensive rests and bags are available in Hoppe's brand, the same people who make the famous Hoppe's #9 powder solvent. A small bench rest that sells for about $10 is adequate for most hunters. Hoppe's also makes a more sophisticated rest for the shooter who does a lot of shooting, and they make rear and front sandbags in both leather and vinyl.

I never fire more than three shots with any game rifle, because rifles tend to heat up in shooting. Both barrels and stocks move with heat, and this will also affect accuracy. Any game rifle that puts three shots in a tight cluster will be an effective hunting rifle; you do not need a five- or ten-shot group to kill a deer.

Rifles used in deep-woods hunting ought to be sighted to hit point of aim at 100 yards. In most cases this will permit shooting at any deer by holding "right on" within about 125 yards. This is true even with a slow-moving bullet like the .45/70.

If you can't get your rifle/ammunition combination to shoot within the stipulated 3 or 4 inches at 100 yards, you can look for the trouble in several places. The first thing to try would be different brands of ammunition, because most rifles will perform differently with the various brands. It has been my experience that some rifles will shoot as wide as 4 inches with several brands and then will close up to as small as 1 inch with a different brand.

One year I was preparing for a hunt in northern Quebec with Jack Smart, a friend from Maine. We were sighting his rifle at 100 yards on a range near his home outside Augusta. The rifle was a remodeled Springfield .30/06 with a 4× scope. It was delivering groups of around 4 inches, which I didn't consider good enough. I was trying to persuade Jack to use one of my rifles instead, but he didn't want to use another rifle. Some rooting around in my car trunk produced a third brand of ammunition—in this case it was Federal. And the rifle closed down to an inch, so Jack shot his Canadian buck that year with his pet Springfield and Federal ammunition.

Should ammunition not be the trouble, then you should look to the rifle, and I'll have specific comments on various rifles in the appropriate chapters later in this book.

Deep-woods rifles frequently are fired in brushy situations, giving rise to the term "brush-busting." This term is frequently employed by advertising copywriters; rifles with big, fat, slow-

The current Model 94 Winchester, popularly known as the ".30/30 Winchester" or sometimes simply as "the deer rifle."

In 1977, Savage produced a version of their famous Model 99 rifle for the .358 Winchester cartridge. A fine cartridge, almost overlooked for years, it is an excellent choice for any deep-woods hunting situation for deer and larger game in North America.

moving bullets are said to be good brush-busters. They are supposed to plow their way through twigs, branches, trees, and, to hear some say it, cords of stacked wood and still hit the deer.

This is sheer nonsense. Bullets must have an unrestricted path to the target or they aren't going to hit. Moreover, the hunter who thinks he can shoot through anything is apt to try to shoot at a deer he can't see, and this is stupid. Not only does he have little or no idea where the deer is, or what part of the deer may be in the bullet's path, but he may be shooting at a man and not a deer.

This notion, I suspect, came into being because some very light, very fast bullets will blow up when they hit a twig or sometimes even a blade of grass. For example, if you load a light, thinly jacketed bullet in the .220 Swift, it will often fly apart in the air without hitting anything at all. This is due to the high rotational speed, which will make the bullet simply vaporize. It follows that high-velocity bullets are useless if they are at all liable to hit a twig or branch anywhere near the muzzle while they are flying at such speeds.

The very opposite would be the slow-moving, fat, heavy bullet from such rifles as the .358 Winchester and .45/70. The trouble is, a number of hunters as well as some gun writers who ought to know better think this means you can chop wood with such a rifle and still bag a buck. Not so.

It is true that such a bullet will not be much affected by pine needles, leaves, and perhaps small twigs. But you should be able to see what you're shooting at and should find a path through the brush and slip your bullet through that. To encourage hunters to shoot through brush at a target they cannot see clearly is not a responsible practice.

I find a scope to be invaluable for deep-woods hunting, although its use is by no means universal. On many occasions I have been able to sneak a bullet through a hole in a blowdown when a deer was hiding behind it (whitetails are great at that stunt). A scope for this kind of cover should be of low power, for several reasons: you don't need magnification; you often have poor light; the single aiming point is a big advantage; and the lower the power the more light is gathered. Scopes let you see what you cannot see clearly when the light is poor, which is what scope people mean when they use the term "light gathering"; with a scope you can hunt at dawn and dusk, often when you can't even see regular iron sights.

The rifle selected for the deep woods should be one that can be handled fast, fast, fast. This generally means a short-barreled carbine, and popular barrel lengths run from 18 to 20 inches. The choice of action system is up to you, although the most popular styles are lever, pump, and autoloader. A bolt-action is perfectly suitable, because it should be the first shot that does the trick. Even though a bolt is slower for repeat shots, that should not rule it out.

By all odds the most popular cartridge for deep-woods deer hunting is the .30/30, and the most popular rifle style is the lever-action carbine. When you begin to count the .30/30 Winchesters and Marlins, then add the .35 Remington caliber Marlins, you see that there are more of these in use than anything else. And, frankly, I doubt if anything is better for the purpose.

There are, of course, a vast number of cartridges that may be used for deer hunting in heavy cover. It's obvious that any rifle that kills game is a good one, but it's also obvious that some are better than others. I would suggest the following cartridges as top choices for a deer rifle to be used primarily in heavy cover. The list takes into account the type of rifle that these cartridges are available in:

.243 Winchester (100-grain)
6mm Remington (100-grain)
.250 Savage (100-grain)
.30/30 (150- or 170-grain)
.300 Savage (150- or 180-grain)
.308 Winchester (150- or 180-grain)

.35 Remington
.358 Winchester (200-grain)
.44 Remington Magnum
.444 Marlin
.45/70

There are many other suitable cartridges; the above is a list of those regarded as most desirable for hunting in the deep woods. If your favorite is not listed, refer to Chapters 10, 11, and 12 for further details.

Choose any of these cartridges listed, select a modern rifle, and mount a good scope. Then check it well for accuracy, remembering that you must add your aiming error to the basic accuracy (or lack of it) in the rifle itself. Make your first shot count, and do not depend on follow-up shots. That ought to put meat in the pot for you.

2

The Mountains Deer Rifle

Deer hunting in the mountains embraces two types of hunting—close-range and long-range. While you must be prepared for the former, you must also be equipped for the latter. The result is most likely a compromise.

It need not be a complete compromise, for a lot of mountain hunters go equipped only for long-range shooting. Should they happen onto a close shot, they can take it or not at their option. But, I suspect, most deer hunters prefer to take the compromise route with a rifle that will handle both situations reasonably well.

The long-range rifle, the true one, is what I'll cover in the following chapter. The short-range or deep-woods rifle was discussed in the last chapter. What we'll talk about here is the compromise—a rifle that will perform exceptionally well at very long range and yet can be handled fast enough to prove itself on a close and unexpected shot.

First, though, I'd like to briefly mention a type of hunting that is done by a very few sharpshooters in Pennsylvania. They are by no means an ordinary breed but rather are more or less long-range bench-rest shooters using very powerful rifles and shooting deer at ranges often exceeding 1,000 yards. Their rifles are always specially made and are chambered for mammoth wildcat cartridges producing unheard-of velocities. They cruise back roads in vehicles (the rifles are too heavy to carry) and when they spot a deer across a ravine or on the opposite side of a valley, they stop and drag a bench-rest out of the car. The deer is so far away he is undisturbed, so there is ample time for the men (it takes two) to set up. Their "stalk" consists of setting up the gear and estimating the range, which can take quite a while. These people often get their deer despite the range.

While I have never shot at deer at such great distances, I have shot a lot of woodchucks at extreme range, up to about 800 yards. I know that at such distances the game is usually undisturbed by a shot or two landing fairly close, so long as it doesn't kick dirt over them. They seem to think it's a fast-flying bee whipping by their ears. So the first shot at these ranges is often a sighting shot. Here's where the extra man comes in: he spots the shot. (The shooter also can recover in time to spot his own shot at such great distances.) When the miss has been determined it's often relatively easy to bring the next shot on target.

Such shooting is only for a few with the proper equipment; others should not try it.

The mountains of the East offer some sections where long-range shooting can be employed and the "mountain rifle" is appropriate. But this is much more common in the West and Southwest, primarily because a great deal of that land is more or less arid and one can see a lot farther. Some of those Pennsylvania bench-rest shooters can shoot a deer as far as they can see it, but the rest of us may have to stalk to get close enough to make a telling shot.

The Western deer hunter will be able to get shots as far as he can legitimately shoot with hope of connecting. This can happen often during a single hunt. I've been on hunts in the West where several dozen mule deer were spotted in a single day—and I've been there when you didn't see anything too! In some of these cases it's simply a matter of sizing up the animals and taking a careful shot.

It's not too often the Easterner has such an opportunity, because of the terrain and the habits of the whitetail in typical Eastern country. Nevertheless it does happen on occasion that an Easterner will be on a side hill and have the opportunity of surveying the whole other side of a mountain. If he could see a whitetail over there he could shoot him—with a long-range rifle.

One of the main problems in shooting over long distances is that of range estimation. This is a complex subject and not really the subject of this book, yet some mention of it is appropriate. During the past ten or fifteen years there have appeared several gadgets to estimate range based on the common rangefinder. Some of these work fairly well, others do not. The optical rangefinder is based on the triangulation method; you look into the lens and adjust until the two objects you see are superimposed. Then you can read the range directly off the scale. If you remember anything about your high school math you know that given one side and two angles of a triangle, you can find the other dimensions. The rangefinder uses this method and gets your answer for you. But it's no cure-all; it's not always that accurate, simply because you can't place the extreme ends very far apart. In World War II, antiaircraft artillery units employed similar rangefinders whose extremes were 30 feet apart. These were pretty accurate.

There also have been scopes designed with various rangefinding devices built in. Usually these are variable scopes so you can move a pair of parallel wires closer together or farther apart, then read the range from a scale that appears in the scope. Such a gadget is based on an object of known size where the game is standing. For example, if it's a deer precisely 3 feet high, you can bracket him with the wires and read your range. But how do you know the deer is exactly 3 feet high? Maybe he's standing in water. Or grass. Maybe he's a tiny deer, or a giant. Unless you know all these things this sort of rangefinding gadget is useless.

Another gadget supposedly designed for long-range sighting employs a cam in the scope's adjustment to compensate for long range. In use, you first sight the rifle for 100 yards. Then, using the appropriate cam, you can turn the dial to 200 yards and be on at that distance. You can do the same thing to 500 yards. This is fine if—and it's a big *if*—the cam is precisely right for your rifle. (These cams are made to accommodate a range of cartridges, and they can't be right for all of them. Moreover, your rifle may shoot a little different than the average.) These scopes generally come with several cams for different cartridge classifications. If you happen to get the right combination, you're in business. If not, you're where you were. And, keep in mind, you still have to guess the range right! I have been shooting one of these scopes, a Bushnell, on a .300 Winchester Magnum caliber Ruger Model 77 rifle that seems to work very well. I like being able to turn the scope to the range rather than holding over by "Kentucky windage." It's much more precise.

Rifles for mountain hunting can be of any action style you

A Winchester Model 70 Magnum, available in numerous chamberings, is a frequent choice for the mountain hunter. Naturally, the rifle should be fitted with a suitable scope.

Winchester's Model 70 standard rifle, which is available for a wide range of standard cartridges such as the .243, .270, .30/06, etc. This rifle has been a perennial favorite ever since its introduction in 1937.

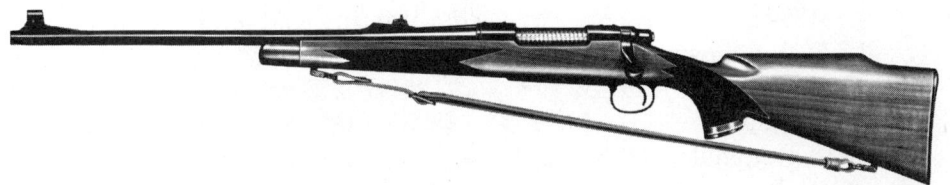

The Remington Model 700, shown here in deluxe grade left-handed version. The Model 700 is available in a wide array of calibers, in standard and deluxe models, and in both right-hand and left-hand versions.

choose within the proper cartridge limitations. Today's pump and autoloading rifles will shoot with comparable accuracy to any bolt action as you receive the rifle. Of course, you must practice with your own rifle to learn what it does, and why, before making the determination of how far you can kill a deer with it. A rifle that shoots 4-inch groups from the steady bench at 100 yards isn't worth a damn at 300 yards. Add the errors in aiming, holding, and range estimation, and you'll soon see what I mean. If, depending on your sights, your aiming error is 4 inches, and if you can't hold within another 4 inches, you have to add these to the inherent inaccuracy of the rifle. Three times four is 12, and an error of 12 inches at 100 yards will likely miss a big deer at that distance. Sometimes these errors are in opposite directions, in which case they wash each other out. But you cannot depend on that.

Under no circumstances do I recommend you shoot at any distance beyond 300 yards. That's a long shot. And that should only be taken by a man who knows his rifle and can shoot it, and who can judge range with some precision. And it assumes your deer is cooperating by standing still and that you have a steady rest. Otherwise, do not try such a shot.

If you qualify on all those counts, here are cartridges you may use:

.243 Winchester (100-grain)
6mm Remington (100-grain)
.25/06 Remington (117- or 120-grain)
.250 Savage (100-grain)
.257 Roberts (100-grain)
.264 Winchester Magnum (140-grain)
6.5mm Remington Magnum (120-grain)
.270 Winchester (130-grain)
7mm Mauser (139- or 175-grain)
.280 Remington (150-grain)
7mm Remington Magnum (150-grain)
.30/06 (150- or 180-grain)
.30/40 Krag (180-grain)
.300 H&H Magnum (150- or 180-grain)
.300 Winchester Magnum (150- or 180-grain)
.300 Savage (150- or 180-grain)
.308 Winchester (150- or 180-grain)
8mm Mauser (170-grain)
8mm Remington Magnum (185- or 220-grain)
.338 Winchester Magnum (200-grain)
.358 Winchester (200-grain)
.375 H&H Magnum (270-grain)

And of course the .240, .257, .270, 7mm, .300, and .340 Weatherby Magnums are superb rifles for long-range shooting.

A very few hunters are capable of shooting at ranges beyond 300 yards, but in no case should any hunter take a shot beyond 500 yards, and then only when every condition is right. For those few, then, the following cartridges from the list above are suitable for this pin-point shooting: .25/06 Remington, .264 Winchester Magnum, .270 Wincester, .280 Remington, 7mm Remington Magnum, .30/06, .300 Winchester Magnum, 8mm Remington Magnum, .338 Winchester Magnum, and all the Weatherby cartridges. This is not a list that's set in concrete, but it's a reasonable list under any circumstances.

When you choose your "mountain rifle," make sure you choose one powerful enough for whatever other game you might run into. This may mean elk or grizzly, in which event you'll want to lean toward a bit higher power.

Your mountain rifle ought to have a variable scope, so that

when you're hunting where the ranges are short, you can wind the power down to its smallest, which will increase the field of view. Then it can be wound up to maximum for your longer shots and for spotting.

Despite the vast choice of fine rifles and cartridges available for deer hunting at long range, you'd be surprised at how many .30/30 carbines are still carried out West. And they successfully shoot muleys and elk.

This is a good place to tell you that barrel length has no bearing on accuracy, other things being equal. Long barrels used to be a lot more popular than they are today; shooters have finally learned that short barrels produce virtually the same results.

The long barrel was necessary in black-powder days to allow the powder to burn completely and achieve full thrust. With smokeless powder, barrel length is much less of a factor in velocity. It is true that a longer barrel will deliver a bit more speed, but this is negligible and you can ignore it for most any deer-hunting purpose.

I can relate one experience that I had to illustrate the point. I had built a .243 Winchester rifle for a woodchuck-shooting companion, the late Doc Bassett of Cobleskill, N. Y. It had a 26-inch barrel, fairly heavy for its full length. It shot with exceptional accuracy, and Doc shot many chucks with it. His chuck-shooting habit was never to shoot at them under 300 yards.

One day he sent me the rifle and asked me to shorten that barrel to 19 inches and turn it down to light-sporter dimensions. I did it and sent the rifle back. Doc phoned me a few days later to say he had replaced the scope and, using the same loads with the same scope setting, the rifle shot exactly the same size groups as it had previously. And the point of impact had not changed either. I have had occasion to cut many barrels shorter, and the result has always been identical accuracy.

3

The Plains Deer Rifle

The plains deer rifle could as well be called the open-country deer rifle. It doesn't depart significantly from the mountain deer rifle except that it need not have the added power necessary for big bears that might be comforting in a mountain rifle if you're hunting in parts of Alaska or Canada.

The plains deer rifle is simply a long-range rifle, much like a varmint rifle except that it is chambered for a cartridge suitable for bagging a deer at long range.

Deer hunting in plains country is far less common than either deep-woods or mountain hunting. There are fewer plains areas, the deer are more scattered and there are fewer per square mile, and the hunters are fewer and more scattered, too.

The rifle used for plains deer hunting should be a flat-shooting, high-velocity rifle with a good scope. You must know how to estimate range, and this is very difficult on the plains, because there usually is nothing to use as a reference. In the mountains you have trees, and it's often not too hard to estimate range closely by referencing a tree.

Plains hunting also often involves stalking, sometimes on your belly as you creep close enough for a shot. The plains hunter will take advantage of every possible rest; you don't shoot at deer 300 yards away without taking every advantage you can.

It will be apparent that the rifle for plains hunting must possess top accuracy and must also be sighted correctly. You must

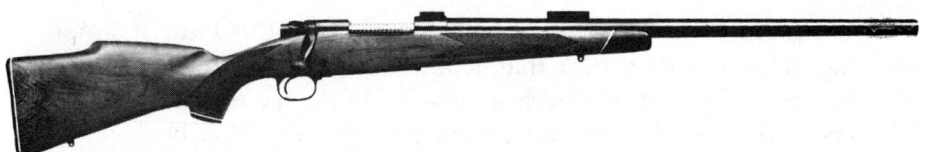

A Winchester Model 70 "varmint" model which is made with a heavy varmint-type barrel. In suitable chamberings, this rifle is an ideal long-range deer rifle when mounted with a suitable scope sight. The added weight and length of the barrel makes holding easier with the result that it can often be shot with greater accuracy.

know its trajectory over any distance you might shoot and be capable of milking every last ounce of accuracy out of the rifle.

Weight of the plains rifle is less of a factor than with either a woods or mountain rifle. You won't be required to unlimber it and get into action fast as with a woods rifle when a deer jumps out of cover at arm's length. Nor will you have to clamber over deadfalls and make like a mountain climber as the mountain hunter is often required to do. So you can tote a 10- pound rifle—as long as it is equipped with a good sling—and can even carry a spotting scope and other equipment if you wish. Slings are useful on all rifles; however, I've missed out on a few shots at deer when walking down a trail with rifle slung over my shoulder. A sling can lull you into daydreaming in deer country, and that's not conducive to good hunting. Cartridges considered most suitable for plains deer hunting would include the following:

.243 Winchester (100-grain)
6mm Remington (100-grain)
.25/06 Remington (117- or 120-grain)
.264 Winchester Magnum (140-grain)
.270 Winchester (130- or 150-grain)
.280 Remington (150-grain)
7mm Remington Magnum (150-grain)
.30/06 (150- or 180-grain)
.300 H&H Magnum (150- or 180-grain)
.300 Winchester Magnum (150- or 180-grain)
.308 Winchester (150- or 180-grain)
8mm Remington Magnum (185- or 220-grain)
.338 Winchester Magnum (200-grain)

and all the Weatherby Magnums from .240 to .340 inclusive.

This is not to suggest that these are the only possible choices for a plains cartridge, but it is the best list of those currently available. You must remember that I'm talking about cartridges capable of hitting and killing a deer at ranges up to 500 yards—

assuming *both* rifle and hunter are capable of this kind of shooting. This means a rifle that will shoot into minute of angle (5 inches at 500 yards) and a man who can achieve that performance consistently and can estimate range very closely.

This by no means should be accepted as a recommendation to take shots at 500 yards. Indeed, the good hunter will try to close the range as much as he can. There are very few rifles and very few men capable of 500-yard shooting. My only purpose here is to point out that there are rifles and cartridges that can do the job. Unfortunately, there are fewer men who can do it.

I suggest that the longest shot one should aspire to take at a deer in the field is closer to 300 yards, which is still a damned long shot. Any of the above cartridges will perform brilliantly at 300 yards, and of course there are other cartridges which could be added.

If you see a deer when you're hunting in open country, do your best to get within range that will assure you a killing shot. If your capability is 100 yards, then get down on your belly and crawl closer. If you can hit to 300 yards, then get within that distance. Then get closer. Make *sure* you are going to score. The way to do that, regardless of where you're hunting or with what rifle, is to be familiar with your rifle and its load and to know your own ability with that rifle.

4

The Farm-Country Deer Rifle

They grow a lot of fat deer in farm country. In fact, you will find bigger, fatter, and better-tasting deer in farm country than anywhere else. It just isn't as much fun—it isn't "deer hunting" in the usual sense—to hunt in farm country. Yet if you want either meat or the reward of a nice trophy then you can often find a solution in what we generally call farm country.

Farm country is usually rolling country in truck-farm or dairy-farm regions. Deer have adapted well to such an easy life, for the eating is good and there are few dangers. However, don't expect always to find farm deer out in the alfalfa field waiting to be shot. This may happen in the summer, but in the fall they smarten up fast and spend most of the daytime in the woodlots.

Deer hunting in farm country can either be deep woods, mountain, or almost plains hunting. It depends on where the farm is. There are many sidehill farms in Vermont and New York state, there are wide-open farms and ranches in country that's flat as a pancake in Ohio and the rest of the Midwest and parts of the Far West, and there are rolling hills, sometimes almost treeless as in Oklahoma and sometimes wooded as in western New York state. Much farm country is restricted to shotgun shooting, so be sure to check local laws; we will discuss shotgun slug shooting in Chapter 16.

If you hunt in farm country, then your choice of a deer rifle should follow one of those already discussed. For example, if you hunt farm country in Vermont or Pennsylvania where most shots will be less than 100 yards, then any rifle suitable for deep-woods hunting will fill the bill nicely. If on the other hand your hunting will take you into country where it's quite hilly, then you may want a rifle with more range and you can choose anything under the mountain-rifle classification. Or if your shooting may be at long range, as you will find on some ranches, you may choose a plains rifle.

Is there any such thing as an "all-round deer rifle"? Sure. Any rifle can be an all-around deer rifle as long as it's used within its limitations. You have to stretch the imagination a little bit, I admit, but it's perfectly acceptable to use one rifle for all your deer hunting no matter where you hunt. That's why the honorable old .30/30 is the nation's favorite. It will do the job acceptably in all types of hunting as long as the gun's capability isn't exceeded. No .30/30 is a long-range sniping rifle—but that can be argued, too. For example, a 200-yard shot in the deep woods is a very long shot. (It happens rarely but is quite possible along a logging road, for instance.) Yet a good .30/30 with a good man behind it can bag a deer easily at 200 yards.

The late Colonel Townsend Whelen, who wrote about rifles in the nation's outdoor press for many years, used to spend quite a lot of words on the subject of an "all-round rifle." I knew the Colonel pretty well during the later years of his life and built a couple of rifles for him. He defined his all-round rifle as one that can be used for any game anywhere. Such a rifle did not exist, of course. It is nigh impossible to produce a rifle that is suitable for both woodchucks and elephant. But that's stretching the point. Maybe you can't define the all-round rifle, but you can find an all-round deer rifle. That's not hard at all.

And you can choose this as well as I, because it requires a personal choice. And it requires a definition. What is your definition? What is a deer rifle? Some claim only the traditional lever-action repeater is worthy of the term "deer rifle." The man who lives his whole life in one area of the country has need of only one deer rifle, and that will fit one of the patterns already discussed. The Vermont resident who hunts the puckerbrush every year doesn't need a bolt-action .300 Winchester Magnum with a variable scope that will reach over into New Hampshire. Similarly, the lad that hunts the canyons of the Western and South-western mountains ought to have that .300 Magnum, or something like it. No matter the kind of rifle that's right for you, we should agree to agree on one thing—the rifle must deliver decent accuracy.

5

The Lever-Action and Single-Shot

Lever-action and single-shot rifles are operated in a similar manner, by moving a lever underneath the action. At one time all firearms were single-shots; the repeater could not be developed until the introduction of metallic cartridges in the mid-1800s. As rifles and cartridges improved, the action systems also improved. It has often been said that the American Civil War was begun with muzzleloaders and ended with the breechloader. This is essentially true, although a bit oversimplified. It is also true that at least one repeater was used in that war (the Spencer, tested by President Lincoln; the company was later purchased by Winchester). Following the Civil War, rifle developments came thick and fast. Most were heavy single-shot rifles like the Sharps and a few others with which the buffalo and Indian were virtually removed from the West.

THE LEVER-ACTION
In 1860, B. Tyler Henry invented a lever-action repeating rifle, and that laid the foundation of the Winchester gun empire. The company was then known as the New Haven Arms Company and was succeeded by the Winchester Repeating Arms Company in 1866. During the next several years the Henry rifle was gradually improved and formed the basis for Winchester's early development.

However, in about 1882 or 1883, a single-shot rifle was brought to the attention of Winchester. It was a rifle invented

The Winchester Model 94 shown here in antiqued finish is the world's all-time leading seller among sporting rifles.

Winchester made this sleek and elegant Model 88 lever rifle for several years, but it has now been discontinued. Available in .243 and .308 calibers, it was typical of modern-design lever-actions.

and made by the Browning brothers, John and Ed, of Ogden, Utah. The rifle was purchased for manufacture by Winchester and became the Model 1885 single-shot. Winchester also acquired rights to another rifle that was to become the famous Model 1886 lever-action. This was the beginning of a long relationship between Winchester and John M. Browning, the greatest firearms inventor the world has ever known. Browning also brought the Model 1894 rifle to Winchester—the single most outstanding gun purchase in history. He produced nearly all Winchester's inventions until about 1900, and all the automatic pistols ever made by Colt; machine guns and automatic rifles bear his name as well as automatic aircraft cannon. John Browning died in 1926, shortly after inventing his last famous gun, the Browning over/under shotgun.

Winchester's Model 94 was rocketed into prominence with the introduction of the .30/30 cartridge in 1895—the first sporting rifle and ammunition loaded with smokeless powder.

Meanwhile another traditional lever-action rifle was also born in New Haven. John Marlin had started his company in 1870 to make revolvers after the Smith & Wesson patent for charge holes drilled clear through the cylinder had expired. But in 1875 Marlin took over manufacture of the famed Ballard single-shot rifle, one of the all-time classic actions. Noting the success Winchester was having with lever-action rifles, and the market that appeared ready-made, Marlin began manufacturing lever-action repeaters. His two designers were not as famous as John Browning but they also produced lasting designs. They were Andrew Burgess and Lewis Hepburn. Based on patents by these men, and with some John Marlin patents, they produced the Model 1889 Marlin. This was the first Marlin with a solid-top receiver. In those days the advantage of a solid top had nothing to do with mounting a scope; it was boosted as a safety feature. Indeed, these early Marlins bore the words "Marlin Safety" on the top of the receiver.

With a few further improvements, this company produced the Marlin Model 1893, a lever rifle chambered for .30/30, .32/40, and .38/55. The Model 1893 was updated in 1936 and renamed the Model 36. Then, in 1947, Marlin again updated the action by changing the old square breechbolt to a round one, which greatly strengthened the action. It became Model 336, which continues today. There are at present more than 3,500,000 Marlin 336 rifles in use.

There is a great deal of similarity between Winchester's Model 94 and the Marlin 336. The Marlin is offered as a straight-grip model like the Winchester, but a pistol-grip Model 336C is also available. The Model 336C is chambered for the two most popular deer cartridges of all time: .30/30 and .35 Remington. The Model 94 Winchester is available as a .30/30 straight-grip-stock carbine. Marlin also has two other rifles built on the basic 336 action: the 444 and the Model 1895 in .45/70 caliber. There also is the Marlin 1894, a shorter and lighter action with old-style square bolt in .44 Magnum caliber.

At about the same approximate time, a Utica, N.Y., street railway superintendent named Arthur Savage developed a rifle action which was produced originally as the Model 1895, then revamped slightly and reissued as the Savage 99 in 1899. Savage had something big going for him: he had no older models, no old factory, no old employees with tradition-bound ideas to hobble him. The Savage Model 99 was a completely new rifle in all ways. It was stronger than any other lever rifle and capable of handling hotter cartridges. The Model 99 Savage is considerably different from the Winchester and Marlin in nearly all respects.

Let us first study the way the Winchester and Marlin actions work. Given a loaded rifle, you pull the trigger to fire; pulling

Marlin's Model 1894 is a lighter version of the famous Marlin 336, except the 1894 has the old-fashioned square bolt and is chambered for the .44 Magnum. This is a very popular woods rifle.

The Marlin Model 444 is chambered for the .444 Marlin cartridge, a heavy cartridge providing good ballistics and excellent power for big game at short range. The rifle has become quite popular among devotees of lever-actions.

The Marlin Model 336A is a rifle version of the company's popular 336 carbine. It features a 24-inch barrel.

The Marlin Model 1895 is a redesigned 336 made for the .45/70 cartridge. The .45/70, first used in 1873, has become popular again, and the Marlin 1895, named for an early Marlin model, is one of the more popular .45/70 rifles.

the trigger moves the trigger nose out of engagement with the hammer and allows the hammer to fly forward and strike the firing pin. The firing pin strikes the primer, which ignites the powder; the latter generates propellant gas which drives the bullet out of the barrel.

Lowering the lever has several results. It first unlocks the action by drawing the locking bolt down out of engagement with the breechbolt. Then the lever pushes the breechbolt to the rear, which extracts the fired cartridge from the barrel and ejects it from the rifle. At the same time, the bolt is moving to the rear; it is pushing the hammer back down so it can again be caught by the trigger and recocked. In the Winchester, the last movement of the lever raises the carrier (sometimes called the lifter), which has a fresh cartridge in position to be chambered. The cartridge was allowed to be pushed into feeding position as the bolt moved back. In the Marlin this feeding cycle occurs on the beginning of the lever's return stroke.

Then, in both rifles, the lever is moved back, driving the breechbolt forward and feeding the fresh cartridge into the barrel's chamber. At the end of the lever stroke the lock is forced up into engagement with the bolt to lock it securely against the impact of firing. Both rifles also feature a two-piece firing pin which assures that the rifle cannot be fired unless the action is fully locked (the lock moves the rear part of the firing pin into position).

These rifles are perfectly sound and safe; more than 7,000,000 of them have been made and most of them are still in service, so it's obvious that these are sound designs. They have a tubular magazine, which some regard as a disadvantage, since you can use only flat or round-nose bullets (a pointed bullet runs the risk of impacting the primer of a cartridge lying ahead of it in the magazine). This is not really a disadvantage. It is a limiting design factor, however. Some years ago Remington devised a spirally fluted magazine tube; it held cartridges in such a position that each bullet's nose could not touch the center of the cartridge in front of it.

Tubular magazines, for such cartridges the .30/30, .35 Remington, and similar, are very handy. They allow you to carry as many rounds as you need for a day's hunting (seven) without taking up pocket room. And they are neat and tidy with no protuberances to get in your way.

The Savage 99 differs from the Winchester and Marlin consid-

The Savage Model 99-A is a copy of the earliest Savage 99 rifles and features a straight grip. This action design dates back to 1895 and is a long-time favorite.

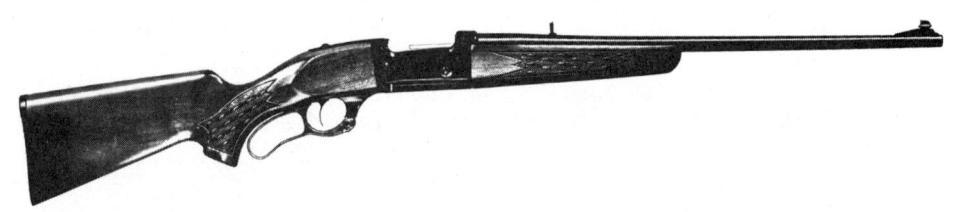

The popular Savage Model 99-C style with pistol grip and fairly new feature—a detachable box magazine. The latter replaces the familiar spool magazine, a feature of this rifle since 1895.

erably. It is a "hammerless" action, and this word needs some explaining. The 94 and 336 are known as "hammer actions," and the term simply means that they have an exposed or visible hammer. Any gun action where you don't see a hammer is called "hammerless"; the term is usually false, since most of them have hammers, but they are inside where you can't see them. This applies even to most of the newest designs. And the reason is that a big hammer is one of the most positive ignition systems ever developed. It takes a good solid blow to give consistent ignition, and the massive hammer is a proved way to accomplish this.

But the Savage is truly a hammerless action. It has a spring-loaded firing pin similar to that in a bolt-action rifle. Equally as positive as a big hammer, this was designed into the earliest Savage 1895 model. The Savage 99 also locks in a different manner. Its breechblock has a large square shoulder at the upper rear end which engages the receiver. The lever forces the breechblock's rear end up to lock, down to unlock. From there on the breechbolt (breechbolt, breechblock, and bolt are three terms used interchangeably) moves back and forth in conventional fashion.

Pressing the 99's trigger pulls the sear down, which releases the spring-loaded firing pin and allows it to fly forward at high

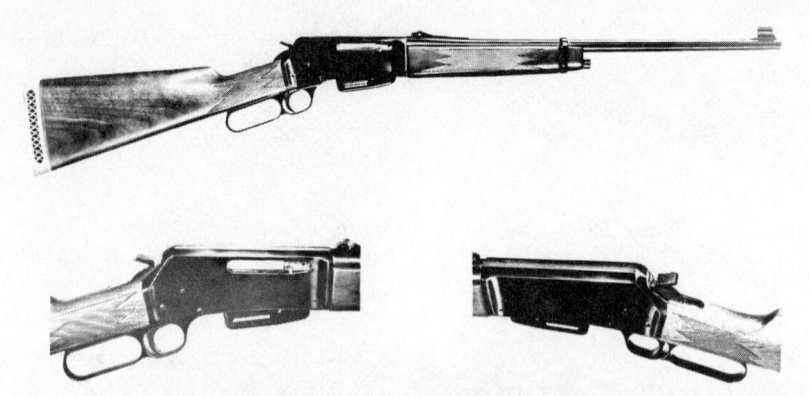

Browning's BLR model features a totally different system than the traditional lever-action but is an excellent rifle available in such popular cartridges as .243, .308, and .358. It has a removable box magazine.

speed to ignite the primer. The 99's feeding system is unique in that it employs a spool which resembles a revolver cylinder with the outside walls cut away. This provides a separate niche for each cartridge, which serves to protect the cartridges from scratching. Savage also adds a little number on the spool which you can view at the left side of the receiver and it tells you how many cartridges remain in the magazine. As far as I know, this spool-type magazine was first used on the Austrian Mannlicher-Schoenauer rifle.

An important point about the Savage action is that it has been able to handle any modern cartridge that has come along and that will fit the action. Among these are the .243, .308, and .358 Winchester cartridges. (Many cartridges are too long to fit this action.)

The remaining lever-action rifle is slightly different than any of these just described. It's the Browning BLR (for Browning Lever Rifle), which employs a rotary locking system similar to that in a bolt-action rifle. Throwing the lever down and up causes the front end of the bolt to rotate so its locking lugs engage and disengage. The lever's movement also moves the bolt back and forth after unlocking. Of recent design, the BLR also has an outside hammer which works much like those on the Winchester and Marlin rifles. The Browning's magazine, however, is a box magazine which is inserted under the action. There is considerable merit to a removable box (Savage also has a Model 99 with detachable box) which allows you to unload the rifle easily without jacking the cartridges through the magazine. It also permits you to buy a spare magazine and carry it, loaded, in your pocket.

The Browning box, however, hangs down right where you want to carry the rifle, at the balance. This is an unfortunate part of the design. It would have been much better to reduce magazine capacity by one cartridge and provide a flush magazine.

The Browning BLR is available in .243, .308, and .358 Winchester calibers. It is a fine rifle except for the magazine protrusion. There are other lever-actions on the market, replicas of older Winchesters. These are chambered for weak cartridges which are not suitable for deer hunting.

The advantage to lever-action carbines is that they are fast. They can be gotten into action in one fluid motion that thumbs the hammer back into cocked position as the gun is shouldered, and repeat shots can also be very fast. They are chambered for cartridges that will handle any game in North America (the .358 Winchester) as well as those perennial favorites the .30/30 and .35 Remington. All of them can be scoped except the Winchester 94 (the 94 can be scoped but its top ejection means an offset mounting or too-far-forward mounting, neither of which is desirable). Most lever rifles will deliver far better accuracy than you have been led to believe. The Savage 99 has always been accepted as an accurate rifle, but many have put down the traditional rifles as being something less than accurate. They cite a two-piece stock as a disadvantage. This is unsupported by any shooting tests and, presumbably, those who brand them as inaccurate have never really tried them out. I have on many an occasion, and these rifles are capable of very fine accuracy. In fact, I have a Marlin .30/30 Model 336 with a 2½× scope that will shoot into 1¼ inches at 100 yards with factory ammunition. That's better shooting than many bolt-actions will do right out of the box. I have had similar results with any number of other rifles with two-piece stocks in autoloading and pump actions as well as levers.

Lever-actions do have disadvantages, though. Among them is that none of them are chambered for big magnum cartridges, though that's hardly a loss for the deer hunter, who doesn't really need that kind of power. The two traditional lever rifles do not have what is called "primary extraction," which is defined as the breaking loose of the expanded cartridge. This is not necessary with such cartridges as the .30/30, but it is essential with high-pressure cases such as the .243 Winchester. These

The inside of an English Farquharson action made by Westley Richards of London. This has always been regarded as one of the finest single-shot actions ever made.

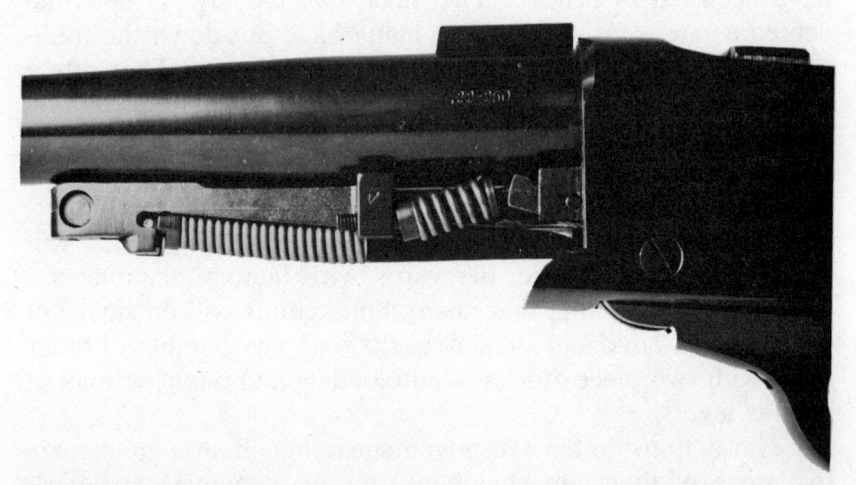

The Ruger Number One, shown here with forend removed, employs a modern system of attaching the forend to the rifle. The springs visible are for hammer and ejector.

cases swell and grab the chamber walls tightly. They must be loosened by a powerful camming action. This is available in the Savage 99 and the Browning BLR but not in the Winchester 94 or Marlin 336. It's not needed in these two rifles, although it does present a limiting factor. For example, if either of these actions were long enough to handle the .243, they could not because of the lack of primary extraction.

THE SINGLE-SHOT
There has been an awakening of interest in the single-shot rifle during the past few years for hunting. It is an acknowledgment of the fact that the most important shot is that single aimed shot, as well as the fact that it's a more sporting proposition. It's a movement that deserves support.

The single-shot rifle, as the word implies, is one that fires one shot and then must be emptied and reloaded in order to fire again. Such rifles generally resemble lever-actions because they are usually operated by a lever under the action. Lowering the lever withdraws the firing pin, then drops the wedge breechblock. At the same time the hammer is cocked and the cartridge extracted with a powerful motion and ejected. You slip a new cartridge directly into the barrel's chamber and pull the lever back up, which relocks the rifle.

If more hunters used single-shots there would be more game killed and less crippled. This argument has been voiced by many, and it's probably true. It is a good way to teach that the first shot is the most important and not to rely on a magazineful for follow-up shots. I think it's safe to say that the ordinary deer hunter who shoulders his rifle once or twice a year rips his first shot in the general direction and hopes to connect with subsequent shots. This is stupid. You should shoot as though there were no more shots in your rifle and no more cartridges in your pocket or belt. The youngsters of America ought to be taught with single-shot rifles instead of the autoloaders most of them seem to be using.

Today we have several fine single-shot rifles in manufacture that make excellent deer rifles. These are led by the Ruger Number One, which is available in a long list of cartridges starting with the .22/250 and running up to the .458 Winchester Magnum. There also are several variations in the Ruger Number One, depending on the caliber. Ruger also has a Number Three rifle at about $100 less which is chambered for the .22 Hornet, .30/40

Harrington & Richardson is currently manufacturing replicas of the original "trapdoor" Springfield rifles. They are known by this name because the breech is hinged at its front and opens up and forward like a cellar door.

Krag, and .45/70. I have one of these chambered for the .30/40, which is an excellent deer rifle.

Browning has a pair of single-shot rifles on the market, including a standard model in a variety of calibers up to the .30/06 and a .45/70 model with octagon barrel and old-style buttstock. One of the more interesting things about the Browning single-shot is that John Browning's first invention was a single-shot rifle very similar to the one now offered.

Harrington & Richardson has long had a barrel for their popular Topper model single-barrel shotgun in .30/30 caliber. This is a very utilitarian rifle no matter how you slice it, and it's priced low. For less than $80 (in 1977) you can get this rifle plus a 20-gauge shotgun barrel that fits the same action, which is a pretty good deal. H&R also offers a number they call the Model 155 Shikari. It's based on the Topper action (similar to a break-open double shotgun) and is available in .44 Remington Magnum or .45/70. And H&R is offering a replica of the 1871 and 1873 Springfield .45/70s with the "trapdoor" action. The name was derived from the fact that the breechblock is hinged at the front and opens up like a cellar door by swinging up and forward. These are not very strong actions, however.

Another single-shot rifle is known as the Wickliffe. It resembles one of the old Stevens models and is available in .243 and .308 Winchester. This is a good-looking rifle, though I have not fired one of them.

One advantage of using a single-shot rifle is that it gives you a good gut feeling of satisfaction if you can bag your buck with a single shot—something your ancestors did, except you have the advantage of a better rifle, more powerful cartridge, and, most likely, a scope. You can select a single-shot in whatever caliber you like. The .30/40 and .45/70 would certainly rate high

In 1885 John Browning brought his first invention to Winchester; it became the Winchester Single Shot rifle and was in the company's line for years. Today, Browning is manufacturing a rifle along similar lines; this is the current Browning single-shot. It is an excellent rifle and delivers fine accuracy.

on anybody's list for a deep-woods deer rifle. And the .25/06, 7mm Remington Magnum, .30/06, .300 Winchester Magnum, and other available chamberings would fill the bill for deer at whatever range you wish to shoot them.

A single-shot has the obvious disadvantage of no repeat shots, at least not very fast ones, although you may learn to work that action fast if necessary. A single-shot is not especially fast to swing into action, at least not for me. The design favors deliberate shooting. I would not choose a single-shot for deep-woods hunting unless I planned to sit on a stand, in which event they're as good as any other rifle. But if you are moving and spook a deer, I think a single-shot would put you at a decided disadvantage. Still, a single-shot is a challenge and adds a lot to the hunt.

Old they may be, and they may be derided by some who should know better. But the single-shot, like the lever-action, is going to stay with us for a long time to come. It ought to, because it's still as good as anything else for many kinds of deer hunting.

BLACK-POWDER SINGLE-SHOTS
In recent years there has been another step backward into history. This is the sport of black-powder hunting. A number of states have established special seasons for what they often refer to as "primitive weapons." (Incidentally, I never use the word "weapon" when referring to sporting firearms. I feel the word is legitimate when referring to military or law-enforcement arms, but has no place whatever in sporting jargon.)

Black-powder guns are single-shot by definition; most of the popular ones are replicas of the old Hawken or plains rifles. "Plains rifles" is the generic name given to those rifles that opened up the West. They were adapted from the graceful Ken-

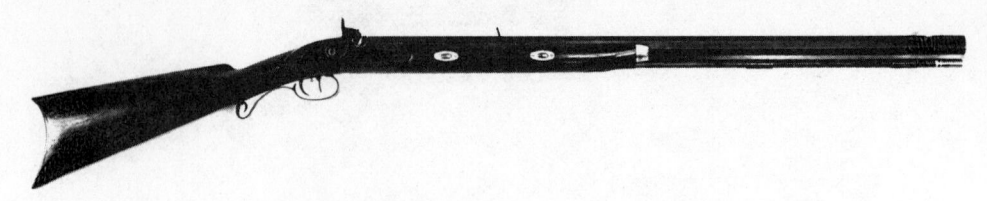

There is today a great interest in hunting with "primitive" firearms. Best-known of the modern replicas are the various versions of "Hawken" rifles, named after the brothers Sam and Jake. Shown is an Ithaca Hawken, a muzzleloading percussion rifle.

tucky, because that elegant rifle was too small in bore and too long and fragile for the rigors of the West.

What was needed was a thicker stock so it wouldn't break in a fall from a horse, a shorter barrel that could be carried on the saddle, and a heavier charge, with larger bore, because the game was tougher in the West. Some also said the Indians were tougher too. This need was met by a number of gunsmiths in St. Louis, the jumping-off place. Among them, the Hawken brothers, Jake and Sam, were the best-known.

Most of today's black-powder hunting rifles use round balls for bullets. A round ball is the most miserable shape you can try to drive through the air. It lacks stability, its wind resistance is fearful, and its ability to kill is limited to relatively short range. These rifles will usually do fairly well when using an elongated slug, but performance will suffer when a round ball is employed.

Used within its limits, a primitive sporting firearm is an effective deer rifle. But it's not a modern rifle by any means, and if you learn one thing from shooting it, you'll learn that our ancestors had it a lot tougher than we do. Of course, these are really single-shot propositions. There's no way you're going to get another shot off. Moreover, your target will be obscured for a while by the huge cloud of stinky smoke you put out.

ACCURACY SECRETS WITH LEVER-ACTIONS AND SINGLE-SHOTS

Rifle accuracy is a tricky thing. Suddenly a good-shooting rifle spatters its shots like a shot gun pattern and you wonder what happened. I wish I had a dollar for every shot I've taken when the sights had loosened up and that was the last thing I looked for. The first thing you should look for is a loose scope or loose sights. The next thing is loose screws—the screws that hold the buttstock to the action. One of the most vital things in the accuracy of any rifle with a two-piece stock is that the action must bear tightly and evenly against the buttstock. This is easy to check. Remove the stock and look where metal meets the wood. It will always show up as a shiny place. This is not so easy to correct, though. If you don't know how to do it, I'm not going to tell you, because you won't be able to do it properly. Instead, find a good gunsmith and ask him to do it for you.

No rifle will deliver its best accuracy unless it has a good trigger pull. This is defined as a pull with as little movement as possible (ideally, you shouldn't feel any movement, but this is often impossible). You should take up the trigger pressure gradually and should feel nothing until the rifle fires. This is sometimes described as feeling like breaking a glass rod or an icicle. And that is a good analogy. The weight of a trigger pull is of less importance than these other factors. A trigger with any creep—a pull that stops, starts, and stops again—is intolerable under any circumstances.

Unfortunately most lever-action rifles come equipped with more than their fair share of creep. You can remove it from any hammer rifle, though, quite easily. Take a wide-bladed screwdriver and place it behind the cocked hammer—with the rifle unloaded, of course. Then try to force the hammer off while you pull the trigger. This will cause the mating surfaces to be honed after you've repeated the treatment a few times. Place a couple pieces of stiff cardboard between the screwdriver and the metal parts before this rough treatment to protect them.

The weight of a trigger pull for such a hunting rifle should not be lighter than about 4 pounds and it can be as heavy as 6. Weight is measured by a scale made for the purpose or by hanging a weight of the proper amount on the trigger.

The lash-up of forend and magazine tube to receiver is a subject of considerable mystery when it comes to accuracy. In most cases this has not proved detrimental to good accuracy with tubular magazines. Other lever-action rifles, such as those with rotary or box magazines and single-shot rifles perform best when a "forend hanger" is built into the rifle. Ruger employs this system, which consists of a metal piece attached to the front of the frame to which the forend is attached, leaving the stock itself free of the barrel.

Many lever rifles and single-shots have their buttstocks secured to the action by a through-bolt from inside the buttstock under the buttplate into the rear of the action. This is the best system, and the screw must be kept tight. Winchester 94 and Marlin lever rifles do not use a throughbolt but depend on the tapered tang screw to hold things together. This is as good when it's assembled right—it usually is, but it can loosen, and you must be aware of the system.

A very few rifles in these action systems have adjustable triggers, like the Ruger, and these can be adjusted easily by following directions.

Some of the older rifles that have seen a lot of hard service have developed some setback, and excessive headspace results. Headspace is the fore-and-aft dimension for the cartridge in the chamber. You can easily tell if this condition exists because the fired cartridges will show primer protrusion. If your fired primers are raised above the head of the case, your rifle has excess headspace. This condition is detrimental to accuracy and it can be dangerous, allowing a case to rupture. Such a rifle should be repaired or replaced. It should not be fired without getting an expert opinion.

6

The Bolt-Action

Bolt-action rifles are quite a bit older than you may think. The first is generally credited to a Prussian, Johann Nikolaus von Dreyse, who in the early 1800s patented the Prussian needle gun. It was so named because the firing pin was long and thin, like a needle, to penetrate the entire "cartridge" and reach the primer, which was located forward of the powder charge and just behind the bullet. That was in the days before metallic cartridges, when the powder, primer, and bullet were enclosed in a paper wrapper.

While there were a couple of attempts to market bolt-action sporting rifles in the United States in the late 1800s, they never achieved any popularity until after World War I, when returning servicemen came home from France with an admiration for the Springfield rifle and the .30/06 cartridge. Until then, hunting in America was a lever-action and single-shot affair.

The first really modern bolt-action rifle was the Model 1898 German rifle perfected by Peter Paul Mauser. Earlier Mausers had led to the evolution of the Model 98 as the truly modern design. In fact, eighty years later, the Model 98 Mauser is still as up to date as just about any action made. It has some of the same features possessed by the most modern bolt-actions, and it has some features that are superior to those in some modern actions! Just about the only really important improvement on the basic Mauser 98 is the use of better steels today. There are refinements—improved triggers, lowered bolt handles, low safeties, and similar cosmetic changes—but basic improvements are few.

One of the first actions adapted from the Mauser was the U.S.

The famous Mauser action is still available and is still branded Mauser, now Mark X, and imported by Interarms. This modern version is as up-to-date as any other rifle and is an excellent choice.

Rifle Model 1903, the popular Springfield. It departed from the Mauser in several important respects, few of which are considered real improvements. Most of these alterations were designed to evade Mauser patents (they were not entirely successful and the U.S. government paid a royalty to Mauser for a number of years). But the Springfield was a great rifle; it possessed extraordinary accuracy and was a favorite of several early bolt-action hunters.

Among these early riflemen were President Theodore Roosevelt and the famous author Stewart Edward White. Both Roosevelt and White took custom sporting rifles made from Springfields to Africa and hunted extensively in the United States as well. The first Springfield sporters, as they became known, were made by Louis Wundhammer, a Bavarian who emigrated to the United States. It may be said with accuracy that the first of the modern sporting bolt-action rifles was the one Wundhammer made for Teddy Roosevelt. Later, Roosevelt had a rifle made up for him at Springfield Armory while he was President. It is refreshing to note that he paid for the rifle.

After the Springfield was adopted by the government, surplus Krag rifles were sold by the DCM (Director of Civilian Marksmanship), of the Department of the Army. These were sold to NRA members for $1.50 each. As a matter of fact, most surplus military rifles (and some pistols) have been sold this way ever since 1900. The intention has been to make the rifles available to civilians at low cost for rifle marksmanship practice as part of the preparedness program. The reason the NRA is involved is that the DCM needs an organization through which to dispose of the material; otherwise it would have to be accomplished at the taxpayers' expense. Hundreds of thousands of rifles and pistols (1903, 1917, and Garand rifles, M1 carbines, and .45 automatic pistols in addition to the Krag rifles) have been funneled into civilian hands by this route.

At the end of World War I both Winchester and Remington had many tons of spare parts on hand for the 1917 Enfield rifle. This rifle had been under contract by Remington for Britain before the U.S. entry into the war. Once we became involved, it was impossible to produce enough Springfield rifles, because it was a complicated rifle to manufacture and the tooling would have required too much time. It was not so complicated to alter the tooling for the Enfield from .303 British caliber to our .30/06, and this is what was done. Rifles were made by Remington in two plants—the main factory in Ilion, N.Y., and a plant leased from Baldwin Locomotive Works at Eddystone, Pa.

Remington was reluctant to dump all those parts and tooling when the war ended, so they adapted the 1917 military rifle into a sporter announced in 1921 and designated the Model 30. It was a good rifle, although it had some features that needed changing, the most glaring of which was the cock-on-closing bolt. This was changed a few years later, a new and rather handsome stock was supplied, and the rifle was redesignated the Model 30-S. Remington never sold vast numbers of these rifles, although they were really good. In 1940, with World War II almost at hand, they again updated the same old Enfield and called the new model the 720. This is probably the longest single run ever from one set of spare parts. It was a mistake, too. In 1925 Winchester introduced the Model 54 rifle along with the exciting .270 cartridge.

The Model 54 Winchester was an improved action—it was essentially an improved Springfield. But it was only improved in certain respects, because it used a cheap, stamped trigger-guard unit; it used the trigger as a bolt stop and its bolt handle and safety would not clear a scope. These deficiencies were corrected in 1936 when the Model 70 was introduced. Winchester's Model 70 became the bolt-action by which other bolt-actions were judged—a position it held for many years.

In the meantime, Savage had been in and out of the market with two high-power bolt-action offerings. The Model 20 was introduced in 1920 and was chambered for the .250/3000 and .300 Savage cartridges. The rifle was dropped in 1928 and replaced by the Model 40 and Model 45, one a standard and the other a special grade. These were never very popular and did not return after the war.

A bolt action's heart is the locking system, which greatly re-

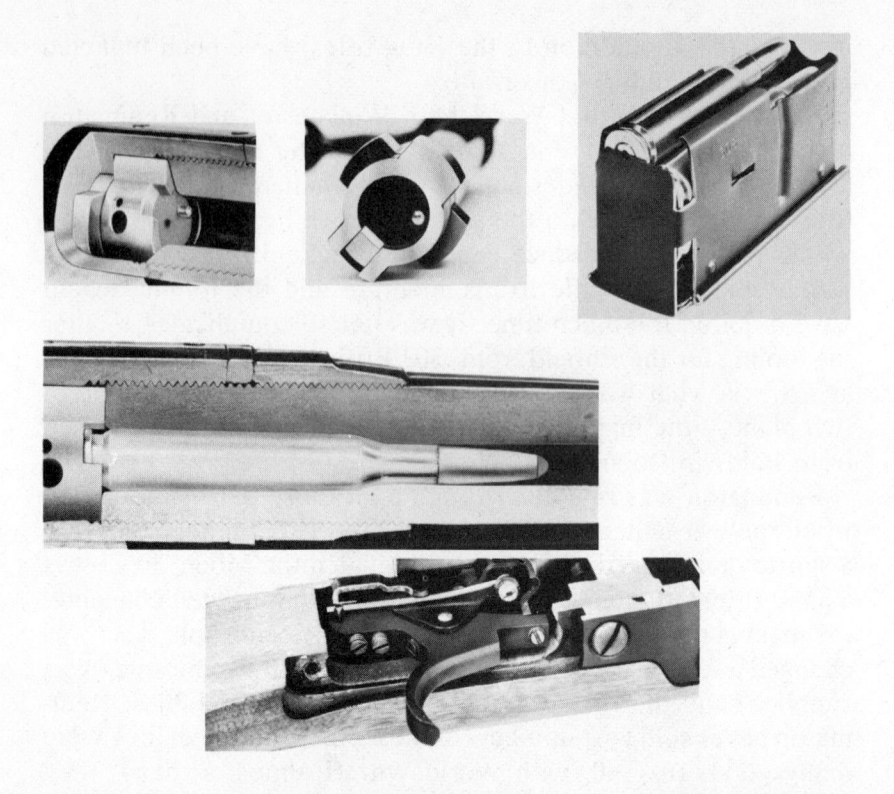

Various cutaway views of the Savage Model 110 action, showing the locking lugs in position, the bolt face with extractor claw and ejector (the round, shiny button) the separate magazine box which is removable, a cartridge lying in the chamber, and the adjustable trigger. Note that high-power rifle barrels are snugly and securely threaded into their receivers.

sembles a common door-locking bolt. The main difference is that the door lock is designed to withstand pressure from the side, while the rifle lock bears its stress in line with the bolt. Turning the bolt handle closed in a rifle securely locks the big lugs into recesses in the receiver that provide an ample margin of strength. In fact, the bolt lockup is among the strongest in the whole world of guns.

    The bolt action also has enormous camming power to close the handle on a dirty or battered cartridge. This is a by-product of a military requirement, because service ammunition can get dirty or dirt can work its way into the action. The opening stroke is also important, and a bolt action exerts a powerful camming action to slowly break the grip a magnum cartridge has gotten on the chamber walls. This is known as primary extraction—the breaking loose of the seal. It frequently requires very powerful camming.

Raising the bolt handle unlocks the action and provides primary extraction at the same time. The same motion also cocks the firing-pin spring inside the bolt. Drawing the bolt to the rear extracts the empty cartridge from the chamber and, at the end of the bolt's stroke, ejects the empty from the rifle. Moving the bolt forward strips a cartridge from the magazine and shoves it into the chamber. Turning the handle down completes cocking and relocks the action for the next firing.

After World War II, Winchester began making Model 70 rifles again, much as they had before the war. In 1964, however, they reached a point where the rifle was too costly to produce, so it was redesigned. This act set up a chorus of complaint among the shooters of America. They claimed that the Model 70 was not nearly as good as the pre-1964 Model 70.

The Model 70 was again redesigned in 1968. This 1968 rifle (still manufactured) had a number of important internal changes which are not very noticeable to the uninitiated. But it also has new stock configurations, which was a big step forward. Generally speaking, the present Model 70 (1968 to date) is considered to be a better rifle than the pre-1964, though you'll have a hard time proving this to any Model 70 enthusiast. There is still a charisma about the older rifle that has driven prices of all early models sky-high.

Let's set things straight on this Model 70 business. I much prefer the pre-1964 rifle myself, chiefly because I think the styling of the metal parts and their workmanship is superior. I wish I had a barn full of them. However, I do have a 1964 Model 70 which is said to be among the worst of all. It is chambered for a cartridge known as the .225 Winchester, which was supposed to replace the .220 Swift but which is now obsolete, while the Swift is coming back. Still, this "rotten" rifle shoots groups as small as ½ inch at 100 yards with factory ammunition. Now that's not at all bad—in fact it's damned good, and while I'm not impressed with the rifle's looks, I am impressed with the way it shoots.

I also have a .264 Winchester Magnum .30/06 and a .458 Magnum, both Model 70s of current manufacture. These rifles shoot well; the .264 is an especially fine shooter with a Leupold 24X scope. Still, you may not think they look as good as the pre-1964 Model 70s.

The Winchester Model 70 in four of its styles. First is the Model 670, a style with the basic Model 70 action but with walnut-finished hardwood stock and with a blind magazine bottom. Next is the Model 70 rifle with varmint barrel and stock and scope bases for a target-type scope. This rifle, in appropriate caliber, would be a choice for the deer hunter who shoots from a rest and does not have to carry the rifle. Next is the Model 70 Magnum, which is the same as the standard rifle except it has a recoil pad. Finally, the big Model 70 African, chambered for the mammoth .458 Winchester Magnum.

Any Model 70 needs its trigger adjusted before it will shoot its best. This trigger, with few changes, has been made the same way since 1937, but those who assemble the rifles do not know how to adjust the trigger. Properly adjusted, the Model 70 trigger is as fine as any. (See Chapter 15 for suggested Model 70 trigger adjustment.)

Meanwhile, Remington finally got the old 1917 Enfield out of its system and began to make some changes after the war. They completely restyled their bolt-action line with a design team headed by Mike Walker. The first rifles were the Model 721 and Model 722, introduced in 1948. Both were very plain rifles with no checkering and no frills of any kind. The Model 721 had a

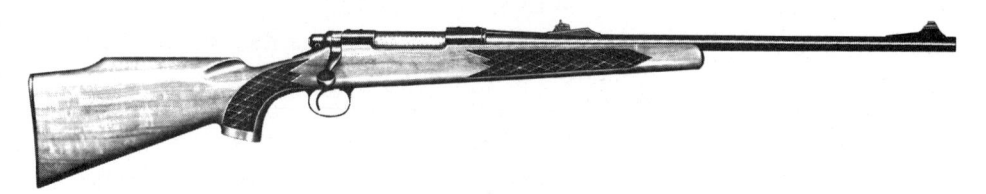

The Model 700 ADL (standard) Remington is the largest-selling bolt-action rifle on today's market. Available in a wide range of calibers, it is an excellent choice. In this rifle Remington has eliminated the conventional floorplate; the magazine has a blind bottom.

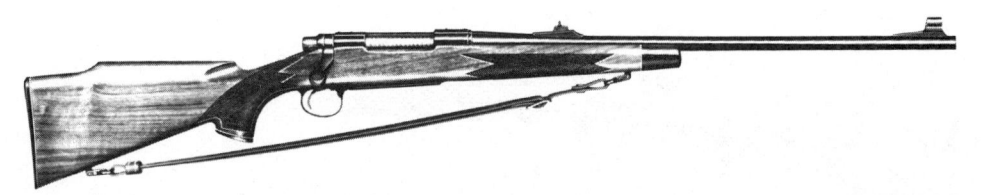

Remington's deluxe grade, BDL, of the Model 700 rifle. Basically identical with the 700 ADL, except a sling is included, the rifle has a floorplate (which appeals to many shooters), and the checkering is better.

standard-length action for cartridges like the .30/06, while the 722 was shorter. The 722 was accompanied by the .222 Remington cartridge, which was another winner. Remington made an awful lot of these rifles before they redesigned and produced the Model 725 with the same basic action but a much prettier stock made to better dimensions. Then in 1962, the 725 was again restyled and emerged as the present Model 700, which is the biggest-selling bolt rifle on today's market.

Remington designed something else into (or out of!) its 700 when it used a blind magazine. The designers simply eliminated the common floorplate and used a simple washer for the front guard screw in the Model 700 ADL, the standard rifle. The bottom of the magazine itself is simply a blind cut in the stock that does not extend through the bottom. Nothing whatever is wrong with the concept; if you want a floorplate you buy the BDL (deluxe) version. Winchester and others have since followed the Remington lead and have eliminated floorplates on their standard models. A modification of this type makes sense because it reduces cost but doesn't affect functioning of the rifle.

Staking a claim in yet another part of the market, Remington introduced their Model 788 in 1967. This had a completely new bolt action, the most notable feature of which is its rear locking lug system. The 788 action also features a rather massive receiver, a major result of the rear locking, which does not require the usual longitudinal cuts for front locking lugs.

The Model 788 is a very plain rifle with no frills. It is available in several deer-rifle chamberings (.243 Winchester, 6mm Remington, .308 Winchester). A blind magazine, nonadjustable trigger, and a few other obviously plain features help make it a low-cost rifle. The 788 is a rugged, plain, and inexpensive bolt-action

Remington's Model 788 is made in several deer-rifle chamberings, and the action is characterized by its rear locking lugs, great strength, fine accuracy, and low cost. It's a rather plain rifle but it takes a back seat to nothing in the shooting department.

This close-up shows the rear locking lugs on the Remington 788 bolt-action. The nine lugs offer exceptional strength and the rear location provides a smoother bolt travel because the receiver is not slotted for front-mounted lugs.

rifle. Its basic action is so sound that it is becoming increasingly popular for target rifles.

Remington designed yet another *different* bolt-action rifle in the early 1960s; it was a shortened version of the Model 700 and its original purpose was the XP-100 single-shot pistol. This strange gun is chambered for the hot (for a handgun) .221 Remington cartridge—a shortened .222. Shortly after, the same action showed up as the Model 600 rifle, which was announced in 1964. Along with that new rifle, Remington introduced two new belted Magnum cartridges, the 6.5mm and .350 Remington Magnums. These were shortened cartridges that provided enormous power (see the descriptions in Chapters 10 and 12). The rifles were very short and very light and delivered very heavy recoil. They were not pleasant to shoot, and moreover they were ugly as sin. In 1968 the Model 600 underwent some changes and was reissued as the Model 660. It was short-lived, however, and the rifle, along with its cartridges, went out of the line shortly after.

In 1971, Remington began manufacturing and marketing the Mohawk 600. This is the same action, but the rifle is chambered for .243 and .308 Winchester and 6mm Remington. "Mohawk" is what the trade calls a "promotional" brand, which means it is not sold through regular channels, but rather through discount houses. It's a neat way to bypass list-price regulations and it avoids the stigma of having your brand name associated with price cutting. It also affords a good bargain for the consumer, and many manufacturers follow the practice.

Dick Dietz, a good friend and occasional hunting companion who is on Remington's public-relations staff, has chosen the Mohawk 600 in caliber .308 Winchester as his favorite deer rifle. Here's a guy who could choose any rifle in the Remington line, but Dietz prefers the light, handy Mohawk 600. On his recommendation, I got one from the factory and fitted it with a Lyman 2½× scope and Lyman mounts (very few mounts are made for this short action). After shooting this little carbine awhile I can see what Dick Dietz means. It's far from pretty, but it sure is a useful little rifle, with power aplenty in .308 to bag anything in North America, although I consider it a bit light for the big bears in Alaska. I can't tell you what it costs because Remington doesn't set a retail price on the Mohawk. You'll find it at K-Mart and similar stores.

Sturm, Ruger's Model 77 rifle is a recent model which incorporates the design genius of the firm's founding father, Bill

Ruger, with classic appearance. All Ruger firearms evidence striking design, and all are engineered to be sold at reasonable prices. The Model 77, for example, is competitive with the biggest-selling bolt-action, Remington's 700. Yet the Ruger has some features not found in other rifles.

One example is the classic stock—the opposite of the style popularized by Roy Weatherby and often referred to as the California school of stock design. Classic features a combination of straight lines and curves, and employs no Monte Carlo, flared grip, rolled-over comb, or slanted forend tip.

The Monte Carlo is that little drop you see at the rear of the top line, just ahead of the top of the butt plate. The usual justification given for the Monte Carlo is that it helps get the stock high enough for scope sighting. This is not true. The elevation of a shooter's face is governed by the height of the comb of the stock (the top line), and the nose or front end of the comb cannot be higher than will clear the bolt on a bolt-action rifle. Thus the governing factor for this dimension is the bolt itself. It is also interesting to note that the thickness of the comb's nose will raise or lower your face. Translating this into stock-design language, it means you also do not need a cheekpiece; the same thing can be accomplished by making the comb wider.

This is what Ruger has done with his Model 77—no Monte Carlo and no cheekpiece. Yet the rifle is just as functional with a scope as the Weatherby itself. Moreover, Ruger has also eliminated that "forward-slanting cheekpiece" which is supposed to let the rifle slip away from you in recoil. This is pure bunk. When a rifle recoils, your head goes right along with the rest of you. If it slips away from the stock you're going to be sorry when it catches up, because it'll whack you sharply in the jaw.

The elimination of these nonfunctional frills allows a bit less costly manufacture, since the necessity of sanding is removed. The Ruger 77 is a superb rifle, very high in manufacturing quality and outstanding in its design. It's available in most any caliber imaginable. Remington in 1978 began production of a "classic" version of its Model 700. Closely paralleling the Ruger pattern just described, the new model is also available in popular calibers.

Savage expanded its product line shortly after World War II with a sound, new bolt-action design. The initial production of these rifles was pretty ugly, but the company kept improving them, and present Savage Model 110 series rifles are not bad-

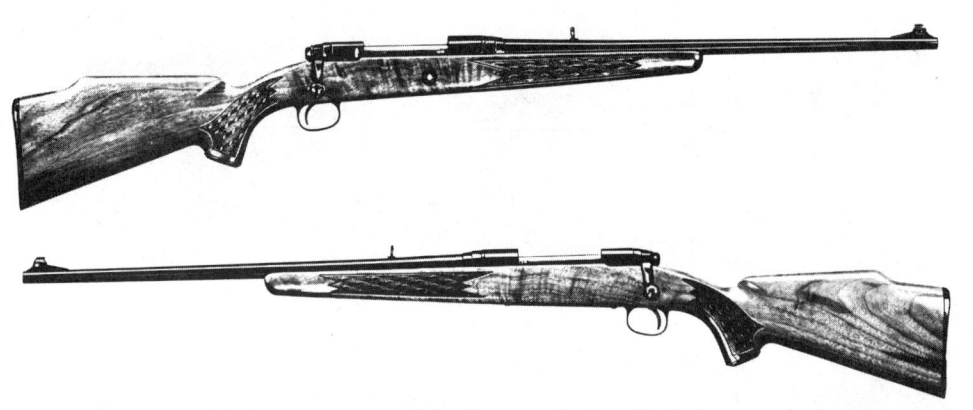

Right- and left-hand versions of the Savage Model 110 high-power bolt-action rifle. Savage was the first company to offer a standard left-hand rifle.

looking rifles that shoot quite well. A few years after the rifle was announced, Savage began marketing a left-hand version. It was the first left-hand action made by one of the large producers of American firearms, and the move has been copied by many others since that time.

Savage first claimed that 10 percent of all Americans were left-handed, but I have since seen figures all the way up to 25 percent. The Savage move to aid "lefty" pulled its whole Model 110 line along.

I've been doing quite a bit of shooting with a Savage Model 111 chambered for the 7×57mm Mauser, one of the finest cartridges to ever come along. This rifle is very impressive. It has a 22-inch barrel, which I think is long enough for most any hunting rifle, and it has the Savage detachable box magazine, which is handy—much handier, in my opinion, than a hinged floorplate. Both will let you empty the rifle quickly, but the detachable magazine is a lot neater and it has the added advantage that you can carry a spare magazine loaded in your pocket. That eliminates loose cartridges, makes reloading faster, and is a much tidier way to reload.

Savage also produces the inexpensive Model 340 chambered for the .30/30, .22 Hornet, .222, and .223. In .30/30, it is a suitable deer rifle, if you want a bolt-action. It must be said that the 340 is just what it is supposed to be—a low-cost, no-frills rifle. It shouldn't be compared with other bolt-action rifles, but it will be found adequate for the purpose. The company also provides, at slight additional cost, a scope mount.

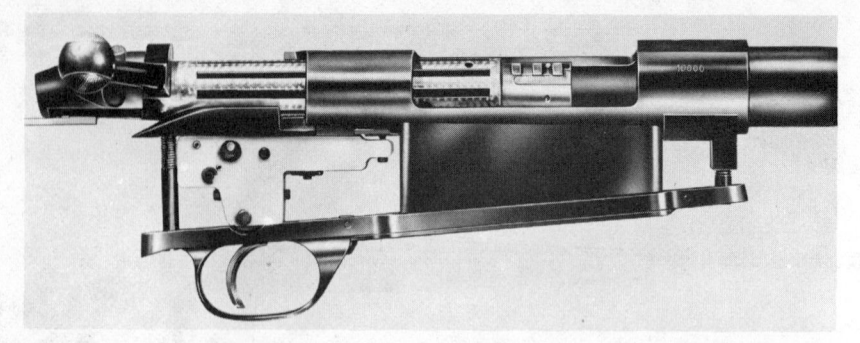

Weatherby's Mark V action is made to handle the line of Weatherby Magnum cartridges up to and including the monstrous .460 Weatherby Magnum, the most powerful shoulder-rifle cartridge in the world. Note that the bolt body is larger than the diameter of the locking lugs, which results in an exceptionally smooth action since the receiver is not slotted for the lugs.

Roy Weatherby began his company with Mauser actions made by Fabrique Nationale in Liège, Belgium. In 1954 he started to design his own action. It was finally completed in 1958 and production got underway in 1959. The first actions were made in California, and production tooling was begun in Germany by J.P. Sauer & Sohn. By the late 1960s German production was too expensive and the manufacture was removed to Nagoya, Japan, where it remains. Many fine rifles and shotguns are being produced in Japan today, including the elegant Winchester Model 101 over/under shotgun.

Weatherby's Mark V action is a rather massive affair, but it is used for cartridges up to and including the whopping .478 Weatherby Magnum that has shoved the .600 Nitro Express off its perch as the world's most powerful shoulder-gun cartridge. You need a lot of beef to hold these cartridges inside the rifle. Weatherby has advertised his action as the "World's Strongest." Remington had used the same words for years with respect to its Model 721 and 722. Just which action is the strongest is unimportant, since both are certainly strong enough. I don't know that anyone really knows, or cares, anyway. The advertised claims and counterclaims were dropped after about a year.

Weatherby elected to try to make his bolt action as smooth as possible. It is generally accepted that a Mauser bolt shakes from side to side when it's fully withdrawn like a dog wagging its head. Its ride back and forth makes you think of a subway car on a bad track. But it must be said that Mauser bolts go back together again. One of the things that makes most bolts sloppy (if that's the right word) is that the receiver must have two long grooves cut on either side for the locking lugs to ride back and forth. Weatherby eliminated these grooves completely by making his bolt oversize, and cutting nine small locking lugs in the front which are of smaller overall diameter than the bolt body. The result is that his action is bored out to the round shape of the bolt body and the only cuts are those necessary for ejection, trigger, and magazine.

The nine lugs are placed in rows of three each, as opposed to the two massive lugs opposite each other in actions like the Mauser, Winchester 70, Remington 700, etc. The latter require a bolt-handle lift of 90 degrees before the bolt can be withdrawn after unlocking. The Weatherby needs a shorter lift—actually 56 degrees—because of the spacing of these lugs. A shorter lift means faster action when all other things are equal, but they are not equal because the shorter lift of the Weatherby means that cocking and extraction must now be performed in a shorter arc. Similarly, less camming is available to close the bolt on a cartridge. These are minor inconveniences of little importance to the average hunter, but they are a fact of the design. Other bolts with multiple locking lugs are on the market too; some of these are probably based on the success Weatherby has enjoyed with his Mark V action. The most prominent of these is the rear-lugged remington Model 788, which also has nine lugs in three banks of three lugs. Other rotating-bolt rifles employing multiple lugs are found in a number of pump and autoloading actions.

Weatherby has recently produced another rifle, called the Vanguard, which he uses for standard chamberings. The Weatherby philosophy is that the proprietary cartridges (the "Weatherby Magnums") are only for the Weatherby Mark V rifle, not the Vanguard; the latter action was developed to allow the company to market rifles in conventional chamberings.

The Vanguard has a pretty conventional action. It's a two-lugged affair quite like other conventional actions. The Vanguard does have many typical Weatherby features, such as adjustable trigger, hinged floorplate, and American walnut stock with hand-cut checkering. While the Mark V rifle is available in a left-hand version, the Vanguard is not.

I've been doing a good deal of shooting with a Mark V rifle in .340 Weatherby Magnum and with a Vanguard in .30/06. Both rifles are equipped with Weatherby 3-9× Premier scopes. The

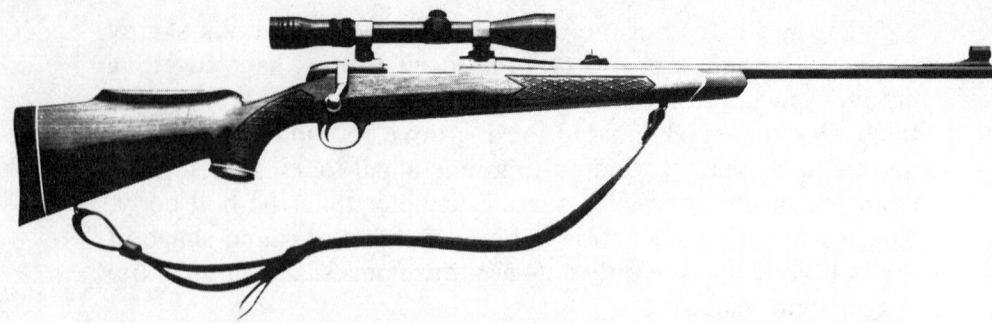

Ithaca imports a rifle under its brand that is made in England by BSA (Birmingham Small Arms, a company which also makes motorcycles and bicycles). The company also imports another bolt-action made in Finland and known as the Ithaca-LSA.

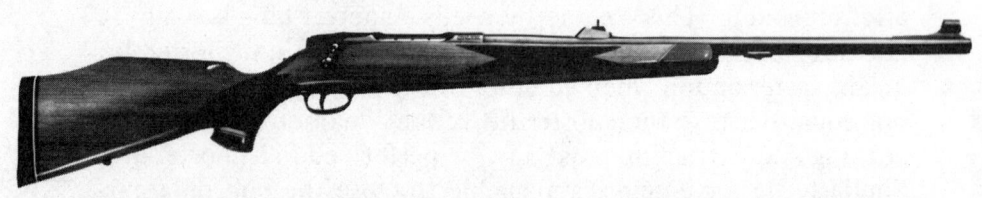

The Colt Sauer, made for Colt by Sauer & Sohn in Germany, is an exceptionally streamlined rifle and has a most unusual locking-lug system. Shown is the magnum model with barrel heavy enough for the .458 Winchester Magnum.

.340, of course, is a powerhouse that belts the hell out of you when shooting from the bench. But it's the most powerful of a number of cartridges in this class (.338 Winchester Magnum and 8mm Remington Magnum) and therefore is fun to pound away at long range. This rifle really excels at ranges out to 500 yards. These are excellent rifles in all respects. If you like their styling, if their cartridges appeal to you, and if you can spend a little more, I have no reluctance whatever in recommending Weatherby's rifles.

The Sako rifle is a popular action that has been in this country for many years, having been imported from Finland by Firearms International, Garcia, and now Stoeger. It is to be hoped that the distribution will settle down and that Stoeger will keep it. The Sako is a fine rifle, made in several action sizes. It has a more or less conventional two-lugged bolt action, a hinged floorplate, and dovetail scope bases machined right into the receiver. Another and fairly similar-appearing Finnish import is marketed by Ithaca. This is the LSA-55, with a squarish receiver contour which also has an integral dovetail. You can either buy bases that will fit these rifles from makers such as Redfield, or you can get them from the importer to fit the dovetails. The LSA-55 has a removable magazine box.

A most unusual rifle is the Colt Sauer bolt-action available in standard and magnum styles. It is made in West Germany by Sauer & Sohn. The rifle's most unusual feature is its locking lugs, which consist of three rather small flaps which are extended into lug recesses in the receiver when the handle is closed. When the bolt is raised, these flaps are tucked in and the bolt becomes a cylinder. Since the lugs are near the rear of the bolt and lock into the receiver at the rear ring, it follows that the hole the bolt rides in is a perfect cylinder without the lug raceways. The result is a snug bolt movement that's entirely free of the "Mauser wobble." The Colt also employs a removable box magazine, although the box is a single-row style as opposed to the staggered box used by Mauser and most other rifles. This reduces the magazine capacity, which might be a factor in your buying decision. Using three lugs, the Colt has a bolt lift similar to that of the Weatherby Mark V and Remington 788—about 55 degrees. One of the more unusual features of this Colt Sauer is its streamlining, which swoops out metal in great chunks of the receiver. You may like this or not; it's a matter of personal taste. The stock is French walnut, the best stock wood available for a gunstock, and the Colt is a very well made rifle that shoots as good as it's made. The styling is a bit unusual, departing from both the classic and the California school.

Ever since 1967 I've been shooting a prototype of a new bolt-action that may not ever be marketed. It appeared for a while that it would, but now I'm beginning to have my doubts. I can't name the maker except to say that he's a major producer of sporting firearms. The action is unique in that it uses a locking-lug system of interrupted threads. This was used earlier by Charles Newton in the rifle bearing his name before World War I, so there's nothing new about it. The system is an excellent one in all respects. An interrupted-thread locking-lug system could be compared to machining a buttress thread (with square rear surface, angled front) on the front end of a bolt, then machining off the top and bottom just as it's done with a conventional bolt. The result is an "interrupted" thread, the interrupter being that part cut away. Then the same thread is cut in female version inside the receiver so the thread lugs turn into the recesses. Similar locking has been used for years in artillery to secure the breech against firing such huge projectiles as the awesome 16-inch naval shells.

This particular prototype was built in .30/06 caliber; the barreled action was handed to me with instructions to make a rifle out of it the way I thought it should be done. Since I've been out of the active gunmaking business for some years, I turned the project over to Al Biesen, one of the country's top gunmakers for more years than he probably wants to remember. Biesen and I collaborated on the design of metal and wood, and he did the work. The result is a gem of a rifle that shoots into ½ inch at 100 yards with my hunting load, using a 180-grain Nosler partition jacketed bullet. I've killed deer, both whitetails and muley, several trophy caribou, and two arctic wolves with it. I used to mount a Redfield 2-7× scope but have switched to a fixed-power 4× Redfield Widefield.

I hope this rifle gets on the market, because I think there's a place for it. Unfortunately I'm afraid it never will.

Though the credit for the first really successful bolt-action rifle belongs to Peter Paul Mauser, development of the bolt-action *sporting* rifle to its present high state of excellence is strictly American. That's true despite the fact that London's famous gunmakers, such as Holland & Holland, Westley Richards, John Rigby, and others well known for their fabulous work on shotguns, also made bolt-action rifles. They made these on commercial Mauser bolt actions obtained from Germany before World War I. Great as the English shotgun is, English bolt-action rifles (which they call magazine rifles) don't hold a candle to ours. In fact, many of them try to copy some of our styling. This sometimes goes to the point of being ridiculous, an example being the British attempt at the flamboyant styling. Any given gunmaker ought to stick to what he knows best.

The styling given rifle stocks over the years has varied considerably. Early in the bolt-action's history, the open iron sight was used primarily. Then the peep or aperture sight became fairly popular. And then the scope began to appear on American rifles by the tens of thousands. Early rifle stocks had considerably more drop than today's because the line of sight is much lower with iron sights than with a scope. That means your head should be positioned lower. Or, to put it the other way, when a scope is used, your stock ought to be higher (less drop). Since a stock

There is a style of bolt-action stock known as the "Mannlicher"; the wood runs clear to the muzzle. The name comes from the old Mannlicher-Schoenauer rifle, a famous sporting and military rifle of years gone by. This is a current Steyr-Mannlicher Model M, the newest of the famous line. The fine action system dates to around 1900.

at the comb can only be as high as the open bolt will allow, that becomes the upper limit. Using the axis of the bore as a center line, the drop from center line to stock comb is a given dimension, and the additional drop at the heel should not be more than another ½ to ⅝ inch. There are several reasons for this, the most important being that your butt should be as close to the center line as possible because that will be the pivot point for recoil. The lower the pivot point, the more the rifle will roll up in recoil. And the more it rises, the harder it's going to kick. This is one of the prime reasons the classic stock is preferred by so many.

Bolt-action rifle stocks evolved over the years as shooters and shooting conditions changed. The move from iron sights to scopes was a drastic change, while other changes were much more subtle. The requirements of use have always dictated rifle and gun design.

The advantages of a bolt-action are several. They should be carefully calculated in your choice of a rifle but may not in themselves be decisive. A bolt is the strongest breech action (with the possible exception of a modern single-shot), which means you can handle more powerful cartridges in a bolt than in other types. Such a point becomes moot if your choice is a .30/06, however.

In a rifle correctly tuned, the bolt action will probably deliver slightly better accuracy than other actions. It also can offer a better trigger pull, which is essential to good accuracy. Its enormous camming power is one of the biggest advantages of the bolt, because it gives you the ability to chamber, or extract, sticky and stubborn cartridges that would jam another type of rifle.

An "advantage" often credited to the bolt-action is that it is more accurate because it has a one-piece stock. This isn't true. *Some* bolts are more accurate, but not because they have a one-piece stock. Not at all. In fact, I think I've fired enough rifles as they come out of the box to make a good case for two-piece-stock rifles over the average bolt-action. I've gotten to the point where I very rarely fire any bolt just as you buy it because many of them need some attention for them to perform at their best (see Chapter 15).

If a bolt-action has any disadvantage it would be that it is slower to operate than other types when it comes to repeat shots. It might be mentioned also that is is particularly hard for a lefty to handle a bolt unless it's a left-handed action.

Some of the things you may want to try if you don't think your bolt-action is performing to a standard you expect are quite simple to do. The trigger pull is quite likely the most important. It should be around 3 to 4 pounds in weight and free of any creep or follow-through. In most rifles, this can be adjusted simply by following the directions that come with the rifle. On others, you'll have to remove the stock and work on the trigger itself. Some, like the Remington 788, have no adjustment, and the only solution is to replace the unit with a trigger like the Canjar.

The next thing to do is make sure the guard screws are tight. This is most important and is something that should be checked often, because changes in the weather make the wood swell and shrink with resultant differences in bedding tension.

7

The Pump-Action

Pump-actions are sometimes called slide actions and in the past were often called trombone actions, after the action of a slide trombone. By whatever name, they are fast to operate and have long been popular. This popularity, however, is more evident in shotguns than in rifles.

The first practical and popular pump-action shotgun was the Winchester Model 1893, an invention of John M. Browning. The gun was improved and modified in 1897 and redesignated the Model 97. It was a very popular gun, largely because it arrived at a time when game was plentiful and market hunting was pretty much at its peak. Market gunners took to the 97 like a duck to water.

Pump-action .22 rifles were quite the rage at one time and were often seen at shooting galleries, which used to be one of the most popular events at carnivals. Among those early favorites were such as the Winchester Model 1890, 1906, 61 and 62. Nearly every major company made a .22 pump rifle but only Remington made a high-power pump.

Remington's high-power pump rifle was the Pedersen-designed Model 14, introduced in 1912. It was improved in 1935 and redesignated the Model 141. It was dropped in 1950 in favor of the present Model 760. Actually the 141 never came back after the war; it proved too costly to manufacture and Remington undertook a massive retooling and reengineering program.

J. D. Pedersen was a prolific gun inventor. Had he lived in another time his name would be well known today, but he was a contemporary of John Browning and nobody could shine in his

Remington's Model 760 BDL deluxe, a centerfire pump-action rifle available in some fine deer cartridges. The model succeeded Remington's older Models 14 and Model 141, which were favorite deer rifles in the Northeast's pucker-brush from about 1912 until World War II when they were discontinued.

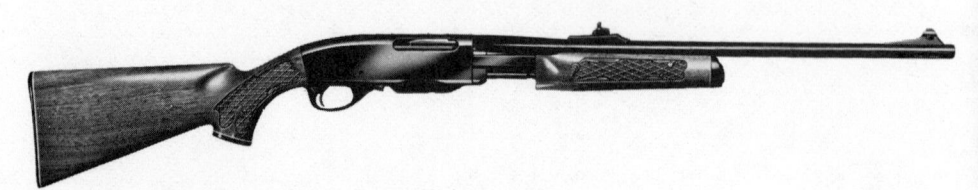

The same Remington Model 760 pump in standard version. The list of available deer cartridges in this popular rifle includes 6mm Remington, .243 Winchester, .308 Winchester, .270 Winchester, and .30/06. A short-barreled carbine version is also available.

shadow. Pedersen invented Remington's first pump shotgun, the Model 10, and the company's .22 pump rifles too. His Model 14 high-powered rifle was one of his most important, and it began a trend that has been virtually a Remington exclusive since 1912 —the pump-action deer rifle.

The Model 14 was strictly a deer rifle. It was chambered for those Remington rimless cartridges meant to compete with Winchester's .25/35, .30/30, and .32 Special. Remington's comparable cartridges were the .25, .30, and .32 Remington. Remington added the .35 Remington, today's only survivor, which became the most popular of the line.

A pump-action rifle—or shotgun—is very fast-operating. It can often be worked faster than an autoloader (for what that's worth). All the functions of the operating cycle except firing are performed by stroking the pump handle back and forth. The first motion is to unlock the action. Remington's Model 14 employed a lock where the rear of the bolt was forced up and into a recess in the receiver. Further rearward movement of the operating handle extracts and ejects the fired cartridge. It also forces the hammer down into cocked position, and it releases a cartridge

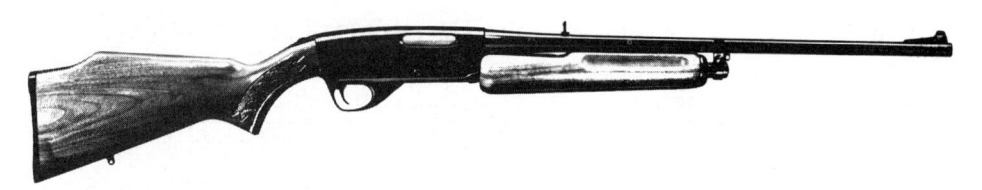

The Savage Model 170 is listed as a "dependable, rapid-fire rifle at a modest price." It's no beauty, but it's just what it claims to be, and it's available in two of the most popular chamberings of all time, the .30/30 Winchester and .35 Remington.

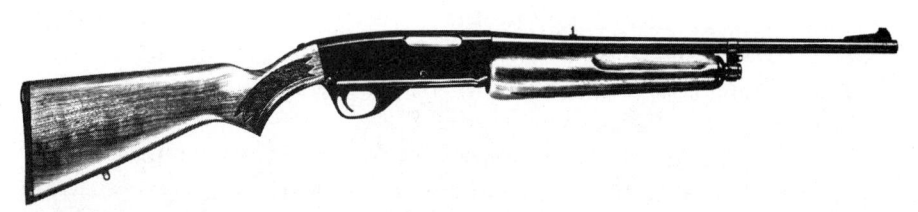

The Savage 170 in carbine form. "Carbine" simply means short-barreled, and it's a hangover from scabbard days in the military. A handy, fast rifle for use in the brush.

lying in the magazine tube so it can move back onto the carrier.

Once the empty is ejected from the rifle, the pump operation moves the carrier up to position the new cartridge for feeding. Forward movement of the handle drives the new cartridge into the chamber and relocks the action ready to be fired again. A small part called the "action slide lock" keeps the action closed until it is fired or until the action slide release is pushed. This is necessary; otherwise the hand on the operating handle might urge the handle rearward and unlock the action.

The Model 14, and the Model 141 which replaced it in 1935, was one of the most popular rifles in the wooded sections of America for many years, especially in .35 Remington caliber. The rifle suffered from two major faults in the years after World War II, however: it could not handle a cartridge more powerful than .35 Remington and it was too expensive to manufacture. Machine tools and manufacturing methods had been improved considerably between its introduction in 1912 and the late 1940s.

In 1952 Remington introduced a vastly different high-power pump-action rifle to replace the 141. Designated the Model 760, the new rifle had a rotary locking bolt, which made it similar to the Mauser, since any action using a rotary bolt, or turn bolt, is by definition a takeoff on the bolt action. Remington also replaced the old tubular magazine with a removable box magazine. It was a big surprise at the time when the rifle was introduced in the powerful .30/06 caliber.

I very well remember the first 760 I ever saw. At the time I was a gunmaker in upstate New York and a guy dragged in his new 760 along with a scope and mount. He wanted me to mount the scope. My attitude was that it was pretty silly to put a scope on this rifle because no pump-action could be accurate enough to use a scope. But I mounted it anyway and tried a few shots to verify the sighting. The rifle shot amazingly well, and I became a believer. As I remember, the 100-yard group was around 1¼ inches.

Today's 760 is advanced somewhat from the first versions and the model is available in a wide choice of cartridges. It is an excellent deer rifle and the choice of many pump-action shotgunners.

A relative newcomer to the ranks of high-power pump-action rifles is the Savage Model 170. Savage calls this rifle a "dependable, rapid-fire rifle at a modest price." It is that all right. The 170, available in rifle style with 22-inch barrel or carbine with 18½-inch barrel, is chambered for either .30/30 or .35 Remington, the two most popular deer-rifle cartridges of all time.

The 170 is not a gun lover's rifle. It's too crude for that, but it is an honest rifle selling at a low price that will most certainly get the job done.

The chief advantage of a pump-action rifle is its speed of action resulting in fast repeat shots. It is simple to use for either a right- or left-handed shooter; it's only necessary to reverse the safety on the Remington. The Savage has a top tang safety that works from either side like a double shotgun's. Any disadvantage to a pump is more difficult to pinpoint. Some of them rattle a bit, some do not. Needless to say, no hunting rifle should be noisy.

I have never hunted with a pump-action rifle, although I have been in the company of hunters who have used them. The only reason is that I'm not especially turned on by the pump, which is just a personal feeling. But I have no hesitation whatever in recommending a pump to any deer hunter, either the Remington or Savage according to caliber choice and pocketbook.

8

The Autoloader

Autoloading guns and rifles are often called "automatics." The word is incorrectly used, but it's hard to fight the uphill battle against it. "Self-loading" and "semiautomatic" are correct words for the system, and what they mean is that all the operational steps of firing firearms are performed by the forces generated within the gun except one—firing. (Those operational steps are firing, unlocking, extraction, ejection, feeding, cocking, and locking. Each must be performed for every shot fired by any firearm.)

There are two principal forces employed in autoloading firearms: recoil and gas. A recoil-operated gun is one in which the kick of firing is harnessed to activate the action. To visualize how recoil operation works, make a mental picture of a lever-action Winchester Model 94 with its lever fastened to a fixed object. Fire the rifle and it will kick or recoil in such a way that the gun jerks away from the fastened lever. The result will be that all the operations which occur when the lever is thrown down are performed.

Now place a heavy spring behind the butt and fire the rifle again. This time it will store energy in the spring, which will force the gun forward again and complete the operation. The rifle will now be reloaded, cocked, and ready to fire. If we added a means of tripping the trigger after closing the lever it would also fire, and we would have a machine gun, or truly "automatic" operation. Recoil operation is just that simple—except that you can't tie your rifle to a fixed object when you want to fire it, so gun designers have figured how to allow the barrel to recoil *within the gun*. And that's one definition of a recoil-operated firearm: its barrel moves.

Some examples of recoil-operated guns are the Colt .45 automatic pistol, the Browning machine guns in .30, .50, and 37mm caliber, the Remington Model 8 and Model 81 rifles, and, of course, the famous Browning Auto-5 shotgun. Sir Hiram Maxim invented recoil operation, and John Browning put it on the map.

Gas operation is said to have originated when John Browning was observing another shooter on the range. He noted how the muzzle blast moved the nearby vegetation and reasoned that this force could be utilized to operate an action. So he altered an old Winchester lever-action rifle by placing a cup over the muzzle with a small hole for the bullet to pass through. Then the cup was connected by means of rods to the lever. When the rifle was fired, the gas blew the cup away and that force operated the action via the rods and lever. Soon after he perfected a machine gun that was made by Colt and used in the Spanish-American War and the famous BAR rifle (Model 1918) of World War I.

Gas operation is the virtual standard today among rifles, for a very good reason which we'll come to in a few moments. There is another autoloading system used in low-powered guns known as "blowback." This differs in two important respects: the barrel does not move and there is no positive mechanical lock. Blowback is employed today only in .22 rifles and a few low-powered autoloading pistols. It is not suited to any high-power rifle.

A lot of people dislike auto rifles (and guns) because they think they are merely "shooting machines" and are not sporting. This is a matter of personal judgment. I have a great respect for these guns and an interest in how they work.

The first major popular autoloading sporting rifle in high-power calibers was the Remington Model 8, based on Browning patents and introduced in 1906. It was updated in 1936 and designated the Model 81, finally being dropped in 1950 in favor of a brand-new gas-operated rifle.

The Model 8 was a recoil-operated rifle. Its barrel moved all the way to the rear like the Browning Auto-5 shotgun's. The barrel was enclosed in a jacket and a long-recoil spring was placed between barrel and jacket. Chambered for the same cartridges

In 1906 Remington first marketed an autoloading high-power rifle based on a John Browning design; it was known as the Model 8 and was most famous in .35 Remington caliber. It was too costly to manufacture after World War II, and the company replaced it with this present Model 742, shown here in standard grade. These rifles are gas-operated and capable of fine accuracy. Available calibers include several excellent deer-rifle choices, among them the popular .30/06.

as the Model 14 pump rifle, the Model 8 was most popular in .35 Remington caliber.

I can remember long ago when hunting in New York's Adirondacks near Gui Pond that a local lad used to hunt the same mountains with a Model 8 Remington. The lad was memorable because he had only one arm and wore a red sweatshirt. The way he negotiated those mountains was something to see; most hunters needed two arms for climbing and a third for carrying a rifle, but this guy did everything with one. How he got into action with that rifle I don't know, because I never saw him shoot, but he surely did on occasion.

Like the pump rifle, the high-power autoloader was strictly a Remington proposition until after World War II. Then the competition began. Remington adopted a new rifle in 1955 known as the Model 740, which was changed a few years later to correct some deficiencies and produce better accuracy. The present Model 742 is a fine shooting rifle. It is gas-operated, as are all the rest that are on today's market. The locking system is a rotary bolt like that on the pump-action Model 760; locking lugs on both rifles are interrupted threads. This is a very powerful lockup and permits the use of high-power, high-pressure cartridges. The fact is that the Remington 760 and 742 are very close in looks, appearance, and operation. The main difference is that one is operated by the shooter's arm while the other is worked by gas bled from the barrel.

In the modern gas rifle, a tiny amount of gas is allowed to bleed from the barrel after the bullet has passed. Contrary to some notions, this amount is insufficient to rob any of the propellant force from driving the bullet. There is no difference

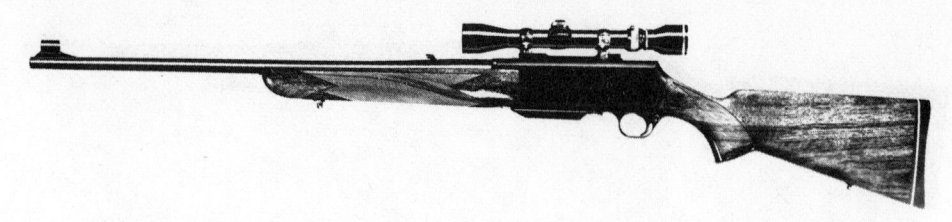

You would expect an autoloading rifle from the company that bears the name of the man who put autoloaders on the market. This is the Browning BAR (Browning Automatic Rifle); it is available in several popular chamberings including several magnums. Its "soft" recoil, resulting from the gas system of operation, makes it comfortable to shoot even in some whopping calibers.

Winchester briefly marketed the Model 100 gas-operated rifle, in .243 and .308 calibers. It did not achieve sales goals and was dropped.

whatever in the velocity of a given cartridge from a gas-operated auto and a solid-breech rifle. The gas thus diverted pours into a small cylinder under the barrel, where it shoves a piston back to operate the action—which is why, if you put a pump handle on that piston rod, you'd have a pump-action rifle!

It will be evident that when the gas moves the piston it does so in a violent and fast manner. This is what makes the design of an autoloading rifle a tough proposition. The rifle must be light enough to carry all day in the deer woods, and its operation cannot be so violent that it tears the rim out of a cartridge instead of extracting the fired case. This means that the bolt must be slowly (comparatively) accelerated to the speed of the operating rod by a camming action. It's a simple matter to design a rifle that will operate, but quite another thing to make one that will work properly and keep on working.

One of the most interesting autoloading rifles on today's market is the light Ruger 44 in .44 Magnum caliber. This little carbine weighs only 5¾ pounds, has an 18½ inch barrel, and is but 36¾ inches long overall. It's one of the fastest handling of all rifles and was designed to be a 100-yard deer rifle. This is cer-

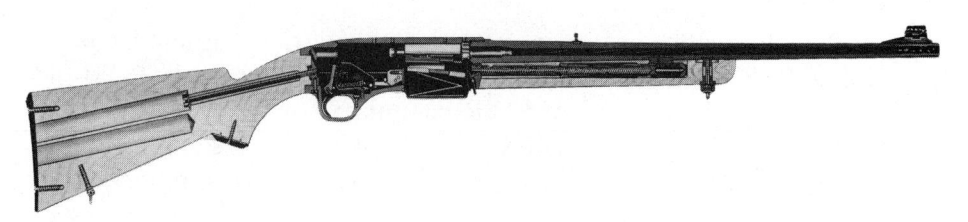

A schematic drawing of the Winchester Model 100 operational system, which was defined as a "metering" system; it allowed a small spurt of gas to enter the cylinder under the barrel and then closed off the supply.

tainly one of the most useful woods rifles to come along in years and has become quite popular.

Browning has added an autoloading high-power rifle to its line in some potent chamberings, including the 7mm Remington Magnum and .300 Winchester Magnum. It is also available in some smaller calibers like the .30/06 and .243. My BAR, as the rifle is called, is in .388 Winchester Magnum, a caliber which has been dropped. This rifle shoots with very good accuracy and is a great deal pleasanter to shoot than a bolt-action. This is one of the big bonuses you get with a gas gun—lower recoil. The reason is that when it's fired, the operating parts are set in motion and are still in motion when you begin to feel the kick. Thus you feel only part of the kick in the beginning, but the remainder comes along a fraction of a second later. The result is that while you still get the same total amount of recoil, you get it over a slightly longer period of time, and it doesn't hurt nearly as much. In fact, the .338 BAR is really fun to shoot, and that's something I can't say about the bolt-action.

During the period 1960 to 1964, Winchester marketed the Model 100 autoloader in .243 and .308 caliber. It also was briefly available in .284 Winchester caliber. This rifle, along with the lever-action Model 88 available in the same calibers, never excited the market. I suspect the chief reason was that its accuracy wasn't all that much, due primarily to the lashup that held the metal to the wood. Using a one-piece stock, the Model 100's receiver hooked into a plug that was attached to the stock, then the barrel was fastened to the stock's forend. The result wasn't very satisfactory from an accuracy viewpoint, and given the calibers the rifle was chambered for, it failed to penetrate the market in sufficient numbers to keep the gun alive.

Harrington & Richardson, which did most of the engineering

on the M-14 rifle, has been manufacturing a fine autoloader in .243 and .308 calibers for a number of years. President C. Edward "Ted" Rowe, Jr., of H&R has taken a number of trophy heads with one of these rifles in .243 caliber. The sample rifle I have in .243 delivers fine accuracy and can be recommended highly.

There are a number of other autoloading rifles on the market. Some of them so much resemble military assault rifles that I refuse to consider them sporting firearms. Others are chambered for that weak pipsqueak the .30/M1 Carbine, which is not suitable for deer hunting. None of them are of sufficient importance to list.

Every semiautomatic firearm has to provide a means of disconnecting the trigger after firing so the gun can be recocked. Failure to disconnect simply means the gun won't be cocked; it won't render it fully automatic. Various methods of achieving this disconnect are in use, although the most common is probably that used in the Browning Auto-5 shotgun. The method was invented by John Browning for the Auto-5, which was patented in 1900.

Autoloading rifles are sometimes longer through the action than some other types, which results in an overly long rifle. And some of them do not balance as well as they might. It should be noted that Pennsylvania as well as the Canadian provinces do not allow hunting with any autoloading firearm.

I've always felt the main objection to an autoloader is that it tends to make a shooter think he can rely on the cartridges in reserve rather than making the first shot count. This does happen, and it is self-defeating. There's nothing wrong with the auto rifle (or shotgun), it's the way it's used. If an auto is your choice for whatever reason, use it with the thought in mind that you have only the one shot in the chamber. You'll kill more deer than if you try to blast down the woods.

9

Custom Deer Rifles

The most important part of any discussion of custom rifles is to define the term itself. "Custom" implies that the rifle is made specifically for one person, meaning that the stock is tailored to be a perfect fit to that person. When he throws it to his shoulder, even with closed eyes, it will point at the target. Moreover, the man for whom the rifle was made, and who paid the bill, will probably have asked for certain embellishments which will further personalize the finished product. These may take the form of initials engraved on a small plate in the stock, possibly a touch of engraving on the metal, a checkering pattern chosen by him, and perhaps certain alterations to the triggerguard, floorplate, safety, or other metal parts.

But the the word "custom" has been abused; it is used improperly at least 90 percent of the time. It has come to the point where any rifle stock not turned out by one of the major factories as a commercial production item is called "custom." Some of this work is fairly good; most of it is absolute trash. The hell of it is that owners get tired of these guns sooner or later and put them up for sale. Often the poor unsuspecting buyer is snowed by the words "custom rifle" and he pays many times what the thing is really worth. Just the other day a guy tried to swap one of these rifles to me that was of average quality but was by no stretch of the imagination a custom rifle. Not by my definition.

The average guy is better off with a rifle produced by one of the major factories than he is with something branded "custom"

A closeup of grip checkering as performed by Phil Pilkington of Enid, Okla. The rifle is a 1909 Argentine Mauser barreled for the 6mm Remington cartridge. Workmanship of this quality deserves the use of the word "custom."

but which is really a piece of crap. Most—I'd say at least 95 percent—of the stuff being peddled as "custom" is worth far less money than a commercial rifle. And the latter has a better and more realistic resale value.

This average rifle we're talking about is generally a German Mauser military rifle that has been rebarreled to either a standard or wildcat cartridge. Most likely, whoever installed the barrel never marked it with the correct caliber designation. The barrel might or might not be a decent job. Any analysis of its quality is beyond the casual observer, and chances are that its contour is ugly.

Then this average rifle is polished on a buffing wheel, which "breaks" every square corner and "pulls" every hole and all the lettering so it looks awful. The bolt handle is altered by someone who hasn't the slightest idea what a proper shape ought to be. The trigger is probably diddled with until it's unsafe, or maybe the guy had sense enough to buy a Canjar or one of the other replacement triggers.

But the worst part, the most visible part, comes when someone tries to stick the metal into a piece of wood. This is often

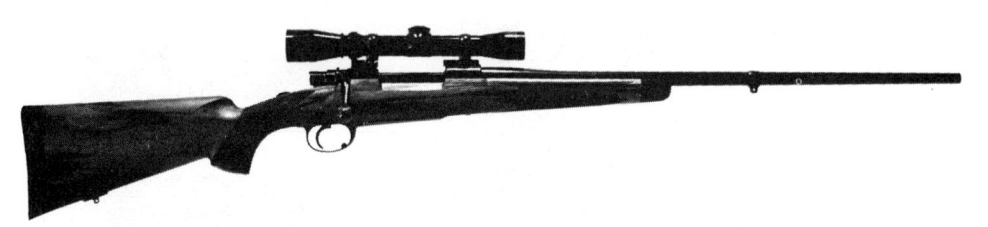

Another Phil Pilkington product, a Mauser action barreled for the .300 Winchester Magnum. A rifle of this quality is made to order for a particular person and thus is truly a custom product.

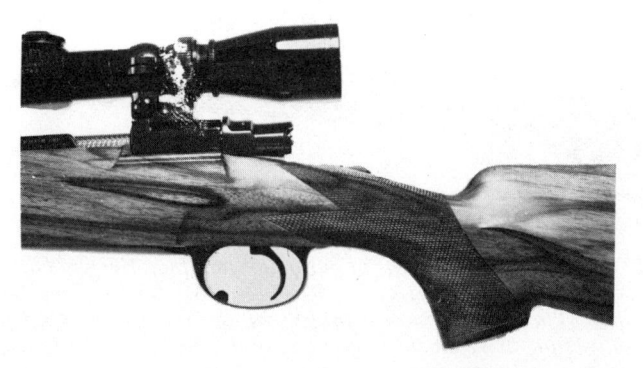

This closeup of the left side of the Pilkington-Mauser .300 Winchester Magnum shows the fine checkering and the excellent metalsmithing, which includes a tang safety. Note the way the wood is shaped under the bolt stop (below the rear scope base).

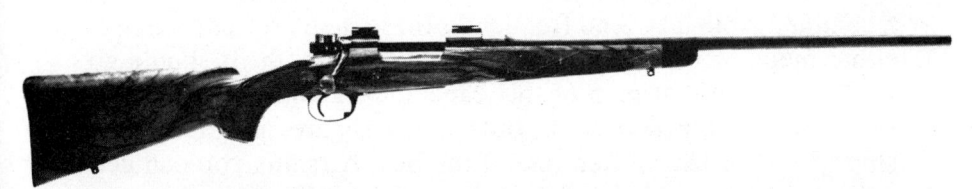

Woodwork by Phil Pilkington, metalwork by Ron Lampert. The rifle is a 6mm Remington built on a Mauser action. Stock is an exhibition grade of English walnut from New Zealand. The checkering, too fine even to see in this photo, is 24 lines per inch.

accomplished by buying one of those "inletted blanks" that generally come preshaped. In all truth, this is the best way to proceed, since the guy who does the stocking hasn't the foggiest idea of how to proceed anyway. At least this will keep him within certain guidelines. But the result will be a long way from our definition of a custom rifle.

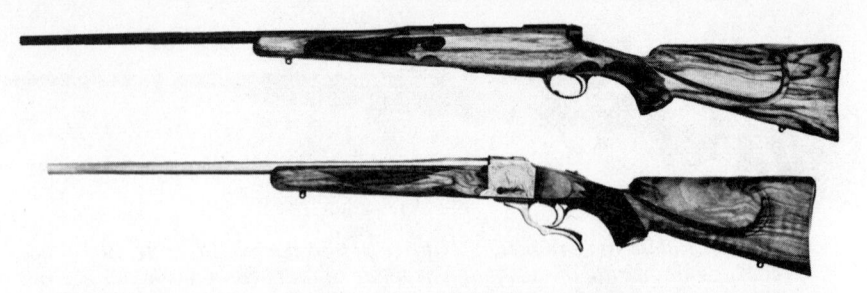

Two handsome rifles stocked by Joe Balickie of Raleigh, N.C. Above is a Winchester Model 70 stocked with as fine a piece of presentation English walnut as you are likely to see. Below is an engraved Ruger Number One single-shot.

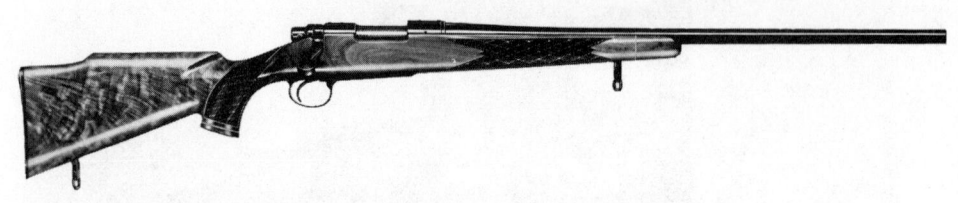

The custom departments of our major gun factories are capable of turning out some fine work too. Here is a Remington Model 700 from Remington's custom shop. The shop has also worked with the U.S. Army's Advanced Marksmanship Unit for years turning out custom rifles for International shooting.

There are a very few men with the artistic flair, the capability of using their hands, the knowledge of tools, the creative expertise, and the experience and knowledge of firearms to turn out a commendable job. And frequently these men are specialists in either metal or wood, although some work in both. It should go without saying that men of this capability ought to be compensated mightily for their work. But they rarely are, and craftsmanship of this order is often one of the best bargains you can get.

On the bright side of real custom work is the fact that there are several young men coming along who are true artisans. One might get the impression that quality custom work is dying out with a few old men. Not so. There are a number of young men coming into the trade with ability—I have to say this—that exceeds most of the older men's.

If your intent is to take the genuine custom rifle route I suggest the best approach is to buy a copy of *Gun Digest* (DBI Books, Inc., 540 Frontage Rd., Northfield, Ill. 60093), an annual which contains the names and addresses of virtually all custom makers and contains many illustrations of custom rifles so you

This English Farquharson single-shot is my product, both metal and wood. The barrel is chambered for a .30/40 Krag necked to .25 caliber, the scope mounts are handmade, and the stock is fine English walnut from France.

can pick the style you like and write to the correct man. Don't expect to get bargain-basement prices; this kind of work commands a high ticket and is well worth it. I would advise against having this kind of work done by some local character who may be recommended by a friend or relative.

Most hunters who are also riflemen know that there really are no rifles on the market that are suited for women. Hunting is predominantly a male sport, but there are women who enjoy it. I ran into a bright young girl in 1975 who had won a $1,000 savings bond as the winner in Marlin's annual hunter-safety contest. Kim came from Wisconsin, where she hunted deer with her grandfather, and I had the pleasure of meeting her and her family in San Diego, where the NRA had its meetings that year. This youngster shot a Model 70 Winchester .338 Magnum, which is a hell of a lot of rifle for a little gal to shoot.

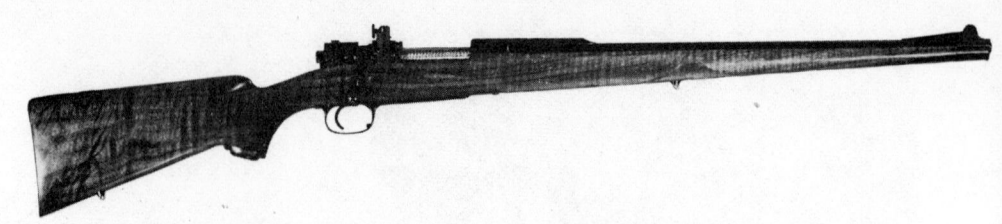

Stocked in the Mannlicher style by Al Biesen of Spokane, Wash., this is a fine Mauser rifle rebarreled for sporting use. Biesen is one of our better-known craftsmen in both metal and wood.

It reminds me of a featherweight gal some years ago who hunted Africa like it was the back pasture. She used a .375 H&H Magnum Winchester Model 70 and bagged everything from elephant down with it. As I recall, the recoil didn't bother her.

In the eighteenth edition of Roy Weatherby's catalog there is a photo of a stunning Italian countess next to an African elephant she had just shot with a .460 Weatherby Magnum. This is the biggest shoulder rifle in the world, and it kicks like hell. If this woman can handle that big a rifle and flatten an elephant with it, then there is little reason a strapping American male can't absorb the recoil of a .30/06 without wincing.

But these are exceptions. The best advice for a woman interested in hunting is to have a custom rifle made for her. There are no factory-made rifles that will really do that job, simply because the market for a woman's deer rifle is too small. No manufacturer could cater to it and make a profit.

A woman should have a rifle stock with shorter dimensions (from trigger to butt) because her arms are shorter; it ought to have a soft pad and should be chambered for a light-recoiling cartridge. Among the best calibers to choose from are ones such as the .243 Winchester and .250/3000 Savage.

Since you're not going to find such a rifle available off the standard racks, you will most likely wind up by patronizing a custom maker. At least you will be served best in this manner, and, while it will cost you some heavy dollars, it will be worth the investment if the woman you're buying it for stays with shooting and hunting.

This is the age of specialization. As I've stated, many of the best gun makers specialize in either wood or metal, and some also specialize in either rifles or shotguns or pistols and revolvers. John Warren, for example, started out as a complete gunsmith by making the total rifle, including engraving. He got so good at the latter, and had so much work, that he had to give up everything but engraving. Alvin White, on the other hand, who may be our best engraver today, has always been an engraver and touches nothing else. Herman Waldron and Tom Burgess are strictly metalsmiths—their work is flawless indeed. Earl Milliron, Maurice Ottmar, and a few others are strictly woodworkers. A few, like Al Biesen, who perhaps is the best known, are complete gunmakers who toil in both metal and wood. Then there are a few small firms that turn out complete rifles, sometimes on an action built by them.

A rather unfortunate trend seems to be developing in the custom field. Phil Pilkington, a young man of exceptional talent in Enid, Okla., has advised me that he is giving up strictly custom work. Phil will complete his present obligations, then will accept no more orders, but will begin to make presentation or exhibition rifles, whichever you wish to call them, and then sell these pieces. I understand several of our other outstanding custom men are following a similar route.

One cannot criticize these men for abandoning a rather tough way to make a living, but what I find disturbing is that some of the most highly skilled artisans seem to be following this procedure. Where will we turn for true custom work if they all take this new route? The usual reasons given for abandoning custom gun work are that it's not a good way to make a living in the gun field and that it's a headache. I've found most things can be a headache—many times, making a living can be a headache no matter what!

Since you will be dealing with an individual, as opposed to an impersonal industrial giant, you should write to several of these men or small firms and make your choice based on what you see and what you like.

You also may alter an existing factory rifle for a woman and have a reasonably good rifle for her. Rifles like the Winchester Model 94 with its small butt area would require a new buttstock with more generous dimensions. Other rifles would simply require shortening the stock; fitting a rubber recoil pad would be advisable too. The common way to determine stock length is to grasp the gun or rifle with the buttplate in the hollow made at the elbow. The hand should now comfortably grasp the grip and trigger. While a rule of thumb, this will suffice closely enough for a rifle stock.

Rifles are aimed, not just pointed like shotguns, which does

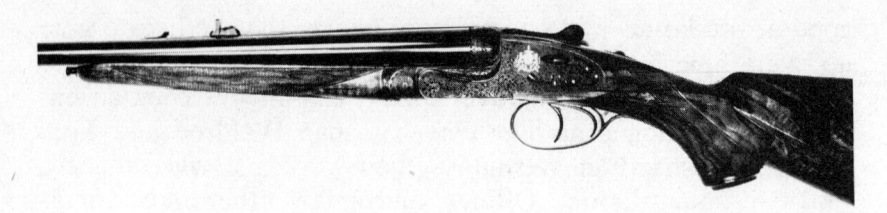

The British firm of Holland & Holland, Ltd. in London has been making the finest in guns since 1835. There may be guns to equal a Holland & Holland but it's generally acknowledged that none surpass them. Shown is a double rifle, caliber .458 Winchester Magnum; the model is Holland's "Royal" model, top of the line. Sideplates are inlaid in three colors of gold with a coat of arms.

require a perfect stock fit for best shooting. As long as a stock is short enough so that a woman (or youngster or any person with shorter-than-normal arms) can handle the rifle without contortions, he or she ought to be able to shoot it.

The only exception is the heavy double rifles carried to follow up wounded dangerous game. These are fired quickly, by pointing as a shotgun, and therefore they require perfect stock fit. But you'll have no need for such shooting in the deer woods. The double rifle is chiefly used in Africa and even there is being slowly phased out because of its high cost and the general excellence and acceptability of the .458 Winchester Magnum in bolt-action rifles.

The British, who make the finest shotguns in the world, do not have that same reputation for rifles. In the first place, you must realize that to the English, a shotgun is a double-barrel gun, period. They recognize nothing else, and in most parts of Europe, as a matter of fact, anything but a double is frowned upon. Some countries absolutely forbid you to enter the country with anything but a double.

The English bend a little when it comes to rifles, however; they acknowledge the bolt-action (which they call a "magazine rifle") and the single-shot. A number of English gunmakers make bolt-action rifles on Mauser actions. But they prefer to make double rifles, and a few Americans, people who must already have everything worth owning, do use double rifles for hunting deer. Of course they don't use a .465 No. 2. They have these rifles made for a cartridge like the .30/06. When made by a top maker, such a rifle is suitable for deer shooting to about 100 yards. Making a double rifle is a tougher proposition than making a double shotgun. The latter is tough enough, because

This is a Holland & Holland magazine rifle, a bolt-action made on a Mauser action. It's a fine piece—the workmanship is equal to that of a Holland & Holland shotgun—but the British do not produce so fine a bolt-action sporting rifle as some of our top custom makers.

its barrels must be "regulated" to center at 40 yards, which means each barrel must be set to shoot slightly toward the center. The reason is that each barrel is a little off the center line and, in recoil, the gun moves a bit in that direction before the load leaves the barrel. (Every gun barrel moves slightly before the bullet or shot charge leaves the muzzle.) A right barrel, for example, will shoot slightly to the right unless it was installed to shoot slightly left, or converge.

This is accomplished by placing spacers between the barrels and actually shooting them to make sure positioning is right. The same thing is done with rifles, but more precision is necessary since you are shooting a single bullet and not a charge of shot that may cover 3 or 4 feet at 40 yards (depending on the choke). Rifles are targeted at 100 yards or a specified distance, and both barrels must shoot to the same point of impact. Gun regulators shoot and fit until they have accomplished that degree of perfection. Then the spacers are brazed and soldered in place.

You can begin to see why a double rifle costs so much when you appreciate what goes into it. This kind of workmanship is disappearing even in England. Building a rifle with a single barrel is far less complicated.

The British Mauser-actioned "magazine rifles" are also quite costly. British gunmakers do not know how to make an inexpensive product. Generally speaking, I think the English make the finest shotguns in the world, but I do not have that high praise for their rifles. Aside from dangerous-game hunting in Africa and India and the occasional Scottish stag, English guns are largely made for export. And here they are dependent upon the customers to tell them what the rifle should look like.

They are a lot farther away from the action than American gunmakers. You can sum it up by saying that while the British

In 1977, the year of Queen Elizabeth's twenty-fifth anniversary as Queen, Holland & Holland made a set of presentation shotguns for Her Majesty that are unparalleled in adornment and value. At the same time, they also made twenty-five presentation "magazine rifles," and this is a photo of the floorplate of the first. These will become collector's items.

make fine magazine rifles that cost a lot of money, they are not as useful as a quality American product. In the first place, the English appear unsure of how these rifles will be used. As a result they tend to add the appurtenances normally found on double rifles. These include folding leaf sights and ribs on the barrel. While these are very attractive and handsome, they are useless and add a hell of a lot to the cost.

The English stocking style also leaves a lot to be desired when it comes to the bolt-action rifle. The checkering usually is not over a broad enough area and generally lacks imagination.

If your desire is for an English rifle, then by all means buy a double. These are absolutely top rifles and the best in their field, bar none. But if it's a top-quality bolt-action rifle you have in mind, you will do much better to buy American. The custom product of such a shop as Griffin & Howe or one of the other small makers in this country will be a far better value.

It is generally acknowledged that any rifle stock ought to be checkered. Some are not, purely as an economy measure, but every custom stock should be checkered and checkered properly. There are a few firms specializing in checkering, and you may want to consider them for what you might call specialized work. A rifle such as the Ruger Number Three single-shot is excellent for deer hunting in either .30/40 or .45/70 calibers, except the rifle comes unchecked. It also comes with the wood too generous around the buttplate and action areas. So this rifle, as

A Savage Model 2400, made for the company in Finland by Valmet, with 12-gauge barrel on top, .308 rifle barrel on the bottom. Many Americans have found such combination guns very useful, depending upon the cover in which they hunt.

one example, needs to have the stock taken down to the metal and refinished and checkered. This is custom work, and a specialist can handle the job for you neatly.

Another specialty is engraving. An engraver is quite possibly the most skilled artisan of all those involved in gun work. He must not only possess the necessary skills to cut gun steel, but he must have the artistic ability to create designs that not only show off an animal or bird with fidelity but are compatible with the particular gun or rifle being worked on. Needless to add, engraving is an expensive addition to custom gun work. And if you like spending money, the engraver can add inlays of gold, silver, ivory, and other precious materials.

While they are not custom products, some very useful combination guns are available. These are guns, usually over/under, combining a shotgun and a rifle barrel; the user can pop a partridge while deer hunting, or the other way around. Perhaps the best known of these guns—you can't call them either a rifle or a shotgun—is the Savage, because that company has long had such a gun in its line.

Today Savage has a sort of "super combination" gun in the Model 2400. Made in Finland, this gun has a 12-gauge shotgun barrel on top and either a .308 Winchester or .222 Remington rifle barrel underneath. These guns are made by Valmet in Finland and are well made; the price is fairly high.

At quite a bit less money, Savage also has the Model 24, which has a .30/30 barrel on top and a 20-gauge shotgun underneath. Both these guns will serve the purpose nicely to bag either type of game, and they are very popular. The Model 24 is also made in .222 Remington/20 gauge, and other variations are made in combinations of .22 rimfire, .410, and 20 gauge. For deer, the .30/30 and .308 are the only two candidates. These guns, if you have use for their specialized feature, will perform nicely.

Other combination guns have been made in Europe for many years; these are generally double shotguns with a single rifle barrel slung between and below the shot barrels. Such three-barreled guns are called "drillings." Some have over/under shotgun barrels with a rifled tube tucked between them at one side. Others feature four barrels—two each shotgun and rifle. These are most often seen in 16-gauge shotguns, while the rifle barrel varies in caliber and chambering over a wide range of cartridges chiefly of European designation.

Should you run across one of these foreign combination guns, make sure it is sound. Make sure the rifle caliber is one for which you can obtain ammunition. Make sure the 16-gauge barrel either has been or can be chambered for 2¾-inch 16-gauge shells—all that are now available. (Most of these guns were for the old 2$^9/_{16}$-inch 16-gauge shell, which is no longer made.) It would be very prudent to buy with the stiuplation that you will have it checked and will return it for full refund if it isn't what you want. Then get a good authority to check it out.

10

Calibers up to .25

The only caliber smaller than .25 that can be recommended for deer hunting is the 6mm or .243. No .22 caliber rifle or cartridge should ever be used on deer or deer-sized animals.

This is true despite the fact that many deer have been downed by .22s. There is no question that a high-velocity .22 rifle, used by a skilled marksman within close range, will dispatch a deer quickly and humanely. But the average hunter isn't in that class.

On a caribou hunt in Quebec's Ungava Bag region, more than 1,000 miles north of Montreal and slightly north of Hudson Bay, I learned what rifles the Eskimos use. These are people who, supposedly, crossed the land bridge from Asia long before recorded history. They are patient hunters, men who can sit by the side of a seal hole cut in the ice for as long as a day until a seal surfaces, whereupon they drive a spear through the seal. Eskimos also have the patience to wait for a caribou to come close enough so they can place a bullet precisely where they want.

The favored rifle in this Eskimo country is the .222 Remington, with the .243 Winchester as second choice. A principal reason for these choices would seem to be that the ammunition is lighter (an important factor in a land where everything must be flown in). A caribou goes down easily and, if shot in the right place with a high-velocity .22, will drop instantly. It makes you wonder when you show up for such a hunt with rifles like the .30/06, .264 Winchester Magnum, or even .338 Winchester Magnum and find the natives shoot the same animals with a .222!

Of course, it's no secret that poachers have long favored the .222. The poacher does his dirty work at night as a rule, gets close to his target, and wants to drop it with as little fuss and muss and noise as possible. A favorite used to be the .22 Hornet, but the Hornet almost disappeared (it's now coming back), and the .222 became the favored illegal rifle.

Long ago, before World War I, Savage produced a very exciting .22 caliber cartridge called the .22 Savage High Power. It stirred up quite a ruckus in the gun world and many pundits suggested its use in the game fields. Some hunters even took it to Africa, where they got in trouble. It was known as "the Imp," and variously called ".22 Savage" or just ".22 High Power." It drove a 70-grain bullet at 2810 feet per second, which was pretty fast for its day. The bullet was not very efficient and tended to blow itself to pieces when it hit brush, and it often broke up on impact with a deer. The result was that it didn't penetrate sufficiently to make a clean kill. This experience, plus that of other hunters on dangerous game where the stakes were higher, led to disillusion with the Imp.

It all happened again in 1935 when Winchester introduced the .220 Swift with a 48-grain bullet at the sensational speed of 4140 fps. Here was an exciting package indeed, especially after the Model 70 Winchester rifle was introduced in 1936. But the same things happened as had happened a generation before with the .22 Savage. Bullets blew up on impacting grass, twigs, skin. They didn't penetrate. Deer were not killed. The message is clear: do not use any .22 caliber rifle for deer hunting (indeed, many states have outlawed them). The smallest bore that should be used on any deer is the 6mm, or .243-inch.

THE FIRST 6mms
The history of the 6mm caliber begins before 1900 with the U.S. Navy rifle known as the Lee Navy. Winchester manufactured 15,000 rifles for the Navy and, in 1897, after the service order was filled, manufactured a similar rifle for the civilian market. The action of this rifle was a "straight-pull" bolt action, meaning that you did not have to raise the bolt handle. You simply pulled it straight back and pushed it straight forward to load and lock it. Locking was accomplished by cams. The action was patented by a man named James Paris Lee, who had sold the rights to Winchester.

But the world was not yet ready for a bolt-action rifle (it has never really been ready for a straight-pull rifle; a number of them have been introduced off and on throughout the years), and less

The .243 Winchester and 6mm Remington, two of the finest cartridges of all time—there's no sound reason to choose either over the other.

than 2,000 were made. The 6mm Lee Navy, as it was called, fired a 112-grain bullet at a muzzle velocity of 2562 fps. One might think today that this might have been a pretty sensational development before 1900. Perhaps it should have been, but those were still lever-action days (the bolt didn't become popular until after World War I) and the bullet's performance was reported as pretty erratic. It has also been pointed out that the retail price, $32, of this rifle was the highest in the Winchester line.

.243 WINCHESTER AND 6mm REMINGTON (.244)
The 6mm was dead in America from the ill-fated Lee Navy until the mid-1950s, when Winchester announced the .243 Winchester and Remington the .244 Remington (the rifles have identical bore dimensions despite the different numbers). The announcements were made at the same time and it was clear that a horse race for popularity was imminent.

Credit for the 6mm goes to the late Warren Page. At that time Warren was shooting editor of *Field & Stream* magazine, and it was he who pushed and goaded the two industrial giants into developing 6mm cartridges by writing about his results with rifles in this bore size. Warren was not alone; there were a number of others experimenting with the caliber, including Fred Huntington of RCBS, Mike Walker of Remington, and many custom gun shops across the country. No matter, it was Warren Page who fathered these two cartridges and it is he who deserves the credit.

The introduction of these cartridges is interesting history. At the time I was a member of the technical staff of the *American Rifleman,* and General Hatcher, then technical editor, asked me to review both the Winchester and Remington offerings. Accordingly, both companies sent me rifles and ammunition in advance of the public announcement.

Winchester had developed a different concept for the 6mm, and this was manifested by the ammunition they produced—an 80-grain bullet at an announced velocity of 3500 fps and a 100-grain bullet at 3070 fps. (Both velocities have since been shaved to the more realistic figures of 3420 and 2960.) The 80-grain bullet was constructed with a thin gilding-metal jacket for rapid expansion on varmints, and the 100-grain was made for deer with a heavier jacket metal. Thus the concept was a combination rifle to be used for varmints with one bullet weight and for game of the deer class with another bullet.

Remington, on the other hand, opted for the .244 as a varmint rifle, and the rifle they produced, a Model 722, was made with a rather heavy barrel. Their ammunition was loaded with a 75-grain bullet at an announced 3500 fps and a 90-grain at 3200. (These loads are no longer in the line; they are replaced by 80- and 100-grain loads.)

Using the same scope on both rifles, I put them through their paces with the factory ammunition supplied and with some handloads. The accuracy of the little Winchester Model 70 featherweight rifle, even with factory ammunition, astounded me. It was the most accurate rifle/ammo combination I had ever run across. Reloading proved simple too, and I was able to get fine performance with handloads right from the beginning.

But the Remington was another story. It did not shoot very well with factory ammunition, although it did shoot better with handloads. But it would not handle 100-grain bullets, because Remington had gone the varmint route—planned on bullets lighter than 100-grains and used a rifling twist that was too slow to stabilize 100-grain slugs.

The result of this horse race was an absolute runaway for Winchester. Remington's .244 died on the vine. The company, which really doesn't make many mistakes, withdrew the .244 from the market and later reintroduced the rifle as the 6mm Remington. Thus the two cartridges (.244 and 6mm Remington) are identical and may be interchanged. Should you find a rifle chambered for the .244, be advised that it will not handle some 100-grain bullets. They will tumble. That is, they will turn end over end like a badly thrown forward pass, because the rotational speed isn't fast enough. A 6mm Remington rifle will handle any ammunition stamped either 6mm Rem. or .244. The new rifle has finally come into its own and it may be said that the .243 Winchester and 6mm Remington are equal in all respects.

There are some who prefer one over the other, and they are entitled to their opinion. For example, I've always preferred the .243, for no solid reason. I suspect it's from my early love and appreciation for that very first rifle I had, but it can't be supported by facts. Those who say the .243 is more difficult to reload and that it doesn't produce as much velocity as the .244 are full of beans. This is pure nonsense. The .243 is a super cartridge to reload when you know how to reload and, believe it or not, I still have some of the original cartridges I got with the first .243 in the 1950s.

When used with the proper bullets, the two 6mm cartridges are superb deer rifles. They offer very light recoil (but a pronounced, sharp muzzle blast) and accuracy that must be seen to be believed (provided the rifle is tuned up to produce its best). This makes them a perfect choice for people who don't care for recoil, women and youngsters included. When shot from the bench, of course, you had better insist on ear protection, lest they equate noise with recoil.

And the 6mms are the ideal combination rifle, just as Winchester conceived in the first place. I've made shots at varmints with a .243 that you won't believe, including a fox at an estimated 800 yards, and many chucks at 500 and 600, when I did my part.

The 6mm is also a superb deer killer. Over the years I've had reports on many deer killed with .243 and 6mm rifles, and the story is always the same—what gets hit goes down. There have been many hunters who have successfully bagged elk with these rifles, although elk ought to be considered a mite on the big side for 6mm.

In the late '40s and '50s when I was building custom rifles, I long admired the .240 Apex, a 6mm cartridge produced by the great London firm of Holland & Holland Ltd. This company is best known for its shotguns, which, along with those by Woodward, Boss, Purdey, and a few others, are to guns what the

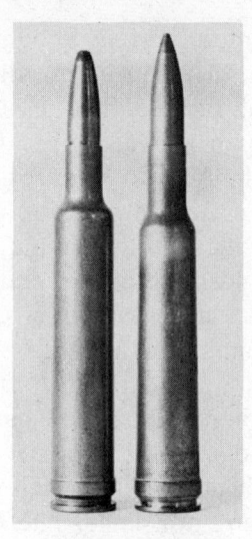

On the left is the .240 Weatherby Magnum, which I consider the finest 6mm cartridge for long-range shooting. On the right is the .240 Apex, a cartridge long used by Holland & Holland of London. However, the H&H cartridge never got the popularity it deserved. As you can see, the cartridges are very similar, but the Weatherby is a bit larger and is a standard while the English cartridge is obsolete.

Rolls-Royce is to automobiles. Holland & Holland also makes rifles—not very many, because they work only to one high standard. In addition to double shotguns, the company also makes double-barrel rifles, chiefly for the African hunter, a few "magazine rifles" (meaning bolt-action).

Holland & Holland is best known in the U.S. as the H&H in .375 H&H Magnum, a cartridge developed in 1912. This company's little .240 Apex is a belted cartridge like the .375 (and many other magnums today, such as the .300 and .458 Winchesters). But the .240 has a smaller diameter, the same base diameter as a .30/06. It drives a 100-grain bullet at 2900 fps in the factory load, which is loaded down, as are all British loads, for use in the tropics where excessive heat raises pressures.

.240 WEATHERBY MAGNUM

It remained for Roy Weatherby to heed the .240 Apex from Holland & Holland. Weatherby produces what has come to be my favorite 6mm—the .240 Weatherby Magnum. It's nearly a dead-ringer for the .240 and it can drive a 100-grain bullet as fast as

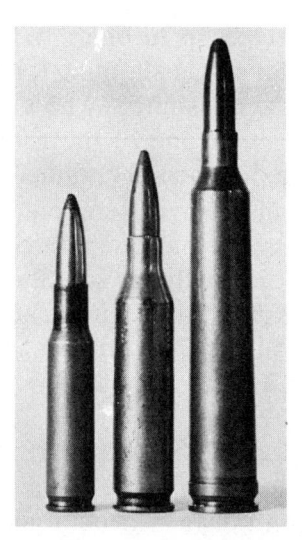

Three extremes in 6mm cartridges. On the left is a wildcat made by me in 1955 and named the .240 Wallack. It is based on the .222 Remington necked up to 6mm, and it drove an 85-grain bullet at 2628 fps. In the middle for comparison is the familiar .243 Winchester, and on the right is a monstrous mistake created by Holland & Holland by necking its .375 H&H Magnum to 6mm. The big case got some early publicity but was so ridiculously over-capacity for the bore size that it died a very quick death.

3200 fps with most reloads (Weatherby claims 3395 fps for his 100-grain factory load).

A long time ago I shipped a Mauser action and a barrel to Weatherby to be fitted and chambered for the .240 Weatherby Magnum. I made the stock myself, and ended up with one of the sweetest-shooting rifles I've ever fired. It likes hot loads and it shoots them awfully well. I suspect the reasons the .240 Weatherby isn't more popular are that the rifle is available only in Weatherby brand, which is somewhat high ticket, and that the ammunition isn't in wide distribution. Nevertheless, if it's a really hot 6mm you want, I don't think you can beat the .240 Weatherby Magnum.

WILDCAT 6mms

At the very opposite end of the spectrum lies a very small wildcat cartridge (identified as any cartridge which is not commercially loaded by one of the ammunition companies like Winchester, Remington, Federal, Norma, Frontier, CIL, etc.). This is most commonly called the 6mm/.222 and is made by necking the

.222 Remington cartridge up to 6mm. While the cartridge was originally developed for target shooting it has recently been used for a deer rifle by some gunsmiths, who claim it does the job.

When I first read about one of these little rifles only a few months ago, it sparked a memory, and I dug out my records, which showed that I made an experimental rifle in this identical cartridge more than twenty years before. I have chronograph records from the old Shenandoah Gun Shop dated September 2, 1955, proving that the rifle I made drove an 85-grain Sierra bullet an average of 2628 fps using 20½ grains of DuPont 4198 powder. And another load of 21 grains of 4198 pushed a 75-grain bullet 2826 fps.

What's interesting about this little cartridge is that it drives a bullet that fast with so little powder. The word is "efficiency," and it proves you don't always need a giant boiler room to deliver decent results. I called my little case the ".240 Wallack." It never went very far in the '50s; maybe the world is more ready for it now. I can't vouch for it as a deer cartridge—in fact, I wouldn't use it—but it has considerable promise for target shooting.

MAKING A CHOICE
If your choice for a deer rifle lies with the 6mm, you can choose either the .243 Winchester or the 6mm Remington by tossing a coin. They are like two peas in a pod when it comes to performance, and they are available in a wide variety of rifles. Don't pay attention to anyone who claims one is better than the other. That is not true.

If you want more power, go to the .240 Weatherby. It's hotter than either of the others by a little bit and will produce excellent results.

The main reason for a 6mm, it seems to me, is that you can use the same rifle for varmints and deer. And you will be superbly armed for either. This is no compromise. It's as good a choice as you can make for either kind of shooting.

You may ask, with justification, "if the Army uses a .22 caliber rifle, why isn't it heavy enough for deer?" The Army uses a cartridge known as the 5.56mm, which is the .223 Remington in civilian terms (the cartridges are interchangeable). This was the rifle of Vietnam and it is available in a number of commercially produced rifles.

Despite the fact that the Army has adopted this cartridge, it is not suitable for deer hunting. The .223 Remington drives a 55-grain bullet at 3240 fps, the .222 Remington (which is just a tiny bit smaller cartridge) drives a 50-grain bullet at 3140, and the .22/250, which is the big daddy of the .22s, drives a 55-grain bullet at 3730 fps. *None* of these cartridges can be regarded as suitable for deer hunting.

In fact, I think the Army has made a serious error in adopting what I regard as a woodchuck rifle for basic infantry use. If this nation ever gets into another war, we will be badly outgunned by whatever enemy we face. Those who believe wars have moved to another plane of weaponry, namely the big bomb and other missiles, have not studied their history. Big bombs may have their place in some future war, but once the big boom is over, the ground will have to be occupied by men with rifles—and to arm them with chuck rifles is foolish.

11

Calibers from .25 to .30

This broad and popular range of cartridges covers many favorites both old and new. All the .25 caliber rifles use the same diameter bullet regardless of the name—all the way from the puny .256 Winchester to the potent .257 Weatherby Magnum. The bullet diameter is .257 inch. There are a couple 6.5mm cartridges, a pair of .270s, and several in 7mm size which, like the .25s, all use the same diameter bullet (.284 inch).

Most of these cartridges are suitable for deer hunting; some of them can be excellent rifles for varmints with the appropriate loads. Some of them are available in military rifles from other nations, and a few are hangovers from the days of black powder.

.25 CALIBER
.256 Winchester Magnum. This was a unique cartridge that was designed for pistol shooting. It was introduced first in the Ruger Hawkeye single-shot pistol in 1961, but its life span was so brief that Ruger Hawkeye pistols are valuable collector's items today because of their rarity. The cartridge lingers on in the Thompson/Center pistol, also a single-shot.

Winchester designed the cartridge by necking down the .357 Magnum revolver case to .25 caliber. There was no handgun and no rifle available when they did it. I've understood that both Smith & Wesson and Colt tried to chamber revolvers for the .256 but that it was too hot to hold. The only rifle ever made for this cartridge was the Marlin Model 56; Marlin added the .256 in 1962.

There was no real use for the .256 and little imagined use. It is difficult to understand why Winchester ever bothered. That the company did so without producing a rifle for it also adds to the mystery and confusion. In any event, the .256 was very short-lived and is gone today except for a few Thompson/Center guns. The cartridge is totally unacceptable for deer hunting under any circumstances.

This cartridge also brings up the corruption of the word "magnum." Literally, the word simply means something large, as in magnum of champagne. As far as I know the first popular use of the word in the world of guns occurred when Holland & Holland produced their .300 and .375 Magnum cartridges. Since then the word has been carved into stone by Roy Weatherby. Its use for a pipsqueak such as the .256 is absurd and degrading.

A reason for this development by Winchester may have been that Remington had just produced a cartridge called the .22 Remington Jet (known as the .22 Centerfire Magnum by Smith & Wesson, who produced a revolver for it). Also based on the .357 Magnum revolver cartridge, this was as big a dud as the .256. I had a Smith & Wesson .22 Jet for a while and the best thing I can say about it is that I should have kept the gun. It's worth a small fortune today because so few of them were made that gun collectors pay gobs of cash when they can find one!

.25/20 WCF. Here's one of the holdovers from the days of black powder. You can tell these because of the double-digit number designation; the second set of numbers indicates the charge of black powder, in grains. Often a third set of numbers was used, and that indicated the bullet weight, also in grains. An example is the .45/70/500, which translates into a .45-inch-diameter bullet weighing 500 grains and pushed by a charge of 70 grains of black powder.

The letters "WCF" are also a holdover. They indicate Winchester Center Fire as opposed to rimfire. Modern cartridge nomenclature no longer uses either the double digit nor the WCF type of designation, so you can always recognize an old-timer when you see it.

The .25/20 was introduced around 1893 and was popular for many years as a combination rifle for small game and varmints. About the biggest game that should be tackled by such a rifle is the turkey. Under no circumstances should it ever be considered as a deer rifle.

Adding to the confusion, there was at one time a cartridge known as the .25/20 single-shot. It was a bigger cartridge and is not interchangeable with the .25/20 WCF, or .25/20 repeater. This was a cartridge with a little more power and was introduced in 1882 by J. Francis Rabbeth, an experimental rifleman. The first rifles were made for it by Maynard, followed by Stevens, Winchester, and Remington.

The .25/20 WCF was developed later to accommodate Winchester and Marlin lever-actions. There are no firearms being produced in either .25/20 version today, and it is most unlikely there will ever be again.

.25/35 WCF. Here's another black-powder cartridge still with us but going fast. There are no rifles being made today, but the Thompson/Center single-shot pistol is made in .25/35. (The Thompson/Center is a unique pistol featuring interchangeable barrels. You can change calibers quickly by switching barrels.)

I've always liked the .25/35. It's a small, relatively low-powered cartridge which can drop a deer like a stone if you use the rifle within its limitations. Used in the old Winchester Model 94 rifle (if you're lucky enough to find one) it will put meat in the pot just as it used to.

The .25/35 was introduced in 1895. Most experts regard it as a has-been, do not advise its use on deer, and in general suggest it's best left on the wall or in the closet. I don't see it that way at all. If you have a .25/35 in good condition, you will find that it shoots well. And if you use it at relatively short range and place your shot right, you'll have a buck hanging by sundown. Today's only available load is in 117-grain at a velocity of 2300 fps. Plenty potent for a whitetail or muley.

Shortly after the introduction of the .25/35 by Winchester, Marlin followed with a cartridge known as the .25/36 in its Model 93 rifle. John Marlin was a feisty type; he was feuding with Winchester at the time—and he used to say so in his catalogs, actually running down the competition. So he produced a cartridge that was just enough different to be different. For any practical purpose the two were alike in performance and what is said for one may be said for the other. Except you won't see many of the Marlin .25/36 rifles.

A little later, Remington also produced a similar cartridge for their autoloading and pump-action rifles. It was known as the .25 Remington and was a rimless cartridge which worked best in their action. (Remington also had .30 and .32 caliber cartridges to compete directly with Winchester's .30/30 and .32 Special; none of these are around today.)

For any purpose whatever, what is said about the .25/35 also applies to the .25/36 and to the .25 Remington, except that ammunition for the Marlin and Remington is no longer made. It should also be noted that a number of European rifles were chambered for the .25/35, especially some of those handsome drillings. In European designation, the .25/35 is the 6.5×52R—which means 6.5mm caliber, cartridge case 52mm long, and a rimmed case.

.250/3000 Savage. I said that in double-digit cartridge names the second figure indicates the powder charge. Not always. Here is a departure. The .250 Savage was introduced in 1915 in the Savage Model 99 rifle; the cartridge was designed by Charles Newton, the man who also produced the famed Newton rifles for a short period. It was loaded with an 87-grain bullet that achieved the velocity of 3000 feet per second. And that's what this second set of digits means—the velocity.

This is one of the finest cartridges ever produced. It has retained its popularity since 1915, and a few years ago when the 6mms came along and pushed all the .25s into oblivion, it was the .250/3000 that came back. And it's rather unlikely that the old .250 will be submerged again in the near future.

While the .250/3000 was introduced with the 3000-fps 87-grain bullet, it was soon realized that this was not a good bullet for deer hunting. So a 100-grain bullet was developed for this cartridge in 1921 by Western Cartridge Company, now a part of Winchester-Western. The result was that the .250 became the first major cartridge that could be employed equally well on varmints, with 87-grain bullets, as well as on deer, with the new 100-grain load.

Take note now that no .25 caliber rifle should ever be used on deer with any bullet lighter than 100 grains. Carve these words in stone if you own a .25 caliber and do not deviate from the pronouncement.

Many riflemen have a love affair with the .250 Savage. Considerable emotion is devoted to the cartridge among those who have used it or who own rifles in this chambering. It has been made in bolt-action and lever-action rifles for many years. Among its many virtues is the fact that it can be made into a very light custom rifle, which has not gone unnoticed by many gunsmiths who have produced such rifles. As a result, the .250 is popular among women, because it produces less recoil than many others and the rifle can be made light in weight.

With a muzzle velocity of 2820 fps, the 100-grain .250 Savage load is more than adequate for deer and deer-class game (which means deer, both whitetail and mule, black bear, and antelope). It produces quick, humane kills, assuming a decently placed bullet. And it has always been an easy matter to get the bullet where you want, as long as you do your part. Most rifles in this caliber have been good shooters.

Accuracy is something that's a little hard to define and pinpoint. A rifle that delivers its shots into a minute of angle is usually considered to be a very accurate rifle. Years ago it was something of a rarity; today it's fairly common. A minute of angle is defined as 1 inch for each 100 yards of range—an inch at 100 yards, 2 inches at 200, and so on. Just how accurate you need your rifle to be depends on many things, not the least of which are your ability, your sighting equipment, and the range over which you will shoot.

For reasons that are hard to determine, rifles in .250 Savage caliber have always shot better than rifles chambered for the .257 Roberts. This is a hard one to figure, because the shape or size of a cartridge case really has nothing to do with accuracy, within reasonable limits. This is one of the things many .250 Savage owners like about their rifles. They can be depended upon to put a bullet right where the sights are, and you can't say that about every rifle.

.257 Roberts. This cartridge was developed by Ned H. Roberts, an experimental rifleman. I met Roberts at the first bench-rest match I attended in Johnstown, N.Y., in 1947. He died shortly after, so I was coming into the game just as he went out. His career spanned the blackpowder and Schuetzen days and just barely embraced modern rifles.

Roberts simply necked the 7×57mm Mauser cartridge case down to .25 caliber to produce his case. He did this in the 1920s, and the first rifles were made by the old Niedner Rifle Co. in Dowagiac, Mich. Griffin & Howe of New York City made rifles later. In 1934, Remington became interested and took the .257 Roberts into its family. When they did so, however, they changed the shape very slightly to make manufacture easier and to differentiate from other .25 caliber rifles. Ned Roberts always claimed that Remington screwed up his cartridge, but the charge was probably sour grapes.

Remington chambered the Model 30s rifle for the .257 in 1934, and Winchester followed suit in 1937 in the new Model 70 rifle. Other rifles, many of them over the years, have been chambered for the .257, and the cartridge has been generally satisfactory as a decent combination for varmints and deer-sized game. In my opinion it is not as good a cartridge as either the .243 Winchester or 6mm Remington, the two cartridges which drove the .257 into obsolesence. It is only fair to point out, however, that my opinion is not shared by everyone. There are many who think the .257 is as good, and there are those who think it better.

I have shot a good many .257 rifles, and I have never had one that would hold a candle to the .250 Savage, nor to any of the 6mms. I have also experimented at great length with improved versions of the .257.

An "improved" version of a cartridge is a wildcat, not available in factory ammunition or rifles. It is made by a custom gunsmith who makes a special reamer to cut the chamber oversize. The standard cartridge is fired in the improved rifle, whereupon the gas generated by firing swells the case out to fit the expanded chamber. Then you can reload with a heavier powder charge and improve performance.

Sometimes it's a moot point whether or not performance is really improved. Sometimes it's just another way to sell something. However, there is little doubt in my mind that the .257 can be improved, and I proved this to myself a number of times by taking a standard .257 rifle and improving the chamber for a case I called the ".250 Helldiver." This permitted a heavier powder charge, and by changing the shoulder angle to a steeper design, I caused the gas to stay in the boiler room longer and develop more thrust. At least that was the theory, but I have no way of knowing that it worked that way. I do know that Helldiver rifles outperformed standard .257s by a wide margin. And so did several other versions of improved .257 Roberts.

Another version of the improved .257 I worked on was the .250 Donaldson, developed by the late Harvey Donaldson, but I did the experimental work for him. Harvey wanted this to be a target cartridge, but it didn't set the world afire. Then we went to a shorter case (based on the same brass but shortened), which he called the .250 Donaldson Ace. It shot well but never became very popular. As far as I know only a few rifles were ever produced in these calibers.

The .257 is a good deer rifle. It is not a bad varmint rifle either, and may be used as a combination rifle with good results. Use 100- or 117-grain bullets for your deer shooting and 87-grain for varmint shooting. There are no rifles being manufactured today for this cartridge, and I consider it unlikely that there ever will be. I also see this as no loss.

.25/06 Remington. In about 1920, A. O. Niedner necked the .30/06 cartridge case down to .25 caliber and produced a cartridge which has ever since been known as the .25/06. It wasn't all that big a success in the early days because propellant powders then were not entirely suitable. Today it's another story entirely; since the last war DuPont and Hodgdon have offered powders that were slow enough in burning to squeeze the full potential out of this big boiler room.

The .25/06 was a custom-rifle proposition until 1969, when Remington adopted the cartridge and gave it legitimacy. It also gave it standardization, which was of no small importance. Some custom gunmakers have the ability to make accurate chamber reamers, and others have sense enough to buy reamers from a reliable source which are accurately made. Alas, others just set out to make a reamer by guess and by God, then quit when they get tired, and the result is what they call their "version" of the .25/06. Without standarization, they have as much right to call it that as anyone else. All that nonsense came to an end when Remington adopted the concept and produced an industry standard.

The .25/06 is loaded with a 90-grain bullet at 3440 fps, a 120-grain at 3050 fps, and a 117-grain Federal at 3060 fps. Those who handload will find 100-grain bullets can be driven at speeds as fast as 3300 fps; the 100-grain is not available in over-the-counter ammunition. This is sizzling performance. It is a perfect rifle for the varmint and deer combination; in fact, it seriously rivals the 6mms for this purpose. The .25/06 I have is a Model 700 Remington and it shoots awfully well for me.

More than twenty years ago I chambered a barrel for the .25/06 for Bruce Hodgdon of the powder company. He has recently told me that this rifle is still performing well and that it has always been one of his best-shooting rifles.

For reasons I have never been able to fathom, you can rechamber a .257 Roberts rifle to the .25/06 and it will shoot significantly better. You can make this conversion with any bolt-action rifle; the magazine can usually be altered to accommodate the newer cartridge. However, it's wise to consult your gunsmith first, because there are some rifles with actions too short to handle the longer .25/06 cartridges.

Why Remington saw fit to add its name to this cartridge is more than I can say. The company did the same with the .22/250. Both cartridges had been around for generations. Remington gave them respectability and removed their bastard status, so presumably there is justification. But since the first .25/06, so far as is known, was produced by Niedner and the first .22/250 by Grove Wotkyns, the name Remington seems odd to me.

You may regard the .25/06 as a superb rifle for deer shooting, and with power enough to drop large game as long as the proper bullets are used.

.257 Weatherby Magnum. Roy Weatherby designed his .257 cartridge around the end of World War II by shortening the .300 H&H Magnum to approximately .30/06 length (so it would feed through standard-length actions) and blowing out the body in approved wildcat fashion. The result was a fast cartridge which became very popular in the game fields over the world. Hunters have used .257 Weatherby rifles for tough African plains game with considerable success; they have even been used on Cape buffalo.

As a deer rifle the .257 Weatherby is needlessly powerful, though it does the job. It would be a good long-range cartridge but is vastly more than is needed for the ordinary shot at less than 200 yards. It develops about 200 fps more velocity than the .25/06, and consumes about 20 percent more powder to achieve that higher speed.

The .257 Weatherby Magnum is recommended for long-range deer shooting but not for ordinary hunting. If you anticipate shots in excess of 200 yards, you might add this one to your list for consideration.

.25 Krag. This is a wildcat cartridge made by necking the old .30/40 Krag cartridge down to .25 caliber. The .30/40 was our

military rifle adopted in 1892 and abandoned in favor of the .30/06 in 1906. A rimmed cartridge, it works very well in single-shot rifles.

I built myself one of these rifles some years ago on an English Farquharson action which had been made by Westley Richards of London and chambered for the .303 British. I fitted the new barrel and built a nice-looking rifle which shoots very well with a Redfield 2-7× variable scope.

This cartridge is recommended for the person with a good single-shot action that he wants made into a deer rifle. There is no other use for the cartridge. It gives performance at about the level of the .257 Roberts.

6.5mm CALIBER

6.5mm Remington Magnum. 6.5mm is .264 inches, and bullets of that diameter are used in all 6.5 mm rifles. In 1966, Remington introduced two new cartridges in a new, powerful rifle. These were the 6.5mm and .350 Remington Magnums. The rifle was the Model 600; it came with an 18½-inch barrel and was an ugly rifle no matter how one looked at it. It also was a very light, very handy, very accurate rifle, except it kicked like hell. I have one of these in .350 Remington Magnum but have no experience with the 6.5mm. Not many shooters have, and neither cartridge lasted very long.

Should you run across one of these Remington rifles in the used-gun department, it will make a good deer rifle. Remington still offers the ammunition, but it would be wise to buy a decent supply along with the rifle.

The 6.5 Remington is a little more powerful than the 6.5mm military cartridges that we'll come to in a few moments but is far less powerful than the .264 Winchester Magnum. It is suitable for all but the biggest North American game; use it on deer with complete reliability.

6.5mm Japanese. When World War II started, the newspapers were full of rather contemptuous scribblings about the puny ".25 caliber Jap rifle." That was pretty dumb. The Japanese had introduced this service cartridge in 1897 and the Type 38 rifle in 1905. Known as the Arisaka, the Japanese rifle in this caliber was loaded with a 139-grain bullet at a muzzle velocity of 2500 fps. While that was not a sensational performance it certainly was ample and was on a par with or better than 6.5mm cartridges used by such nations as Sweden, Norway, Greece, Italy, Holland, Rumania, and others. No sporting rifle was ever made for this cartridge.

In 1939 the Japanese replaced both the Type 38 rifle and its cartridge with the 7.7mm cartridge in the Type 99 rifle. These will be discussed in the following chapter.

Japanese rifles in 6.5mm were brought back by World War II servicemen. Ammunition is available factory-loaded in Norma brand and, of course, may be reloaded. The 6.5mm Japanese is close to an ideal deer cartridge and, assuming a decent rifle, will perform along with the best. However, these rifles were very crude and most difficult to sporterize. In fact, I don't consider them worth working on; it's worse than trying to make a silk purse from a sow's ear. Still, the action is a strong one, and if you have such a rifle, it may be kept as a "loaner."

6.5mm Carcano. The Italian service rifle and its cartridge. Vast quantities of these rifles were bulldozed into piles on battlefields and imported into the United States in the years after World War II; there are many of them in this country. Even though they were offered at very low prices it is generally felt that they were overpriced, because the rifles are crude. The extra margin of safety existing in most military actions is not present, and the finish of the rifle is sloppy. Most Italian rifles are not capable of decent accuracy, and fitting a scope (which is difficult) isn't worth the effort.

Ammunition is available in Norma brand. The cartridge is suitable, but the rifle is not recommended, even as a "loaner." But should you be fortunate enough to have one that shoots well, it will provide a suitable deer rifle.

6.5mm Mannlicher-Schoenauer. This has been one of the world's fine game cartridges for many years, even though it has never been particularly popular in the United States. The cartridge was first adopted by the Greek army in 1903. Sporting rifles have been produced for years in the great Austrian Steyr Works and sold around the world. Stoeger imported Mannlicher-Schoenauer rifles for many years. The chief distinguishing features of these game rifles are their short barrels (usually 18 inches in 6.5mm caliber) and full-length stocks—hence today's "Mannlicher-style" stocks.

These rifles—that is, the Mannlicher-Schoenauer sporters—were made with great care and their workmanship was superb. And the cartridge has been widely respected around the globe for game, even in Africa. There is no question whatsoever that this little rifle and cartridge are ideal for deer hunting. Norma lists two loads: a 139-grain bullet at 2580 fps and a 156-grain at 2461 fps.

6.5×55 Swedish Mauser. Adopted by Sweden in 1894, the same cartridge is used in Norway. It was used in Mauser rifles by the Swedish forces and in Krag-Jorgenson rifles in Norway. Norma loads the same two bullets it offers for the 6.5mm Mannlicher, 139- and 156-grain, except that the velocities are 2789 and 2493, respectively.

A fine cartridge in every respect, the 6.5×55 was boosted a few years ago by target shooters, although that particular group has now turned to other fields. It remains a suitable deer cartridge in a rifle capable of good accuracy. You can handload for all these imports, of course; loads and dies are available from most sources. However, it will pay to be prudent if you have one of the older rifles. They are not capable of handling excessive pressures and you should heed the loading tables.

.264 Winchester Magnum. This is a real hummer. It zings a 100-grain varmint bullet at 3620 fps and a 140-grain at 3140 fps. Both are flying. The cartridge was introduced in 1958 and achieved quite a bit of popularity at once. In 1962 Remington introduced its 7mm Magnum, and that had the effect of diminishing the .264's popularity.

I had one of the first rifles in this caliber, and it shot with exceptional accuracy. Now I have a new Model 70 in this caliber and, with a Leupold 24× scope, it shoots into about ½ inch at 100 yards. This is superb accuracy for so large a rifle. It's good enough to hit a mouse at 200 yards with consistency.

The deer hunter won't need such a rifle for any ordinary hunting unless he expects a long-range shot, in which case the .264 Winchester will prove ideal. And with its lighter load it will fill in nicely on varmints. However, this is a very high-velocity, very high-performance cartridge/rifle combination. You don't achieve such speeds without burning a lot of powder, and the result is short barrel life. You should be very careful not to fire the rifle too fast and get the barrel overheated. Avoid fast shooting at the bench, because this will cause rapid barrel wear. Shoot your .264 properly, taking time between shots and shooting as few shots as you can, and the rifle will last a long time. With the appropriate loads, the .264 will handle all North American game.

.270 CALIBER

.270 Winchester. It would be hard to decide whether the .270 or the .30/30 rates the honor of being the most sensational sporting-cartridge development of all time. The .270 was introduced by Winchester in 1925 along with the Model 54 bolt-action rifle—Winchester's first offering in the field of modern bolt sporting rifles. Both were an instant success, although the cartridge might well have been the more important development. Winchester went on and improved the Model 54 to be issued as the famed Model 70 in 1937. But the .270 cartridge goes on today even more popular than ever.

The .270 is great in its own right, but the boost it got from the late Jack O'Connor certainly did more to publicize it than most other cartridges ever got. Indeed, many referred to Jack as though it were his middle name—Jack .270 O'Connor. O'Connor's approximately fifty years of experience with the cartridge is certainly a significant tribute. He used the rifle to take all the North American big-game species as well as others in Africa, India, and Iran. I knew Jack O'Connor for years and considered his knowledge of guns to be very extensive. Moreover, he, as a writer, had the opportunity to choose most any caliber and rifle.

Developing the .270 was an easy matter for Winchester; they simply followed the common wildcatter's procedure of necking the .30/06 down to .270 caliber. It was that simple. In fact, .270 and .30/06 cartridges are headspaced at the same point and the same gauges are used for each. ("Headspace" is the term used for fore-and-aft dimension of the chamber. In a rimless cartridge like the .270 it is measured from the bolt face to a point on the shoulder slope.) So you can see that there is nothing mysterious about the cartridge.

A .270 is capable of downing any North American big game, although it is considered a bit light by many, including myself, for such as the big bears. Just the same, a good rifleman who is experienced at shooting game will find it adequate for even these beasts.

I remember some years back a friend of mine who was a fine target rifleman hunted Quebec deer with a .270. When he came back he was determined to sell the .270 and get himself a heavier rifle. The reason was that he'd lost a nice whitetail which, he claimed, he'd hit well. He got a .35 Whelen, which is the .30/06 necked up to .35 caliber and handloaded with .35 caliber bullets. The point here is that this chap would not have been any better off with a howitzer. You must hit the game in a vital spot to kill it. And, despite his claim, this man did not, or he would have had his buck. No rifle can compensate for a poorly placed shot.

Many claim the .270 is a good varmint/deer combination rifle. I do not. While you can shoot chucks with a .270, I think it is far too large a rifle for them. If you shoot many chucks or other varmints you should have a smaller-bore rifle. If a .270 is your only rifle, then you will find it perfectly acceptable to shoot a few varmints with it.

Most claim that the .270 will do anything a .30/06 will do, and I'd say this statement is about right. The cartidges are very close in performance. Given my druthers, I'd take the .30/06, but I would be hard pressed to substantiate my choice with a logical argument. At one time the .270 was nearly on a par with the .30/06 in sales of American rifles. But I think it is slipping now because of the introduction of newer and higher-performance cartridges. A couple samples of the latter are the 7mm Remington Magnum and the .300 Winchester Magnum. But the .270 is still right up there, and that's where it should be.

.270 Weatherby Magnum. This one is most notable for the fact that it's the only other .270 caliber cartridge in existence. This has not been one of Roy Weatherby's all-time winners. The cartridge is available only in the Weatherby Mark V rifle. Naturally, this cartridge out-zings the .270 Winchester, by some 200-300 fps, but it's moot whether this added zip is necessary or not. It certainly isn't for deer, but it would be very welcome if you're facing a brown bear or grizzly.

Over the years there have been a number of wildcat cartridges in .270 caliber, but none of them has achieved much popularity. Should you run across a used rifle in one of these wildcat calibers, you will have a rifle that probably will perform along the lines of the .270 Winchester, though that will depend on the case itself. You should not pay too much for such a rifle; its resale value will be low—it always is with a noncommercial caliber.

7mm CALIBER

The 7mm was never a popular bore in America until the 7mm Remington Magnum was introduced in 1962. We first learned about it, though, under far different circumstances, in the Spanish War in 1898, when the Spaniards walloped us unmercifully.

They were armed with the fairly new (introduced in 1892) 7mm Mauser repeating rifle using smokeless powder. We were armed with black-powder .45/70 single-shot "trap door" Springfields that blasted a great cloud of smoke to obscure the target and expose our positions. It was a bitter lesson.

The very same cartridge, 7mm Mauser or 7×57mm, has been used as a game cartridge for all the years since, but not by many Americans. It is regarded as one of the world's finest cartridges, and many claim it is the equal of the .270. We'll have more to say about this. It is often claimed that the 7mm is a more versatile bore than many others; many bullets are available to handloaders, ranging from slightly over 100 grains to 175.

7×57mm or 7mm Mauser. The European metric designation of a cartridge usually uses two numbers, the first of which indicates the bullet diameter and the second the length of the cartridge in millimeters. A 7mm bullet measures .284 inch.

One of the important things to realize about the 7mm Mauser is that factory ammunition is loaded to pressures that will be safe in the many older rifles still in service. These rifles are not as strong as modern rifles because steels have improved since they were made. As a result, the 7mm suffers from lower performance than can really be built into the load. If you have a modern rifle in good condition you can handload the cartridge to significantly better performance. But if you have one of the older models you are well advised to use factory ammunition or to reload to those standards. (The same thing is true with a number of other cartridges; examples are the .45/70 and 8mm Mauser.)

One of the most often quoted examples of the potency of the 7mm Mauser is that the famed African hunter Karamojo Bell used this cartridge to kill several thousand elephants. Bell hunted early in this century when game was much more plentiful —and he was a superb hunter who got close to his game. He used "solids"—steel-jacketed, round-nose bullets that pursued a straight course through the massive bone structure of an elephant's head.

The 7mm Mauser is a far better cartridge than is generally accepted and, in a fine rifle, will perform right along with the flashier .270. It has long been a favorite of knowledgeable riflemen for a lightweight custom rifle, because the cartridge is a little shorter than a .270 or .30/06. The Mauser actions made for it are shorter and lighter than those for the 8mm, and the whole rifle can be scaled down slightly. With its lower recoil it has been a favorite for those who don't like kick.

There are many surplus 7mm rifles in this country, some of them excellent and some of them awful. A few years ago I ran into a guy at our local range who had bought one at Woolworth's for something like $10. He was robbed. That rifle sprayed its shots over a 3-foot area at a distance of about 30 yards, worse than a cylinder-bore shotgun. The rear sight flapped up and down like a leaf in the breeze, although it didn't matter because the rifle shot so badly.

On the other hand, some 7mm surplus military rifles shoot with fine accuracy when they are fitted with decent sights. Many shooters have had them remodeled into excellent sporting rifles which deliver excellent performance. If it is your plan to buy one of these old military rifles, you should examine it thoroughly, have it checked over by a good gunsmith, and shoot it before you buy if you possibly can.

A good 7mm Mauser rifle makes a fine deer rifle; factory ammunition will do the job nicely, although the 175-grain bullet has a pretty high trajectory and shouldn't be used at ranges over 200 yards. Still, most shots at deer are at far less than 200, so this rifle will do the job in most cases. With proper handloads, the 7mm can be used for varmints, and it also can be used on all North American big game. Additional loadings are available in other bullet weights, such as the Federal 139-grain and a Norma 150-grain, which will be found more versatile than the 175-grain load. Quite possibly other loads will be added as time goes by. The 7mm is most likely going to be with us for many more years.

There is also a rimmed version of this cartridge which is used in a number of Continental double rifles and drillings (three-barrel rifle/shotgun combinations). It is known as the 7×57R.

.284 Winchester. This was a short-lived cartridge expressly designed for the now-obsolete Winchester Model 88 and Model 100, lever-action and autoloading respectively. It was designed to offer a short, fat cartridge that could operate through these short-action rifles. While the head of the cartridge case was of standard size, the same as a .30/06, its body was fatter than the head. This type of cartridge case is called "rebated." The result was that the .284 Winchester developed performance about like that of the .280 Remington, which follows, even though

the case was about ½ inch shorter. Similar cartridge shapes have been used by British and Continental designers, but this was the first American case like it.

Introduced in 1963, the cartridge was also briefly available in Savage Model 99, Ruger Model 77, and Browning High Power rifles. None are available now, and this cartridge is obsolete. You may find a rifle on the used list somewhere, and it could represent a good buy. The price should be low, and you should buy a quantity of ammunition for it, because while it's still being manufactured, it won't be for much longer. The .284 is an excellent deer rifle and is, in fact, capable of handling anything the .270 or .280 will.

When it was first introduced the .284 spawned a whole new group of wildcats by being necked down and up to other calibers. While many of these were quite interesting, they haven't lasted any longer than the parent cartridge.

.280 Remington. Remington introduced this cartridge in 1957. It was thirty-two years too late. Had it been introduced along with the .270 Winchester, or even a few years later, it would most likely have been the survivor. But it will be the .270 that survives, not the .280.

This is a fine cartridge. It is what the .270 should have been, because there was no reason to introduce a new caliber as Winchester did in 1925. The .270 is only .007 inch smaller than the 7mm (the .280 is a 7mm). But that's what they did, and it has been a real winner, while the .280 is headed for obsolescence.

I had a fine Remington Model 725 rifle in .280 Remington for several years that performed brilliantly. I carried it as a spare rifle on a caribou hunt in Quebec one year, but I never killed game with it, though it was capable of superb accuracy.

At this writing, the only rifles chambered for the .280 are the Remington Model 742 autoloader and Ruger 77. This is a shame, but Remington itself helped kill the .280 with the 7mm Remington Magnum. A .280 Remington is suitable for any game in North America. You need not worry about its becoming obsolete, because cartridge cases can always be made from .30/06, since it's nothing more than that case necked to 7mm.

7mm Remington Magnum. One of the most sensational cartridges to come along in years. Evidently Remington was motivated by the .264 Winchester Magnum to develop this cartridge, because both are quite similar in size and appearance. The 7mm, however, has some advantages—greater versatility through more available bullets, less bore heat and wear due to the larger size resulting in longer barrel life. Also, it drives heavier bullets faster than the .264.

As a result of these advantages, and its rapid rise in popularity, this cartridge is being made by virtually every major manufacturer here and abroad and ammunition is available in every brand.

Before the development of this Remington cartridge there were a number of 7mm wildcat cartridges based on belted magnum cartridge cases and similar to the 7mm Remington in size, appearance, and capacity. Among these was the 7mm Mashburn Magnum, which was used extensively by the late Warren Page and with which he killed many trophy heads. Page also wrote the cartridge up frequently in *Field & Stream* magazine, which undoubtedly helped promote the idea of a commercial 7mm magnum. The fact that Remington's designer, Mike Walker, was also a good friend of Page's suggests this possibility strongly.

Any careful study of ballistics charts will show you how good the 7mm Remington cartridge is, and either a few shots with a rifle in this caliber or a few words with an owner of one of these rifles will cement the opinion. It's one of the finest cartridge developments to come along in years.

In terms of its use in a deer rifle, which is the subject of this book, the 7mm Remington Magnum is more than amply powerful. It would not be my choice for a pure deer rifle, assuming the rifle was only to be used for deer. However, if you have larger game in mind with the same rifle, then it should be high on your list for consideration. Similarly it should be on the list for a long-range rifle. But this is a hunting cartridge; it's no real fun to shoot, and you won't want to do any fun shooting with it. Put it on your list—you'll be pushed hard to select a better hunting cartridge.

7mm Weatherby Magnum. Whatever is said about the 7mm Remington can be said about the Weatherby, except that it is only available in Weatherby brand. The cartridge came along long before the Remington, but it never achieved widespread popularity. All things considered, there is little reason to choose this cartridge over the Remington since the latter is in wide distribution and is available in a wider variety of rifles with lower list prices than the Weatherby.

7×61 Sharpe & Hart. In 1953, the late Phil Sharpe and Richard

Hart collaborated on a cartridge design which they pushed along with considerable fanfare and publicity. It was largely puffery. Their claim was that they had discovered an experimental French military cartridge and had adapted it to sporting use. If they were sincere about this developmental work, they wasted time and effort, because the basic cartridge is identical with conventional belted magnums. They could simply have done what Weatherby and Remington did and come up with the same result. One is bound to conclude that they might have just done exactly that and built a story around it.

No matter. They got the Schultz and Larson firm, a Danish company, to manufacture rifles, and quite a few were sold. The cartridge is a good performer, roughly the equivalent of the 7mm Remington and Weatherby Magnums. It's just that I've always hated to see so much pure nonsense accompany the introduction of any cartridge unless it's merited. In this case it wasn't. Norma lists commercial ammunition.

Other 7mm Cartridges. Two additional 7mm cartridges have been on the American scene in small numbers. One is the .275 Holland & Holland Magnum, from the same London firm that gave us the .300 and .375 H&H cartridges. This was once loaded by Western Cartridge Co., and quite a few custom rifles were made during the 1930s by such firms as Hoffman, Griffin & Howe, Niedner, and others. It was a fine cartridge and should have taken hold long ago. The present 7mm Remington is a better cartridge, however. Another import is the 7×64mm Brenneke from Germany, which has received a good amount of publicity in the United States. This is the same firm that developed the famed Brenneke shotgun slug, a current import from Interarms. At one time Norma listed ammunition for the 7×64 but I believe it's an obsolete item now.

7.35mm Carcano. The Italian government, for a brief period, adopted this cartridge, which used a .300-inch-diameter bullet. It is not a .30 caliber rifle by simple definition and so is listed before we get to that caliber.

The 7.35 was adopted in 1938 but was abandoned during World War II in favor of a return to the 6.5mm because of logistical problems supplying two cartridges and rifles. The Italians had enough problems without compounding them this way, so the 7.35mm rifles were stored, although a few saw service with the Finnish army. These rifles were sold in the United States as surplus after the war at very low prices. No matter how low the price, they were no bargain. The action was poor, and the workmanship was terrible.

This rifle is not recommended, but only because it is of such poor quality. The cartridge itself is perfectly all right—it's virtually a necked-up 6.5mm Carcano.

12

Calibers .30 and Over

Rifle calibers from .30 up include a vast number that are far too powerful for deer hunting. Certainly a .458 Winchester Magnum will kill a deer, and without ruining much meat either, but there is little point. Similarly, this group of cartridges includes a number of old-timers that should be put out to pasture. Those who tend to measure the power of a rifle by the size of the hole in the barrel should learn that an antique like the .44/40 isn't worth toting into the woods.

Cartridges in this group will be bracketed by the diameter of their bullets. The first group is entirely within the .308-inch bullet diameter, from .30 carbine to .300 Weatherby Magnum.

.308 CALIBER
.30 M1 Carbine. This little cartridge, and a small rifle to go with it, was developed on a crash basis by Winchester in 1940. Its purpose was to replace the .45 auto pistol as a sidearm by most U.S. Army service troops. (Service troops are those nonfighting branches like Ordnance, Quartermaster, etc. The fighting branches are Infantry, Armor, etc.)

The definition of a carbine is fairly loose. It means a short-barreled light rifle that can be carried on horseback. Since "short barrel" and "light" are difficult words to pin down, the word "carbine" has embraced many variations. The firearms most typically known as carbines today are those with barrels approximately 20 inches long. And since both Winchester and Marlin call their 20-inch-barreled lever-action models carbines, I think it suitable to use this rough definition. Keep in mind that anyone can call anything a carbine and it would be hard to dispute.

The M1 carbine ammunition is factory-loaded with a 100-grain bullet at a muzzle velocity of 1990 fps. This load is not suitable for deer hunting. Most service carbines deliver poor accuracy, which, combined with the impotency of the cartridge, further removes the combination from consideration as a sporting firearm. During World War II, as an Ordnance officer, I worked with a number of carbines to try to achieve a degree of accuracy that would be impressive. It never happened and I gave up the effort.

There are many carbines in use, however. Most of these were service guns sold off as surplus, but many also are of new manufacture. Furthermore, Marlin made a few Model 62 rifles in this caliber, and the Thompson/Center pistol is available in .30 Carbine. No matter, it's still a poor choice, and I can think of no justifiable reason to buy one.

.30/30 Winchester. "The .30/30 is a has-been. It should be retired. It's underpowered by today's standards and nobody buying a new rifle should even consider it."

That's what a lot of folks say; including some who call themselves experts. Absolute nonsense. The .30/30 is as good today as it has ever been. In fact, it's one of my favorites.

You must remember that about 90 percent of the deer shot are at ranges less than 50 yards. And all you need for that kind of shooting is a .30/30. Besides, it's still used, and still bought, in places like the Far West where you might think most shots will be at long range. Not so. Most ranges are still short, and the .30/30 is therefore still adequate.

During 1976-77, Remington ran an advertising campaign designed to "upgrade" hunters to the .30/06 (Remington doesn't make a .30/30). The campaign has been dropped—not because it was a failure, but because Remington hired a new advertising agency. But the campaign won't work, and Remington would be better advised to make a rifle in .30/30 caliber.

Winchester has made more than 4,500,000 Model 94 rifles, most of them in .30/30. Marlin has made close to 3,500,000 Model 336 (including the preceding Models 1893 and 36) rifles, most of them in .30/30. Add the hundreds of thousands made by such other companies as Savage and others long out of business. The total is a staggering number of .30/30 rifles that have been made since Winchester introduced the cartridge in 1895.

Remington asks, in its ad: "Is the .30/30 still the best deer rifle?" The answer is no, it is not the best deer rifle. But you must qualify the answer, because under most deer-hunting situations, the .30/30 is as good as the best deer rifle (for the record, there *is* no "best" deer rifle).

I have a Marlin 336 .30/30 carbine with a 2½ × Marlin scope with which I have shot a number of whitetails in Maine back in the days before they raised the nonresident's license to a preposterous figure. This rifle shoots awfully well, and I have even shot the heads off a number of partridges with it at ranges up to about 40 yards. I also have a Winchester Model 94 that I use when iron sights are called for. I am very fond of these rifles and of the .30/30 cartridge.

I've been in this game long enough, I believe, to know why many writers do not like the .30/30. In fact, there was a time when I thought it a poor cartridge. But that was in earlier days when I was younger and when I accepted the word of others. I had to prove to myself that the .30/30 was a good cartridge. Most people get smarter as they get older and get more experience. One of the things I have learned over the years is that you should not accept the opinions of others without asking questions.

Some years back I was a custom rifle maker working with many of the exotic wildcats of the day. Most of us engaged in that profession—indeed, most of those with whom we came in contact—wouldn't even pay much attention to factory standard cartridges. The .30/06 was a tolerable exception, but the .30/30 was beneath our notice. Gradually, however, it began to be evident that the factory cartridges were not really all that bad. Most of them could do everything that most of our wildcats could do.

Then, in the early 1960s, I got hold of a Marlin Model 336 in conjunction with my advertising work for that company and began to see what the little rifle could do. I hunted that fall with the rifle and popped a deer neatly behind a blowdown near the Allagash River. He went down like a stone. The awakening began, and I would urge my colleagues who write sage advice for hunters to evaluate on the basis of performance with no preconceived notions. You can't argue with success, and the ancient .30/30 has plenty of it.

The cartridge was introduced in 1895 along with the Model 1894 rifle. It was the first smokeless sporting rifle in America and it set the shooting world afire. It's still setting sales records, although I believe the .30/06 has overtaken it in terms of ammunition sales. But the .30/30 was number one for about seventy-five years!

The first load was with a 165-grain bullet at 1870 fps; the powder charge was 30 grains of powder. Just why Winchester saw fit to use the black-powder designation is hard to say at this late date. Today's loads are a 150-grain bullet at 2390 fps and a 170-grain at 2200 fps. I think it may be safe to say that most users of the .30/30 don't even know there are two loads produced! Not that it makes a hell of a lot of difference—a deer at 50 yards is going to drop as fast with one as with the other. At ranges up to 200 yards both will shoot to about the same point of impact, and 200 yards is probably the practical limit of the .30/30 anyway. I'd say the 170-grain load would have a slight edge if you might run into a black bear, but either load will suffice for both animals.

The only enemy of the .30/30 is ignorance. Anyone who has used it has to appreciate the fact that it does its job thoroughly and with dispatch. It is known as "the deer rifle" with good reason—a lever-action .30/30 carbine *is* a deer rifle.

A cartridge that's identical in performance is the .30 Remington, a rimless cartridge produced by Remington to compete with the .30/30 in Remington's pump and auto rifles. The .30 Remington is obsolete now and not very many were ever made. Still, if you happen across one in the used-gun market, regard it as the equal of the .30/30. But be sure to get some ammunition with the rifle or don't buy it. Then save your brass and reload (using .30/30 load data!).

The .30/30 has also been made in a number of bolt-action rifles over the years as well as some single-shots and, currently, the Savage pump-action. In most of these rifles, you can load at slightly higher pressure levels, and you can, by reloading, use pointed bullets. The latter are not suitable for the tubular magazines used on Winchester and Marlin lever-action rifles.

Remington .30/30 Accelerator. Remington announced this cartridge on the heels of the successful .30/06 Accelerator, which has exceeded their wildest sales forecasts.

To oversimplify, the Accelerator is loaded by placing a .22 caliber bullet (.224 inch) in a plastic sabot (the word means shoe and is pronounced without the "t"). Since the sabot is .30 caliber, it takes the rifling perfectly, and since the whole unit is much lighter than a conventional .30 caliber bullet, it leaves the muzzle like a lightning stroke, whereupon the bullet sheds the sabot.

In .30/30, the muzzle velocity according to Remington is 3400 fps from a 24-inch test barrel. The 55-grain softpoint bullet used in this load can safely be used in tubular magazines of the traditional Winchester/Marlin type. Remington further says that the trajectory of this bullet, from a .30/30 rifle, approximates that of the .222 Remington using a 50-grain bullet. Clearly this is not a deer stopper, but ought to make an interesting varmint combination.

The sabot idea is far from new. It has been tried many times in the past and in many countries, but the first successful commercial use was by Remington in the .30/06. This certainly won't be the last! Remington officials are mum about the future, but one doesn't need more than a fuzzy crystal ball to see that the .308 ought to be next. And who knows what will follow. Maybe a 6mm bullet in .30/06. You can take it from there; there are lots of possibilities.

So far the handloader is not included in the fun, but I doubt that he'll be excluded for long. I'd guess that Remington will make sabot-loaded bullets available for reloading, that DuPont (which owns Remington anyway) will produce suggested loads, and that some of the independent bullet makers like Hornady will also provide plastic sabots that you can stick your own bullets in and load in whatever cartridge you please.

7.5 mm Swiss. Officially adopted by the Swiss in 1889, the 7.5 mm Schmidt Rubin is available here as a surplus rifle. Using a straight-pull bolt action, meaning that the bolt handle is pulled and pushed straight back and forth without raising, the rifle is an adequate one for deer hunting. However, ammunition is difficult to find and military ammo should not be used. So this would be a sketchy proposition; the best plan would be to reload if you have one of these rifles.

.300 Savage. This was once a very popular game cartridge, especially in the Savage Model 99 rifle in which the cartridge was introduced in 1920 or 1921. Its 150-grain ballistics were, at that time, about equal to the .30/06 with the same bullet. But the .300 Savage was blasted out of the market by the .308 Winchester, and this latter cartridge has taken its place.

The .300 Savage is an excellent cartridge, and many rifles, including some bolt-action models, are in use. It is likely that ammunition will be loaded for many years to come. This cartridge can be recommended for deer hunting without reservation, but not for larger species.

.308 Winchester. This is the sporting version of the 7.62mm NATO cartridge adopted as standard by all nations belonging to the North Atlantic Treaty Organization. Shorter than the .30/06, and lighter in weight, the .308 is a better military cartridge, especially for use in automatic weapons. Ammunition for 7.6mm NATO and .308 Winchester are interchangeable.

Many people consider the .308 the ballistic equal of the .30/06. But the numbers do not support this contention. The .308 drives a 150-grain bullet at 2820 fps and a 180-grain at 2620. The corresponding figures for the .30/06 are 2920 and 2700. This may not seem like very much, and indeed it is not very much. But the '06 is a superior and more powerful cartridge. When it comes to a heavier bullet the .308 is loaded with a 200-grain at about the same speed as the .30/06's 220-grain. Clearly, the .30/06 has an edge.

But that difference isn't important in a deer rifle. The .308 is an excellent deer rifle and can be used, with 150- or 180-grain loads, on either whitetails or muleys at whatever ranges you can score a good hit.

Rifles in .308 Winchester caliber also have become very popular for target shooting, principally because the recoil is milder than with the '06. Autoloading, pump, lever, and bolt rifles are all available in this caliber, which is rapidly becoming one of the more popular hunting cartridges in America.

.30/40 Krag. Here's an old-timer that still has a lot of appeal, as it should. Even though phased out by the military in 1903 in favor of the "new Springfield" (which was chambered for the .30/03 until the cartridge was changed in 1906 and became the .30/06), the .30/40 is still an excellent cartridge with performance not too far below that of the .308.

The .30/40 was adopted by the Army in 1892 for the Model 1892 Krag rifle, copied from the Danish Krag-Jorgensen. It was the first American cartridge to be loaded with smokeless powder and was known as the .30/Army (it was never adopted by the Navy or Marines). The .30/40 designation followed black-powder practice, with "40" indicating the weight of the powder charge in grains.

Many Krag rifles were sold as surplus for $1.50 each. Because of the smoothness of this fine action, vast numbers of them were used as sporters, and they made a fine hunting rifle suitable for any game in North America. Winchester also made the Model 1895 rifle in this caliber. It was taken out of the line in 1936. Other rifles were made in this caliber by Winchester and Remington. Today, the Ruger Number Three single-shot rifle is made for .30/40 and is a fine rifle combining light weight, easy handling, and excellent accuracy.

The Krag rifle, however, is made with a single locking lug, which means the rifle should be used only with factory-loaded ammunition or its reloaded equivalent. Under no circumstances should any of these older rifles be loaded to maximum. However, the new Ruger may be loaded substantially higher.

7.62mm Russian. This cartridge was adopted by the Russian government in 1891 and rifles were manufactured in quantity during World War I by Remington, Winchester, and New England Westinghouse. Remington loaded ammunition for this cartridge until about 1950; Norma lists ammunition today.

With a 180-grain bullet at 2624 fps in Norma load, the 7.62mm Russian is suitable for any game on the continent. It also has been used for years by Soviet Marksmen in International competition and has sparked some interest among other nations' shooters as well. This is not to suggest that the cartridge is more accurate than another cartridge, because cartridge shape has no bearing on accuracy when other things are the same. But it does prove this a sound cartridge that can be used for deer hunting with total confidence.

.30/06. If this isn't the most famous cartridge in the western hemisphere I'll eat the pages of this book. And the .30/06 has gained this position by virtue of merit. It was developed in 1906 for the 1903 Springfield rifle—or, officially, the "U.S. Rifle, Caliber .30, Model 1903."

When the military adopted the 1903 rifle in that year, they also adopted a .30 caliber rimless cartridge which was loaded with a 220-grain bullet at a velocity of about 2200 fps. It wasn't much better than the .30/40 Krag. The 1903 rifle was actually not issued until 1905, and experiments with the cartridge continued. In 1906 the bullet weight was dropped to 150 grains and the shape changed from a round nose to a sharp pointed nose after the German spitzer designs. The velocity was also boosted to 2700 fps and the case neck was shortened slightly.

In 1906 the new cartridge was formally adopted and all rifles that had been issued were recalled and reworked, which effectively eliminated nearly all the .30/03 rifles in distribution. The .30/06 achieved its early fame during World War I, when millions of Americans were exposed to the bolt-action Springfield .30/06 rifle (the U.S. 1917 Enfield rifle was chambered for the same cartridge and used in the same war). Prior to World War I most hunters preferred the lever-action rifle, and no commercial bolt rifle was yet in production by any American factory. After the war, however, Remington modified the action of the 1917 Enfield .30/06 and, with thousands of parts left over from war production, began marketing its Model 30 bolt-action rifle. This was the first commercial bolt-action rifle of the modern type marketed in this country. In 1925 Winchester followed with its Model 54 rifle, which was substantially upgraded in 1937 and became the Model 70 Winchester.

If I were to be limited to just one rifle it would be a .30/06. And I think almost any serious rifleman would make the same choice. I would be hard pressed to offer reasons for this choice, except to note that the '06 is quite possibly the most versatile of all cartridges. Its ammunition can be found anywhere in the civilized world. And it will handle any game one is ever likely to encounter except Africa's Big Five—elephant, rhino, buffalo, lion, leopard. (It can kill those beasts but is not recommended.) At the opposite end of the spectrum the .30/06 is usable, if not especially suitable, for varmint shooting.

But the subject of this book is deer rifles, and the .30/06 is as good as they come. It will handle deer at long range and at short range. On a recent mule-deer hunt I was carrying my favorite bolt-action .30/06, which is a prototype action not yet announced. The stock is by Al Biesen, one of our top custom stockmakers. The scope is a Redfield and the rifle shoots into ½ inch at 100 yards. I had it sighted so I could handle any shots I was likely to encounter in the New Mexico canyons, which means I was ready to take any shot up to about 500 yards, since I knew exactly where the bullet would be at all distances up to that point. With all that preparation I ran across a trophy buck at a distance of only 10 yards. He saw me the same time I saw him and I caught him in the shoulders as he was taking off. The 180-grain Nosler bullet anchored him in his tracks.

While the .30/06 offers more power than is needed for most deer shooting, it is an excellent choice no matter the terrain in which you'll be hunting. For most deer hunting the 150-grain bullet is the most popular choice, but for long-range shooting you're better off with the 180-grain. Even though the 180-grain starts slower than the 150, it is going faster at 500 yards because the added weight retains its momentum better.

In the late 1940s and 1950s, there was considerable activity in rechambering .30/06 rifles to various versions of the ".30/06 Improved." This means cutting the chamber larger at the front end, then firing standard cartridges and letting them blow out to the larger shape. They could then be reloaded with more powder and, hopefully, deliver more velocity. While this method of improving did actually work with some cartridges it did not work with the .30/06; it was soon confirmed that this alteration merely required the use of more powder to achieve the same velocities that the standard cartridge delivered. In fact, all it accomplished was to add to bore erosion due to more powder burned and more heat generated.

.300 Holland & Holland Magnum. The .300 H&H Magnum cartridge was developed by the famous London firm of gunmakers in 1920. It was available in this country only in custom rifles up until 1937 when Winchester produced the Model 70 rifle in this caliber. A chap named Ben Comfort won the Wimbledon 1,000-yard match at Camp Perry, Ohio, with a .300 Magnum in 1935, and the rifle rode on the coattails of that publicity. Western Cartridge Company began making ammunition in 1925.

This cartridge is known in England as the "Super Thirty" and has been popular there for years. While the .300 H&H was popular for many years, its use has waned in the United States and there is now no commercial rifle made for it. The reason is that newer and better cartridges have come along. The .300 H&H is most notable today because its belted cartridge case has been the basis of all the belted magnums.

A bit on the overpowered side for a deer rifle, the .300 H&H can do the job at long range. It is a little faster than the .30/06. One of the limiting factors with the .300 H&H is that the long cartridge requires a magnum action—that is, one longer than the standard, which is made for cartridges of the same length as the .30/06. Many owners of .300 H&H rifles have had them rechambered for the .300 Weatherby Magnum, which is possible with any good strong action. But that alteration lifts the rifle up and out of the deer-rifle category unless you want to shoot at extra long range.

.308 Norma Magnum. The Swedish ammunition company developed this cartridge about 1961 and actually furnished chamber-

ing reamers to some gunsmiths so they could rechamber .30/06 rifles to handle the cartridge.

Basically the .308 Norma is the same as a .338 Winchester Magnum necked down to .30 caliber. Since the .338 was originally a .300 H&H (or .375—they both had the same origin) but shortened to work through a standard action, the .300 was the basis for this and other belted magnum cartridges.

Since a little bit of the cartridge case must extend from the rear of the barrel in order for the extractor to grasp the case, that case must be very strong. A belted case head is stronger than other types simply because the brass is thicker at that point; hence the superiority of the belted case.

Of course, any standard .30/06 that was rechambered to the .308 Norma, or any other belted case, required its bolt face opened to the larger diameter and some adjustments made to the magazine. Rifles like the Remington Model 721 with its counterbored bolt face and unique extractor were better left alone. The .30/06 barrel has the correct bore and groove dimensions for this cartridge.

A few rifles in this caliber were made and imported by Browning, but the .308 Norma began a fast fall with the introduction of the .300 Winchester Magnum, a very similar cartridge. Today you won't see any new rifles for the .308 Norma, and there would be no reason for them. As a deer rifle, the cartridge is overpowered but well suited to long-range shooting.

.300 Winchester Magnum. Announced in 1963, the .300 was the last in a series of four introduced by Winchester in 1956. First was the .458 in 1956, followed by the .338 in 1958 and the .264 in 1959. All are essentially the same cartridge case which originated with the original .300 H&H Magnum.

This is one of the finer long-range cartridges; it was developed to be just that. The reason for its introduction would seem to be the popularity of custom rifles built around the .338 Winchester necked to .30 caliber, and the .300 Norma. Winchester lengthened the case body slightly and produced the .300 Winchester. It has become exceedingly popular. The same comments made for the Norma cartridge apply here as well; use the .300 Winchester for long-range deer hunting. It is not a short-range rifle and will do *almost* anything the .300 Weatherby will.

.300 Weatherby Magnum. Developed at about the end of

World War II by Roy Weatherby, this has become the long-range cartridge by which all others are measured. That's quite an accomplishment for what began as a small company. Weatherby built his empire on the .300 cartridge. Factory-loaded ammunition became available in about 1948, and Weatherby still imports his ammunition.

I believe that in the early days Roy Weatherby rechambered customers' rifles in .300 H&H Magnum for his cartridge, but with the demise of that factory cartridge I doubt its done any more. It is a simple matter to obtain cases for the .300 Weatherby by simply firing .300 H&H cartridges. The gas pressure will blow out the case to the new dimensions, whereupon it can be reloaded with much more powder to produce much more velocity. The .300 Weatherby began life as a wildcat; you had to "fire-form" your cartridges and reload them. So useful has the cartridge become and so well has Roy Weatherby promoted it that distribution is now worldwide. You can buy .300 Weatherby ammo in some of the most distant parts of the free world.

A comparison of factory ballistics is interesting. The parent .300 H&H Magnum drives a 180-grain bullet at 2880 fps, while the Weatherby drives the same weight bullet at 3245 fps. That's an impressive difference and explains why the Weatherby became so popular. By way of further comparison, the .300 Winchester Magnum drives a bullet of the same weight at 3000 fps. Owners of the .300 Winchester need not hide their heads in the sand.

It's useful to note that Weatherby's factory ammunition is loaded to very high pressures. Very few handloads are listed at anywhere near the same velocity. A common impression about handloads is that they are hotter than factory ammo, but this is not true by any means. The only cases where you can handload to appreciably higher velocities are those few examples of older cartridges which are purposely down-loaded because many older, and weaker, rifles are still in use.

Using a .300 Weatherby Magnum is being way overgunned when hunting deer. It is a very useful rifle for this size game only when shooting at extreme range. If your shots are 300 yards or better, this would make a fine rifle for the purpose—provided that you have the capability and the mental discipline to take only shots where you know you can place the bullet in a vital spot, and that your rifle is capable of delivering minute-of-angle accuracy. Other hunters should take up some other sport. The

.300 Weatherby is one of the finest of all super-long-range rifles and has the power to handle any game in North America. Fact is, it has the power to down any game anywhere in the world.

.312 CALIBER
There are three cartridges using bullets of this diameter: the .303 British, 7.65 Belgian, and 7.7mm Japanese. It is interesting to note that at least one maker of bullets for reloading makes them .311 inch. It doesn't matter—either size will do, since the smaller .311-inch slugs will expand from the sharp push the gas gives them before they begin to move.

.303 British. While this has never been a popular cartridge in the United States, it was the British service cartridge from 1888 until 1950, when the 7.62mm NATO (.308 Winchester) was adopted. As a result, it was used by British sportsmen around the world. For example, tens of thousands of rifles in .303 British went to Africa during the Boer War. Additional thousands were seen in the various British colonies during those years, and, of course, they were widely used for sporting purposes. It's likely the .303 has killed more African game than any other single cartridge—and perhaps wounded more!

Canada also adopted the .303, and therefore it has had considerable use in North America. The British rifle is the SMLE (Short Magazine Lee Enfield), which is no great shakes as a sporting candidate but has proved an effective war rifle through probably more battles, wars, and skirmishes than any other single rifle has endured. Originally loaded with black powder, the .303 was changed to smokeless in 1892. It remains a fine cartridge that can be expected to produce excellent results on deer.

In U.S. terms, the .303 is roughly equivalent to the .30/40 Krag. The biggest problem with the .303 in America is that it is available only in the British military rifle. At one time Winchester made its Model 1895 lever-action for the .303 but there were few of these in existence. Converting the British rifle into a sporter is a waste of time and money; far better rifles exist for that purpose.

7.65mm Belgian Mauser. This cartridge's commercial designation is the 6.5 × 53mm Mauser, and it has been the official cartridge of Belgium, Peru, Turkey, Argentina, Ecuador, and Paraguay. It was the first small-bore, smokeless-powder rifle/

cartridge combination produced by the great Mauser works, officially in the Model 1889 rifle adopted in that year. It is a fine cartridge which was once made in the Winchester Model 54 and Model 70 and the Remington Model 30S as well as the earlier Remington Lee.

German barrels in this caliber run from .310 to .312 inch, while Belgian barrels run .312 to .314 inch. Norma lists a 250-grain bullet at 2920 fps—100 fps faster than the .308 with the same bullet weight. That points up pretty solid performance, and the cartridge will make an excellent deer rifle. Moreover, some of the Mauser rifles in this caliber are excellent, but you should not buy one of the older ones. Get one that is Model 98 or later in style and you will have a fine barrel and action from which to make a fine deer-hunting sporter.

7.7mm Japanese. A lot of these rifles were brought home by servicemen in World War II. The Japanese Type 99 rifle for the 7.7mm cartridge was adopted in 1939 and was the primary military rifle and cartridge of World War II. If there ever was a commercial rifle made in this caliber I never heard of it. Nor did I ever hear of anyone making a custom rifle. But many of the Japanese rifle souvenirs were converted to sporters—of a sort.

This rifle has a very strong action, far stronger than is generally believed. It is also made very cheaply and with terrible workmanship. The rifle was adopted in 1939 and Japan began the war only two years later, so manufacturing quality was not the best. The rifles therefore must be classified as usable but as far from ideal as you can get.

The 7.7mm cartridge is loaded by Norma in 130-grain and 180-grain weights. It is an effective deer cartridge if the rifle is capable of delivering adequate accuracy.

.321 CALIBER

.32 Winchester Special. This cartridge was quite popular in the Winchester Model 94 rifle for many years. It was first announced in 1895, and Winchester finally abandoned it in the early 1970s.

For some strange reason owners of .32 Special rifles thought they were superior to .30/30 rifles, and many was the argument over which was the "hardest hitter." Actually, for any practical purpose, the two are identical in performance.

Everything I said about the .30/30 applies equally to the .32 Special when it comes to performance on deer. Ammunition is still loaded and probably will be for some years to come, since there are still a great many rifles in use in both Winchester and Marlin brands.

A very similar cartridge, the .32 Remington, was developed by that company as a competitor to the Winchester. Its performance is similar but there were very few rifles ever made and you are not too likely to see one.

.323 CALIBER

8×57mm Mauser. The great German service rifle and cartridge. Like the military cartridges of all great nations, this one is used worldwide and has performed brilliantly over the years since its adoption in 1888.

The original cartridge in 1888 rifles was loaded with a bullet measuring .318 inch and a weight of 227 grains. But this was changed in 1905 in favor of a 150-grain spitzer (the German word for "pointed") bullet at much higher velocity. The new bullet was also slightly larger, .323 inch. As a result the earlier rifles are unsafe with modern ammunition (it being risky to drive an oversize bullet through a too-small hole) because pressures are boosted to unsafe levels. To differentiate between the two, the earlier version with smaller bore is known as the 8×57 J, and the later, modern version is known as the 8×57 S. Since there are many older 1888 Mauser rifles in use in this country, the factory-loaded ammunition is loaded down to levels that will be safe in these rifles.

This has been one reason for the lack of popularity of what really is one of the world's finer cartridges. It does not offer top performance with factory loads. The handloader, however, can produce results that bring the 8mm Mauser up to its potential and to a level approximating that of the .30/06. A 150-grain bullet, for example, can be driven at velocities up to 2900 fps. By comparison, the factory load is with a 170-grain bullet at the moderate speed of 2520 fps.

Any 8mm Mauser rifle in good condition will make a fine deer rifle, and there is nothing whatever wrong with the factory-loaded ammunition for this purpose. If you want to tackle larger North American game, Norma has a 196-grain load at 2526 fps, or you can reload for better performance.

There are hundreds of thousands of 8mm Mauser rifles in this

country, the result of souvenir and surplus operations. The cartridge was used by many other nations in addition to Germany
8mm/06. During the years immediately following World War II many owners of liberated 8mm Mauser rifles wanted to use them and found factory ammunition was hard to find; it took the manufacturing giants a long time to supply demand because all the stocks had been depleted. Military ammunition loaded in Europe was primed with the Berdan primer, which could only be replaced with great difficulty and wasn't worth the bother.

The solution was quick, easy, and inexpensive: running a chamber reamer into the barrel and cutting the chamber slightly larger to accommodate the .30/06 cartridge case necked up to 8mm. The result was a fine wildcat cartridge that could be easily reloaded, since .30/06 brass cases were in ample supply. At about the same time the then-new bullet makers Sierra, Hornady, and Speer were embarking on their business ventures and were only too happy to supply such a ready market.

Another bonus was that a little more velocity could be squeezed out of the .30/06 case, since it had a bit more capacity. If you have an 8mm/06, or if you have an 8×57mm Mauser in good condition that can be rechambered, you will find the cartridge a fine one for deer hunting. Its only drawback is that it requires handloading, but so many shooters are reloading today that this is no longer much of a disadvantage. The 8mm/06 is also potent enough for all North American game.

8mm Remington Magnum. This is a 1977 development that is still pretty new and therefore a little difficult to evaluate until more evidence comes in. A genuine hellbender, this cartridge will prove to be an excellent extreme-range number but is vastly overpowered for ordinary deer hunting.

I have been shooting a Remington Model 700 rifle in this caliber for some months and am much impressed with it. It does provide very heavy recoil and is not pleasant to shoot from the bench. However, it performs well and shoots accurately.

Driving a 185-grain bullet at 3080 fps and 220-grain at 2830 fps, the 8mm Remington Magnum is really screaming downrange. While it's difficult to compare apples and oranges, the .300 Winchester Magnum drives a 220-grain bullet at 2680 fps, so there is a margin there. The bullets from both rifles drop about the same out as far as 500 yards, so for any practical purpose there is not too much difference in performance.

I wouldn't recommend the 8mm Remington for deer hunting.

But I would recommend it as a fine all-around long-range game rifle that will anchor a deer as far as you can shoot it accurately. This cartridge will easily handle all game in North America.

.338 CALIBER

.33 Winchester. Winchester's .33 was a favorite of many deer, moose, and bear hunters for years. Introduced in 1902 for the Winchester Model 1886 lever-action rifle, it was abandoned in 1936 when the company revamped that rifle's action and reissued it as the Model 71 chambered for a new cartridge, the .348 Winchester.

A lot of .33 caliber rifles are still around, although the cartridge is no longer available. Owners of these rifles may handload for them, since Hornady makes a flat-pointed bullet of 200 grains for this cartridge and the Model 86's tubular magazine. It can be driven up to 2200 fps, and cases can be made from .45/70 brass.

I have known a number of older hunters who used the .33 for years and swore by it. It earned a reputation as a fine "meat in the pot" rifle. It's highly recommended for deer with the above provisions.

.338 Winchester Magnum. Here's one of my favorite rifles. I obtained a Model 70 rifle in this caliber the year the cartridge was announced. In fact, I had that rifle in 1958 before it was made public and was smart enough to buy it. Today it has been restocked and fitted with a fine Redfield 2-7× variable scope. This rifle shoots amazingly tight groups, as small as ½ inch at 100 yards. (These are three-shot groups, the maximum number of shots I think should be used with any hunting rifle.)

The .338 Magnum was developed by Winchester as a rifle for the biggest North American game, and it succeeds admirably in this regard. It also is very reliable on the plains game of Africa. But where this rifle really shines, in my opinion, is as a long-range deer rifle.

I took my .338 to New Mexico a few years ago on a combination deer and elk hunt, figuring to use it on elk and a .30/06 on deer. Which is just what I did. However, I lent the .338 to a companion on this trip who hunted with a different party one day. I had fully briefed him on its trajectory with my handloaded 210-grain Nosler partition bullets and Hercules Re 21 powder. This chap had a shot at a sleek mule-deer buck at an even 300 yards. Only the back of the deer was visible; the rest was hidden by a rock behind which the buck was standing. At the shot, the deer dropped out of sight and was found stone dead in his tracks.

Most owners of the .338 Winchester Magnum look upon their rifles as heavy guns, suitable for use on big, tough, dangerous game with heavy bullets. And in this they are right. The .338 is superb on game like grizzly, polar bear, and moose with 250- and 300-grain bullets. But these shooters are overlooking one of the finest attributes of the .338 when they don't use it with lighter bullets for long-range shooting. It will astound you with its performance. To sum this up, a .338, using 200- or 210-grain bullets, comes very close to the flat trajectory of the .300 Winchester Magnum—out to 500 yards (using 180-grain bullets in .300).

In addition to the Model 70 I also have a Browning autoloading .338 Magnum (BAR), which shoots very well also. I have not hunted with the BAR but have shot it extensively from the bench, where it performs nicely (and is a lot more comfortable to shoot with its gas operation that provides lower recoil).

I wouldn't advise buying a .338 for a deer rifle, but it's something to think about if you shoot at long range, and if you also have the need for a heavy rifle that will handle all North American game with ease.

.340 Weatherby Magnum. Here's the big buster in this bore size. Despite the name, it also uses .338-inch bullets, and with full-length Magnum cartridges it develops more of everything than the .338 Winchester.

The .340 Weatherby Magnum will do everything with a 225-grain bullet that the .338 Winchester will do with a 200. That means you can add 25 grains of bullet weight to the combination and deliver correspondingly more energy to the target. The .338 excels at long-range shooting, but the .340 betters it. This has to be one of the most effective and authoritative long-range cartridges ever developed. Weatherby produces factory loads in 200-, 210-, and 250-grain bullet weights.

I have a .340 Weatherby rifle with Weatherby Mark V action and Weatherby scope. It is a sensational combination that produces fine accuracy on targets, though I have never shot game with it.

As with the .338 Winchester, I would not recommend this as a deer rifle but invite its consideration for a rifle to handle all North American big game and African plains game. Handloaded with a bullet like the Hornady 250-grain "solid" (which means a copper-plated steel jacket for penetration in such thick-skinned beasts as elephant), it is suitable for Africa's Big Five where the bore size is legal.

.348 CALIBER

.348 Winchester. Just one rifle was ever made for this cartridge, the Model 71 Winchester, which was introduced in 1936 and dropped in 1958. The cartridge replaced the popular .33 Winchester, but the Model 71 proved too costly to manufacture and was dropped from the line for that reason. Moreover, the Model 71 had top ejection, which was fast falling into disfavor because of the difficulty of mounting a scope properly.

A Model 71 .348 is an excellent deer rifle but, should you have one in good condition, I would not recommend using it. The rifle is a valuable collector's item and should be preserved.

.357 CALIBER

.357 Magnum. The .357 Magnum revolver cartridge has been used by a number of custom gunsmiths in converting Winchester Model 92 and Marlin Model 1894 rifles. Both these old rifles have a shorter action than either the Winchester Model 94 or Marlin Model 336. The concept is to provide a rifle/handgun combination where the same ammunition can be used in both.

This concept is far more successful with the .44 Magnum than with the .357. I do not consider the .357 suitable for a deer rifle, though it is acceptable for small varmints. You can also use .38 Special revolver ammunition in a .357 Magnum.

.35 Remington. At one time Remington made rifles and cartridges in .25, .30, .32, and .35 caliber, the first three to compete with popular Winchester cartridges in Winchester's Model 94 rifle. The only Remington survivor is the .35 Remington, and that cartridge has been kept alive by Marlin.

Remington used to make a pair of great favorites—the autoloading Model 8 and Model 81 and the pump-action Model 14 and Model 141. Both rifles were very popular in the wooded sections of the country for deer and bear hunting. Next to the .30/30 the .35 Remington is probably the most popular deer rifle.

But Remington abandoned manufacture of these two rifles in their extensive modernization program immediately following

World War II. While the .35 hung on for a little while in the Remington line it was eventually dropped. But in the meantime, Marlin was closing in on the market with its excellent Model 336 carbine, chambered for the .30/30 and .35 Remington. As it turns out, the excellence of these two cartridges for deer hunting, and the excellence of the Marlin rifle, added up to a vast business for that company with a single rifle model. To date, Marlin has made more than 3,500,000 Model 336 rifles, most of them since the last war.

What's so great about this cartridge? It's an old-timer like the .30/30 that some say ought to have been phased out years ago. It's popular today for two big reasons: it kills deer fast and many think it a great brush buster (I'll have more to say on that subject in the following chapter), and it's available in a popular lever-action rifle, Marlin's 336.

No question that a lot better cartridges have come along since the .35 Remington first saw the light of day in 1906. Its 200-grain bullet moves at 2080 fps at the muzzle. That's terribly slow and should be obsolete by today's standards. But the .35 Remington continues to bag the venison, and that's the name of the game.

As a matter of fact, the .35 is a better deer cartridge than the .30/30 because it's a fatter, heavier bullet that performs better on game than its smaller-bore cousin. The .35 Remington is quite possibly the very best choice for what we generally mean when we use the term "deer rifle." If your deer shooting is average—by which I mean within 100 yards—you have no need of any cartridge bigger than either the .30/30 or the .35 Remington, and you're better off with the latter.

.358 Winchester. Introduced along with the .243 in 1955, the .358 Winchester is based on the .308 cartridge case. To make the .243, Winchester necked the .308 down to 6mm, and to make the .358 they necked the same case up to .35 caliber. It is a fine cartridge and was originally available in the Model 70 bolt-action and the Model 88 lever-action. The cartridge never caught on and was discontinued.

But there is hope. Savage and Browning are both chambering rifles for the .358 now (in 1977), and it can be hoped that it will catch hold this time. The .358 is a great cartridge, considerably better than the .35 Remington. Comparable ballistics for the two show the .35 Remington with a 200-grain bullet at 2080 fps while the .358 gets 2490 with the same weight bullet. Adding to the enticement, the .358 also loads a 250-grain bullet at 2230 fps.

I've recently been shooting a Savage Model 99 in this caliber; it was added to the Savage line in 1976. This is a good rifle, one that will handle deer and black bear very handily and which can be used for such larger game as moose and elk within range. Not a long-range cartridge, the .358 will be found most useful within 200 yards. But that's a pretty fair country distance for most deer shooting.

.35 Whelen. This is an old and pretty well forgotten cartridge today. It was developed by James Howe of Griffin & Howe in 1922 and named in honor of that grand old man of shooting Colonel Townsend Whelen. It was simply the .30/06 necked up the .35 caliber.

Rifles in .35 Whelen were always wildcats, since the cartridge was never adopted by any manufacturer. Should you run across one of these in the used-gun market and it's in good condition, it will make a fine deer rifle, and it has the clout to handle any game in North America. But it will be a handloading proposition.

.350 Remington Magnum. Here's a real screamer that was introduced in 1965 along with the Remington Model 600 rifle. The rifle was one of the ugliest ever made, to my eyes. In any event it was soon dropped; both the rifle and the cartridge are now gone, although the rifle lives on since the same action is used in the Mohawk 600, a promotional brand owned by Remington.

I have one of these Model 600 rifles in .350 Remington and it is one of the nastiest rifles to shoot that I've ever fired. It has a very short barrel, only 18½ inches, which adds to the ruckus when you press the trigger. The rifle also shoots like a house afire; mine has excellent accuracy. I was on a deer hunt one year in Maine with a party that included Joe Widner, then of Lyman and now of Harrington & Richardson. Joe carried a .350 Remington, a lot more rifle than was needed in the Maine woods. As I recall, he shot a fox, partridge, and deer with it.

It is unlikely the .350 Remington will ever stage a comeback; it's probably gone for good. Nevertheless, it was a fine cartridge and will flatten any deer that ever wanders into its sight picture. It will do the same with any North American game and is more than powerful enough for deer.

.358 Norma Magnum. This cartridge was designed and introduced by Norma in 1959. Rifles were made in several imported

brands, but none ever was manufactured here. Brands of rifle that can be found in this caliber are Carl Gustav (formerly Husqvarna or HVA) and Schultz & Larson. I am told that the Omega rifle has been made in this caliber; I have never seen one but this is a very limited-production, high-priced rifle anyway.

The .358 Norma is similar to the .338 Winchester if the latter were necked up to .35 caliber. Ammunition is available in Norma brand. It's suitable for any North American big game and certainly will handle deer.

.375 CALIBER

.375 Winchester. Designed to function in the Model 94 rifle, the cartridge was announced in 1978. Minor alterations to the basic rifle were necessary to make the cartridge feed similar to the way in which Marlin has adapted their Model 336 to several other cartridges. The most visible outward difference in the new Winchester Big Bore 94, as it's been named, is the rubber recoil pad.

I would venture the guess that Winchester developed this cartridge to compete directly with the Marlin 336 in .35 Remington, which has long been a very popular rifle, and with the Savage 99 chambered for .358 Winchester. The .375 Winchester is loaded with a 200-grain Power-Point bullet at 2200 fps muzzle velocity (2150 ft. lbs. muzzle energy) and a 250-grain bullet at 1900 fps muzzle velocity (2005 ft. lbs. muzzle energy). This indicates the 200-grain slug would be proper deer medicine and the 250-grain appropriate for larger game. Still, the rifle would seem to be strictly a deer rifle, and larger game should call for a more powerful rifle. I think it has a good chance to become popular in the 200-grain weight but can see little real need for the heavier bullet.

The .375 Winchester will be a woods rifle; it has very slightly more oomph than the .35 Remington and quite a bit less than the .358. It is a rifle which can be effective to 200 yards although I would suggest 100 as a more reasonable proposition. The 94 rifle is not a satisfactory rifle for scope use and any shot with open sight (as most Model 94s are used) beyond 100 yards is unreliable.

I would further suspect the cartridge will become popular if some other rifles are chambered for it. Since the whole proposition is meant for lever-action woods rifles, will Marlin and Savage also chamber for it? I doubt it. Marlin's 336 in .35 Remington is only inferior on paper; actual field performance won't be worth a gnat's difference. And Savage has the more powerful .358 Winchester in its Model 99.

.375 H&H Magnum. The famous 1912 cartridge from the famed London gunmakers Holland & Holland Ltd. It quickly established a reputation in Africa, where it was found suitable for the largest game. Known as a "medium bore" in African terms, the .375 is vastly more than is necessary in North America. Despite that, it is used by many hunters, and I've known sheep hunters who used it for their long-range specialty.

Western started manufacturing .375 ammunition in 1925, and custom makers such as Griffin & Howe, Hoffman Arms, and others began making rifles in the early days. The first commercial rifle was the Winchester Model 70 in 1937. When that famous rifle was first announced, the .375 was one of its chamberings. Today there are many rifles in .375 H&H and they are quite popular, although the caliber is gradually losing out to the big Weatherby cartridges as well as the .338 Winchester Magnum.

.378 Weatherby Magnum. This is a huge cartridge, bigger than the .375 H&H. It develops 400 fps more than the .375 H&H with the same 270- and 300-grain bullets. That's a lot of increased velocity no matter how you look at it.

It would be ridiculous to hunt deer with such a rifle, about like using a Greyhound bus to run over a mouse. This rifle is capable of slaying the biggest elephant that ever walked the earth.

.429 CALIBER

.44 Remington Magnum. The 1955 introduction of the .44 Magnum revolver and cartridge by Smith & Wesson and Remington did more than produce the world's most powerful handgun. It led Ruger into production of single-action revolvers, which he followed in 1961 with the autoloading carbine that has become very popular in wooded sections of the country for hunting deer.

Shortly after its introduction a number of gunsmiths altered some of the older lever-action rifles to handle the .44 Magnum. This was a difficult conversion. In order for the straight-walled .44 cartridge to feed, it is necessary to elevate it from the magazine in a straight attitude instead of the usual slant. Some time later Marlin began working on its lever-action to develop a .44

Magnum carbine. The result was that Marlin went back in history to its 1894 action and made a modern version of that rifle for the .44. It's shorter and lighter than the 336 and has become increasingly popular. Both the Ruger and Marlin rifles are very popular, in fact.

I've been doing quite a bit of shooting with both Ruger and Marlin .44 rifles. They are impressive. The big, fat bullet moves along nicely at ranges up to 100 yards, which I would call just about the practical limit. Actually, 50 yards is a better limit; the accuracy of these rifles isn't all that great. But most deer are shot under 50 yards anyway. Under no circumstances is a .44 Magnum suitable beyond 100 yards. I've always suspected that the rifling twist was wrong in these rifles, but maybe the research group tried other twists out too.

I do know that when Marlin was working with the cartridge before they announced their rifle, they were having accuracy problems. Marlin was working with a twist of one turn in 38 inches of barrel length, which I thought, and still think, is too slow. I got hold of a bored but unrifled barrel for the 336 Marlin rifle and took it to Bill Gunn, then president at Smith & Wesson, who rifled it for me to the twist used by Smith & Wesson—one turn in 18¾ inches. I returned the barrel to Marlin to be fitted and tested, but the then-production manager (he has since been replaced) wasn't interested and lost the barrel.

Not only is the .44 Magnum bullet not moving at great speed beyond 100 yards, but the accuracy is questionable beyond that. But within the first 100 and especially the first 50, the .44 Magnum is a superb deer rifle, fully on par with the .35 Remington, except not as accurate.

Hornady, the manufacturer of bullets for reloading, has developed a bullet for the .44 Magnum *revolvers* with a metal-cased bullet. This bullet is specifically designed for handguns only and is for metallic silhouette target shooting. Its use should be confined to handguns.

The use of any pointed or metal-cased bullets in any tubular-magazine rifle is to be avoided at all costs. In fact, in testing the bullet, Hornady Manufacturing Co. loaded the magazine of a Ruger .44 Magnum carbine with handloads employing this bullet. Upon firing, the whole magazine was detonated with the result that the entire rifle was blown apart. At this writing, there are three rifles with tubular magazines in this caliber: the Ruger mentioned, a Marlin, and a Browning. It is extremely important

WARNING: *It has long been known that one should never load cartridges with pointed bullets in tubular magazine. The same applies to a round-nosed* full-jacketed *bullet. Hornady Manufacturing Co. makes a round-nosed jacketed bullet exclusively for revolvers. Just to see what would happen, they loaded it in the magazine of a Ruger .44 Magnum carbine. Here's the result. Apparently every cartridge in the magazine tube was fired and blew the rifle into smithereens. You should note the results and heed such warnings, which are not to be taken lightly.*

that readers heed this warning and *never* use any pointed or metal-cased bullets of any type in any tubular magazine where the nose of a bullet may contact the primer of the cartridge lying ahead of it.

.444 Marlin. Introduced in 1964, this was the first cartridge to bear the Marlin name in many years. Earlier Marlin numbers were such as the .32/40, .38/55, and many of the older black-powder cartridges used in the famous Ballard rifles which Marlin manufactured in the 1870s and 1880s. The .444 cartridge was made by taking the basic .30/06 case before it had the extracting groove machined and forming a rim.

Remington worked with Marlin in the development of this cartridge and, to date, is the only manufacturer of ammunition. However, Remington was also responsible for the most glaring weakness of the .444: they loaded the ammunition with the same bullet used in .44 Magnum revolver ammunition. The jacket of these bullets is too thin for the speeds generated by the .444, which is a pretty potent case. Remington should have made a heavier bullet jacket that wouldn't break up at .444 speeds. I remember that early in the life of the .444, two Marlin executives took .444 rifles to Africa, where they found the bullets disintegrated on the hide of zebra. They failed to penetrate and did not inflict a serious wound.

The gap was filled with a bullet especially designed for the .444 by the Hornady Manufacturing Company. A 265-grain slug, it can be driven as fast as 2200 fps with handloaded ammunition and will not break up on impact.

The .444 Marlin is a suitable deer rifle with factory ammunition. It is capable of handling all North American game with the Hornady bullet in handloads. The only rifle made in this caliber is the Marlin Model 444, a 336 revamped to handle the larger cartridge. It was the most powerful lever-action rifle being manufactured until Savage began chambering the Model 99 again in .358 Winchester. There really isn't too much difference between these two cartridges; the .358 is a little more powerful and is a better long-range proposition.

.458 CALIBER

.45/70. It just won't die! This cartridge was introduced in 1873 for the ancient trapdoor Springfield rifle. It was a military cartridge and was very popular in its day. A number of commercial rifles were made for this caliber. Among the more important were the Marlin Model 1895 and Winchester 1886 which lasted until 1935.

Because of the vast numbers of old rifles still in use, ammunition remained in manufacture all these years. Of course, the ammo had to be loaded to a level considered safe in rifles made as long ago as 1873. Gradually, the .45/70 was sinking into oblivion.

When the cartridge approached its centennial, which happened to approximately coincide with the nation's bicentennial and the centennial of Custer's Last Stand (in which the cartridge was used), new interest began to stir. I suspect this was led by C. Edward "Ted" Rowe, Jr., president of Harrington & Richardson, which began making replica .45/70 trapdoor Springfields to honor the occasion. H&R made a great many of these replicas, including a series of commemoratives, richly engraved and bearing the names of all the troopers in the 7th Cavalry that day with Custer. H&R is still making .45/70s.

This wasn't lost on Bill Ruger, who has a vast nostalgic corner in his heart. He began to chamber his Number One single-shot for the .45/70. Nor was it lost on Frank Kenna, Marlin's president, who issued orders to develop a rifle based on the 336 action. Marlin revamped the action a bit to handle the big cartridge, and the rifle was called the Model 1895. It also was patterned to resemble that famous old rifle.

A few years ago I was on a caribou hunt in Quebec's Ungava Bay region with Frank Kenna and some of his Marlin executives. All those in the Marlin party carried .45/70 Model 1895 rifles with factory ammunition. All bagged their caribou successfully with no problems whatever. Most caribou hunters think the .30/06 is minimum. Many of them are armed with super-long-range rifles. But the .45/70 can still do the job.

If you like the .45/70, buy one of the modern rifles. And if you expect peak performance you'll have to handload, because factory loads are loaded down. Under those conditions, the .45/70 will handle any North American game, just as it did in the last century. If you use factory ammunition and confine your shots to reasonable ranges with an old rifle, it will slay your buck fast.

.458 Winchester Magnum. Introduced in 1956 as the first in a new family of Winchester cartridges, the .458 was developed exclusively for African game. Its 500-grain "solid" bullet is meant for penetration of the three feet of bone hiding an elephant's brain. Its 510-grain soft-point bullet is intended for softer-skinned game such as lion. There is no reason on earth why anyone would consider this powerhouse for deer hunting.

.460 Weatherby Magnum. Even more powerful than the .458 Winchester, Weatherby's .460 (which uses .458-inch bullets) was introduced in 1958 and shoved the venerable British .600 Nitro Express from its spot as the world's most powerful shoulder rifle. As with the .458 Winchester, the use of this cartridge on deer would be ridiculous.

OLD AND OBSOLETE

There are a few cartridges in the old and obsolete category that will be encountered on occasion. Generally speaking, they should not be bought, primarily because ammunition is no longer available (in most cases), but sometimes also because they are too weak for deer hunting. Many states have banned use of several of these cartridges.

.303 Savage. The approximate equal of the .30/30, this was a proprietary Savage cartridge for some years but is now gone and

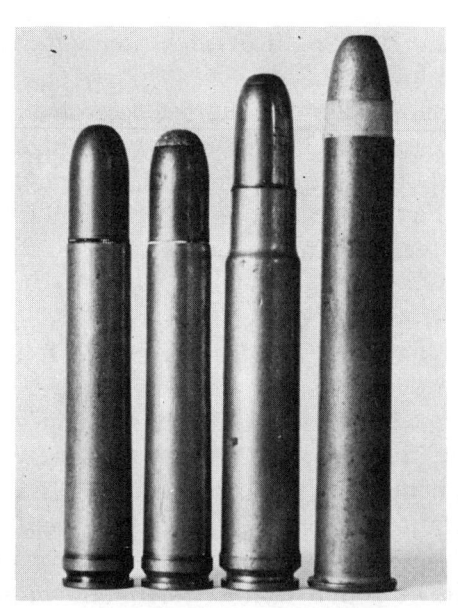

Some whoppers of today and one of yesterday. From left to right, .458 Winchester Magnum with "solid" bullet (mild-steel jacket meant to penetrate an elephant's skull), then the same with soft-nose bullet, and then a .460 Weatherby Magnum, which is the world's most powerful shoulder-rifle cartridge and fires the same-size bullet as the .458 Winchester. At the right is the Sharps "Big Fifty," the .50 caliber 3¼-inch cartridge used by buffalo hunters a century ago. Despite the imposing size of the Sharps case, the other cartridges shown are much more powerful.

largely forgotten. While suitable for deer, its obsolescence and the unavailability of ammunition rule it out.

.32/20. A small, weak cartridge unsuited for deer hunting.

.32 Winchester self-loading. Unsuitable for deer hunting, and ammunition no longer available.

.32/40. A completely adequate deer cartridge, but the ammunition is no longer available and both rifle and ammo must be considered obsolete.

.351 Winchester. Marginal for use on deer. Made for the Model 1907 Winchester self-loading rifle, the ammunition is still listed by Winchester. However, there are very few rifles in use; the rifle was an unbalanced one that was never popular.

.38/40. Too low powered for deer hunting. This is primarily a revolver cartridge for which ammunition is still loaded.

.38/55. An old favorite, and very definitely a deer cartridge, but it's obsolete today and must be forgotten.

.401 Winchester. Like the .351, this is marginal for use in a deer

rifle. It was made for the 1910 Winchester self-loading rifle. The ammunition no longer listed.

.44/40. This was once a pretty famous cartridge that bagged a lot of deer. But there are so many better cartridges today that its use today should not be encouraged. It still makes a fairly powerful revolver load, but even there it is shaded by other and better cartridges. Not recommended.

INTERCHANGEABILITY

Generally speaking, the best rule you can follow is never to chamber a cartridge unless the barrel is stamped the same as the cartridge. If you have any doubt at all, consult a competent gunsmith. If he hesitates, you'd better not use it.

These comments apply particularly to European calibers, where some confusion exists. There are several 6.5mm, 7mm, and 8mm cartridges that are quite different from others. The following list will be found useful; cartridges within each group may be interchanged:

6mm Remington	.30 Army
.244 Remington	.30/40 Krag
	.30/40
.30/30 Savage	
.30/30 Winchester	.30/06
.30/30 Marlin	.30 Springfield
.30/30 Winchester High Speed	.30/06 Springfield
.30 WCF	.30 Government Model 1906
	.30/06 .224 "Accelerator"
.45/70 Government	
.45/70 Marlin	8mm Mauser
.45/70 Winchester	8×57 mm
.45/70/405	7.9mm Mauser
.45/70/500	7.9×57 mm

You must understand that manufacturers often change specifications, and drop and add cartridges as marketing changes dictate. The information here may or may not be entirely accurate when you read it.

There are always some people who think they know better and continue to use cartridges and rifles that are inadequate for the purpose. Fortunately, some states have legislated against some of these cartridges. Some are eliminated by bore diameter, while other states have used muzzle energy as the criterion. These recommendations should be obeyed. It is unfair to game animals to employ a rifle with inadequate power to do the job. Moreover, it's only common sense, since a wounded animal will have to be followed . . . and followed . . . and followed. Choose a rifle that will do the job and do it well.

13

Bores, Bullets, and Ballistics

For about twenty-five years, from 1950 to 1975, there raged a rather spirited word battle between the advocates of a small-bore high-velocity bullet and those who preferred a big, heavy, slow-moving slug. The leading spokesman in the high-velocity camp was Roy Weatherby, and in the big-bullet school it was Elmer Keith.

Weatherby has claimed victory in this debate, and there is substantial evidence to back his claim. On the other side of the coin, Keith is not about to give up the fight. Knowing both these men since the early 1950s, I doubt they will ever change their minds. But there is no question that more people are now in Weatherby's camp than Keith's.

Let's first examine the claims of each side. The high-velocity group claims that cartridges like the .30/30, .45/70, and so forth are obsolete and ought to be abandoned in favor of the higher-power cartridges that produce instantaneous kills by virtue of their speed and shock of impact. This shock of impact has been given various names, the most common one being "hydraulic shock." In other words, the bullet, upon impact, creates so much ruckus that it drives a hydraulic wave of pressure throughout the animal's body. This theory is apparently accurate; there is little doubt that such a shock wave is produced and that it contributes to the instantaneous death that results. One has only to observe the death of an animal when it's hit by a high-velocity bullet to be a believer. And some have captured the effect on film as the bullet hits.

The big-bullet school of thought has a lot of merit on its side because it advocates the use of heavy rifles. You won't ever catch one of these hunters in the woods with an underpowered rifle. They lean toward the opposite extreme. In fact, many of them consider the .30/30 too light for deer, the .270 too light for elk, and so on.

They believe a bullet must be heavy enough not only to open a sizable wound on entrance but also to plow through the body and leave a big hole on the other side. The theory is that the two holes will cause the animal to bleed out faster and die quicker.

All well and good, but both arguments leave out some very important factors. One is that all bullets slow down, and while a .300 Winchester or .300 Weatherby Magnum may deliver enormous speed and cause enormous destruction at 100 yards it has slowed substantially at longer distances. For example, the 150-grain bullet out of a .300 Winchester Magnum has slowed to 1813 fps at 500 yards. A .30/30 with 150-grain bullet is moving at 2018 fps at 100 yards. You could easily deduce from this that the .30/30 at 100 yards is a better killer than the .300 Winchester Magnum is at 500 yards. And you'd be right. So everything is relative, and you must factor other things than sheer flashy performance at the muzzle.

Another factor is that different people react differently to their experiences. For example, a man might have a sour, or good, experience with a certain rifle and cartridge. He will accordingly condemn it to hell or praise it to the skies. It's hard to remain thoroughly objective. I have, for example, a favored .30/30 carbine with which I have taken a number of whitetail deer in the northeastern part of the country. It has not failed me. I also have a similar .30/06 rifle and it has performed in the same way in other parts of the country. So I am very fond of these rifles.

I have not had any unfortunate experiences with rifles while deer hunting, and I suspect this may be because I've always been suitably armed when I went in the woods and have never failed to know precisely where that rifle was shooting. As far as I can recall, I do not know of anyone who ever experienced such problems when he followed that same procedure.

Many calibers are loaded with various bullet weights, some of which are useless for deer hunting. The .30/06, for example, is loaded with a 110-grain bullet with a pretty exciting muzzle velocity of 3380 fps. This bullet is intended for use on varmints and is jacketed with a thin material so it will virtually explode on impact. This bullet is not worth a damn on deer. Another thing to keep in mind with so light a bullet is that it's too light to retain its velocity. The 110-grain .30/06 is only going 1261 fps at 500 yards, while the 220-grain bullet from the same rifle is still trundling along at 1448 fps. The 220-grain has a muzzle velocity of only 2410, nearly 1000 fps slower than the 110-grain.

Generally speaking, the lightweight bullets, when a cartridge is loaded with more than one weight, are intended for smaller game, like varmints. These must not be used on deer because they will fail to penetrate far enough to kill.

You can get the impression that the high-velocity people think you can use any bullet as long as it's fast enough. This is not true at all. They cannot make that claim because many lightweight bullets are so thinly jacketed that they will explode on impact with almost any object. Even a blade of grass will cause some bullets to explode right in the air. But, *other things being the same,* they can make that claim.

When you hear someone blast a cartridge, or when you read someone's criticism of a cartridge, you should take the comments with a grain of salt. Unfortunately many of my colleagues in the writing profession do not have the necessary experience, or "seasoning," to make completely sound judgments, and I have read some awful things in too many magazines that were simply wrong, or which could lead to a totally false impression. There really are no bad cartridges around. There are some that are not powerful enough for deer and there are some that are vastly overpowered. It doesn't take any mental giant to deduce that. When you take any cartridge suitable for deer hunting and combine it with a good rifle and use a load that will deliver decent accuracy, it will be an acceptable combination, as long as you can handle it well enough to extract its full potential.

As I've said, there can be no question that Roy Weatherby's gang has won their long-standing argument with Elmer Keith and his crowd. This is evidenced by the fact that most of Weatherby's theories have been followed. Before Weatherby the only magnum cartridges in existence were those venerable oldies the .300 and .375 H&H Magnums. There was a brief period when the .275 H&H saw a brief flutter among custom gunmakers, although it was never made in any commercial U.S. rifle that I ever heard of. Ammunition was manufactured by Western Cartridge Co. (before that company became associated with Winchester), which ought to give some idea of the flurry of custom activity.

Once Weatherby hit the scene in about 1945 the magnum was here to stay, even though it came along a bit slowly at first. Not until 1956 did Winchester produce its first magnum, the .458, and Remington followed suit in 1962 with the 7mm Remington Magnum. But since that time the factory magnums have been produced somewhat thick and fast. Winchester followed the .458 with the .264, .300, and .338, and Remington with the 8mm Magnum, which followed the 7mm, in 1977. There were two other Remington developments which have flopped, the 6.5mm and .350 Remington Magnums.

You can say, with complete accuracy, that Roy Weatherby alone is responsible for the development and profusion of today's powerful, superior cartridges. And you can say that rifle performance is the better for Weatherby and his dreams. Of course, Weatherby is much more than simply a producer of powerful rifles. He is a superb pitchman, showman, and promoter. Others have produced good cartridges but never caught the spotlight's gleam as Roy Weatherby did. Weatherby made himself highly visible and others had to notice him. They may have disagreed with his direction, and many did, but they could not ignore him. Moreover, the public bought Weatherby's rifles, and that's what it's all about in the final analysis.

The whole situation is somewhat paradoxical, since there is now enormous interest in the old .45/70, a cartridge adopted in 1873 and given up for dead long ago. Today there are a number of rifles being made for it by H&R, Marlin, Ruger, and Browning, and hunters and shooters haven't given up on the grizzled number. Weatherby winds up his dissertation on the subject of high velocity vs. fat bullets in the eighteenth edition of the catalog by stating: "And someday in the not-too-distant future our present high-velocity cartridges will be as obsolete as the old .45/70." I think it likely now that it won't be in my lifetime that any of these types of cartridges will be obsolete. In fact, it's likely that won't happen in the lifetime of anyone now alive.

One of the most important considerations that must be given in any choice of cartridge is that of trajectory—the bullet's flight. A flat trajectory is obtained by high-speed bullets that retain their velocity. A high trajectory is the result of a slow bullet, since that bullet must be fired to a higher elevation to travel farther. To illustrate that point, a fast-balling baseball pitcher can hum his fast, hard one over the plate in a nearly straight line. But when he serves a change-up its flight more nearly resembles a golf ball's because it flies in a higher arc.

Shoot a .300 Winchester Magnum over 300 yards and the bullet rises only 5 inches at mid-range. A .45/70, on the other hand, rises 32 inches over the same distance. To put those numbers in hunting perspective, if your .300 Winchester was sighted to hit point of aim at 300 yards, your bullet would be just 5 inches high at 150 (you should hold low, but a dead-on hold wouldn't miss). But a .45/70 would be 32 inches over the aiming point at 150 yards, and the result would likely be a miss. It is much easier to hit long-range targets with a flat-shooting rifle because it has more tolerance for errors in estimating distance. So the big advantages of the smaller, lighter bullets at high speed are that they kill quicker and better and they are easier to hit with. That adds up to much better performance and explains in a nutshell why such cartridges have achieved popularity. It does not explain the rebirth of the .45/70, but I suspect nothing can explain that phenomenon.

The fat, heavy bullets have their place, though. They hit a deer like a Greyhound bus, they satisfy those who think "brush busting" is a reality, and there is something satisfying about whacking a deer with a .35 Remington, .358 Winchester, .45/70, or one of the other fat boys. I have no hesitation about recommending any one of these three cartridges as being ideal for deer (and some larger game) under conditions where long shots are unlikely to occur.

TYPES OF BULLETS

It is obvious that the most important part of all shooting is the bullet. The rifle is nothing more than a device to propel the bullet to the target. Once the bullet is airborne there is nothing further you can do to control its flight. It must fly true so it hits the target where you want it to hit. And once it arrives, it must do its job satisfactorily. The job of a bullet from a deer rifle is to kill the deer humanely and quickly without allowing it to run off and without destroying more meat than necessary. The latter point should be subordinate to the first point.

The bullet is just the projectile. Calling the whole cartridge a bullet shows ignorance. A fully loaded round of ammunition is called a cartridge; it consists of the brass case, a primer, and a powder charge and it has a bullet seated in the case mouth. But the bullet itself is just the projectile, and that's the part that leaves the rifle bore. The rest stays behind or is consumed.

There are three types of bullets in common use today: jacketed, pure lead, and disintegrating. The last type is loaded only in .22 gallery ammunition; they are made of sintered metal and are designed to disintegrate on impact so they won't ricochet. Of little interest to the average hunter, they turn into dust when they hit their target.

Pure lead (it usually has some antimony added to provide a little hardening, so it really isn't pure lead) is usually found in .22 caliber bullets and in revolver ammunition. There also are lead bullets equipped with a "gas check," a copper base that's fastened to the bullet's base in manufacture to protect the bullet against hot propellant gas. A gas check added to a lead bullet will permit higher velocities. For example, bullets for .357 Magnum revolvers usually are equipped with a gas check because the cartridge is so powerful. Plain lead bullets in the .357 Magnum will cause what is known as "leading," the buildup of lead in the barrel, with resultant loss of accuracy.

Lead bullets must have a special shape to hold a gas check; a little shoulder on the base is provided. They are used in deer rifles only for "reduced-load" target and small-game shooting. Reduced loads are handloads. You can drive a lead bullet, with gas check, out of most deer rifles at moderate speeds which will provide less recoil and less expensive shooting on the target range. Some shooters also like to use these loads for such game as squirrels and turkeys because they destroy little meat. A high-velocity load meant for deer would probably explode a turkey into a feather bomb.

You will occasionally find surplus military ammunition around that requires explanation and that should *never* be used for hunting of any kind. There are four general types of this ammunition: ball, armor-piercing, tracer, and incendiary.

Ball ammunition is just plain old regular ammo used by the military. The term is a hangover from much older days when a musket was either loaded with buck or ball—buckshot for close, nasty work and ball (a round ball) for regular shooting. In today's parlance, ball ammunition is a jacketed military bullet. Bullet jackets are made of a material called gilding metal. It is copper with 5-10 percent zinc added. Jackets are made by punch press, starting with a slug resembling a penny which is gradually formed into a cup, then a deeper cup, and then finally shaped like a bullet.

With military ball ammunition, the jacket is open at the base, leaving the nose solid. The procedure is simply reversed for a hunting bullet because the latter must expand. According to the rules of the Geneva Convention, military ammunition for use in warfare is to be loaded with full-metal-jacketed bullets—or ball ammunition.

We'll get more deeply into expanding bullets in a few moments; the point I wish to make here is that ball ammo is designed *not* to expand. Thus it is no good for deer hunting and ought not to be used. Since there is always a quantity of such ammunition around in military calibers (of several nations) you should know what this is. It is suitable for use on a target range and should be restricted to that use.

The military also uses tracer ammunition. These bullets are much like ball ammunition except there is a pocket of tracer material in the bullet's base that lights up when fired to indicate the bullet's path. Tracer ammo should never be used in any hunting area, because it won't kill any better than ball ammunition and it will set brush afire. Most states ban its use (they also ban any other military ammunition). Tracer ammo is identified by a red tip, painted about ¼ inch down from the nose.

Armor-piercing ammunition looks exactly like ball ammo except the bullet's core is not lead but instead is a hardened steel insert. It's designed to penetrate armor plate. These should *never* be used. Many shooters shoot armor-piercing, or AP as it's known, at the target range. But I advise against this because I have never seen a backstop that would stop AP bullets. They have an uncanny way of getting out of any backstop and flying in strange directions. Do not use AP ammunition. It is painted black on the tip.

The last kind of military ammunition you may find is known as incendiary and is painted blue for identification. This is an explosive bullet designed to explode on impact and set fire to the target, such as the fuel in an enemy aircraft's wing tank.

Incendiary, armor-piercing, and tracer ammunition is generally loaded for use in aircraft machine guns. It is inserted into ammunition belts in a 2-2-1 ratio (two incendiary, two armor-piercing, and one tracer) to be used against other aircraft. There are few planes today equipped with .30 caliber machine guns,

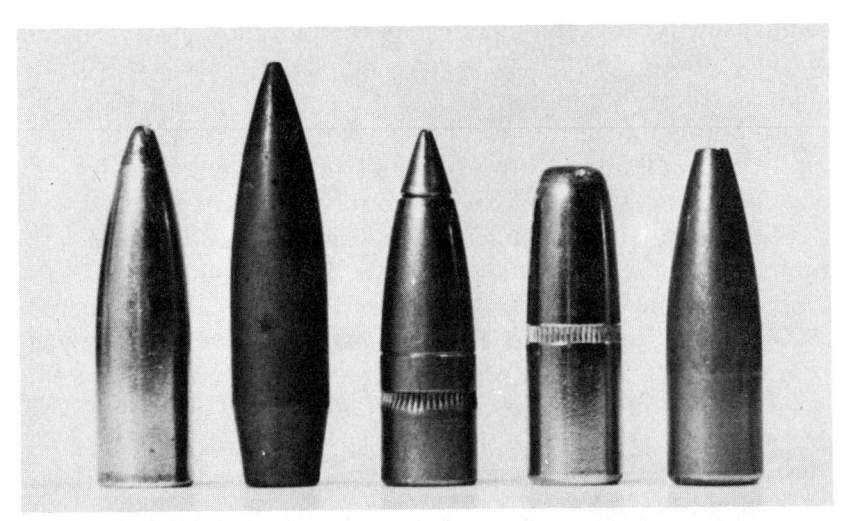

Several common bullet styles. From left to right, soft-point, "spitzer": boat-tail, named for its base shape, which provides better long-range retained velocity; Remington Bronze Point, which has a hard bronze tip; a flat-nosed bullet such as is required in a tubular magazine like that of the .30/30 Winchester; and a hollow point bullet.

and this ammunition is getting scarce. But there is still some around and you should know about it. Moreover, there are some unscrupulous individuals who have no compunction about scraping off the identifying paint from these bullet tips and selling the ammunition. I've even seen dealers do this. The moral is that if you note any military ammo being offered for sale you ought to inspect it carefully. Make sure it does not evidence nose scraping, and if you have any doubt at all, don't buy it.

As stated earlier, sporting bullets for hunting are made with one of a wide number of soft-point tips, often protected by another material, which are designed to expand. It is these bullets which are designed for hunting.

A bullet's weight, shape, and length control its air resistance and therefore its length of flight when other things are the same. Its construction (including balance) controls its accuracy and ability to transmit its energy to the target; that is, its killing power. Bullets are either spherical or conical; there are many versions of the latter.

Bullets are further categorized by their construction beyond the obvious lead and jacketed classifications. For example, there are full-metal-jacketed, boattail, soft-point, pointed soft-point, wadcutter, metal-piercing, jacketed hollow-point, sharp-shoulder, flat-point, round-nose, and metal-cased (solid). In addition, there are proprietary bullets with special types of construction, such as the Winchester-Western Silvertip, Remington Bronze Point and Core-Lokt, and, among the bullets for reloading, Nosler Partition, Speer Grand Slam, and so on.

A full-metal-jacketed bullet is one which is made with the core inserted from the base, and the nose is therefore closed. A boattail bullet is one in which the rear end of the bullet is tapered slightly to reduce tail drag. It has a boatlike shape when viewed from above. Other things being equal, a boattail bullet will retain its velocity better than the ordinary flat-base bullet by reducing air turbulence at the base. It must also be mentioned that it is a little harder to drive a boattail bullet in the bore because there is less base area for the propellant gas to push. Some claim that a boattail reduces barrel life because it's harder to push and because the gas is allowed to push into the gap between bullet base and bore. There is some truth in this, but it's not of vital importance, and many target shooters use boattails exclusively. In a hunting rifle they will provide slightly better long-range ballistics and no appreciable added bore wear. However, their advantage is very slight and consequently need not be any consideration at most hunting ranges.

A soft-point bullet is simply one in which there is lead exposed at the tip; they run from pointed to round-nosed to flat-nosed.

Wadcutter bullets are generally restricted to pistol and revolver ammunition. The wadcutter is simply a bullet with a flat nose; it looks as if it had two bases. The purpose of a wadcutter bullet is to cut clean holes in target paper over the short ranges at which a handgun is generally fired.

Metal-piercing bullets are loaded in a few police loads for use against automobiles. They have no other use.

Hollow-point bullets are made in either all-lead or jacketed construction; their purpose is to promote rapid expansion, although it is debatable whether they really accomplish that purpose better than a soft-point. Moreover, a hollow-point bullet does not retain its velocity as well as a soft-point because it develops more air resistance. Riflemen say a hollow-point bullet "falls off" to describe its velocity loss.

A sharp-shoulder bullet is a sort of combination wadcutter and pointed shape. It is best described as a wadcutter with a small point placed on top. It is for handguns and it combines, to a degree, the paper-cutting aspects of the wadcutter with the better air penetration of the pointed slug. It is a very popular bullet for handgunners and performs well at both target and game.

Flat-point bullets are those made expressly for such tubular-magazine rifles as the Winchester Model 94 carbine. They help prevent the possibility of an accidental discharge should the sharp nose of a bullet whack the primer of the cartridge lying ahead of it in the magazine. This is one of the limiting factors of tubular magazines. (Round-nosed .35 Remington bullets are also acceptable.)

The round-nose is self-evident; it is sometimes called a "semi-spitzer"—*spitzer* being the German word for pointed.

A metal-cased bullet, or "solid" as it's commonly called in the trade, is a bullet with a mild-steel jacket and a very rounded nose fully enclosed in steel which has been plated with gilding metal. It has a lead core in conventional fashion. Solids are used exclusively for the big African dangerous game where deep penetration is necessary. A sharp-pointed bullet will not penetrate in a straight path but will dive off at an angle, the degree of the angle depending upon what it strikes in the way of bones or other resistance. So the rounded nose is necessary for penetration in a straight line. Africa's dangerous animals are rather formidable; the elephant, for example, has approximately 3 feet of bone in front of his brain. You shoot an elephant in the brain or the heart or you don't shoot. If you take the frontal shot, your bullet must penetrate that massive bone structure. This requires a bullet that will retain its shape in addition to plowing a straight path, and it has been learned over the years that a steel-jacketed, round-nosed, full-metal-cased bullet is just the ticket. These are very costly to produce and generally sell for roughly double the cost of ordinary bullets. They are produced in loaded ammunition by Winchester and Remington and are available for handloading from those sources as well as Hornady. The common calibers for solids are .375 H&H and .458 Winchester Magnums, and, in England, several other large calibers.

There is also such a thing as a "steel-jacket" bullet which is primarily found in European ammunition. These steel-jacketed bullets are essentially the same as the bullets with which you are familiar. One of the better known such bullets in this country is the Norma Tri-Clad, produced by Norma of Sweden and sold here by Norma-Precision. Norma manufactures these bullets with a "sandwich" of metal consisting of a mild-steel center with gilding metal on both sides. The gilding metal has two functions: to act as a lubricant in the bore and to prevent rusting. The method is similar to that employed in the manufacture of our dimes, quarters, and half-dollars since "real money" was abandoned in the 1960s. These steel-jacketed bullets are just as good as any others and are not any harder on a rifle barrel.

Early bullets were lead, and before man learned that an elongated bullet was better ballistically, round balls were the projectile. Round balls are still used in a good deal of muzzleloading shooting, both in rifles and pistols. It is interesting to note that the flight of a round ball is terrible. It is undependable and relatively inaccurate when compared to an elongated slug. The oft-quoted accuracy attributed to Kentucky rifles is strictly nonsense, for those rifles fired a round ball and were not accurate in any sense of the word today. They may still spin pretty exciting yarns about the superb accuracy of certain long-gone riflemen armed with the Kentucky flintlock but don't you believe it. If the old rifles had decent accuracy, today's marksmen would be able to perform the same way. But they can't, and the old-timers couldn't either.

A round ball is also an inefficient projectile; in fact, it's the worst possible shape for ballistic efficiency. The air resistance to a round object increases according to the square of the velocity. If you double the velocity, the air resistance will be boosted four times. Treble the velocity and the air resistance is increased nine times. This is a simple law of physics and there is no way around it. The net result is that boosting speeds of round balls really accomplishes nothing because the added air resistance wipes out the gain with a few yards of range. You are right back where you began.

Lead bullets were perfectly suitable in the days of black powder because velocities were relatively slow and the powder did not generate as much heat inside the rifle. But with the advent of smokeless powder, which burns a good deal hotter and develops higher pressures, lead bullets were no longer suitable. They were melted at the base by the heat and they were driven so fast that the soft lead often would not accept the rifling twist and the bullets "skidded." Skidding also resulted in building up lead deposits in the bore, which raised pressures and spoiled accuracy after a few shots.

The approximate date of smokeless powder's introduction and the jacketed bullet was 1885. In fact, there was a UMC

(Union Metallic Cartridge Co., the firm that later bought Remington Arms) cartridge marketed in 1884 using a jacketed bullet for the .45/90 Winchester rifle. Lead was still necessary as a core material because of its weight and low cost, but the bullet required a jacket to withstand the heat and friction and accept the rifling.

An early material used for bullet jackets was the so-called German silver, composed of copper and nickel and also known as "cupronickel." But it was expensive and left a deposit which built up on top of the lands and was perfect hell to get out of a barrel. It soon gave way to what we know today as "gilding metal," a combination of copper and zinc which has proved most satisfactory. The transition from cupronickel to gilding metal occurred shortly after World War I, the approximate beginning of high-velocity performance, when metal fouling with higher velocities was too severe.

Most bullets are constructed along the same lines. Draw a gilding-metal cup from a penny-shaped "blank" in a punch press until it resembles a fired .22 cartridge without the rim. Then slip a lead core inside and shape the unit in a die until it assumes the shape of a bullet. It's about that simple. Metal cases and military bullets are simply made backward, to oversimplify a bit. So their noses are solid and the bases have exposed lead (but which is sufficiently protected so it won't melt).

The only difference between a hollow-point bullet and a soft-nose bullet is that the former is made with less lead in the core. Add a little lead and the same bullet will be formed into a soft-point, because it will force lead out of the cavity to form a nose. Aside from the full-metal-jacketed bullet, all other bullets are of the expanding type. And all perform somewhat along the same lines, despite their obvious differences in appearance and the claims made for them in advertising copy.

CONTROLLING EXPANSION

An expanding bullet is supposed to do just that—expand when it hits the animal. Naturally, it must penetrate for the expansion to accomplish its goal. An expanding bullet is designed to *transmit its energy* to the target.

All the energy on a printed ballistic chart isn't going to kill anything unless the bullet expands in such a way that its energy will be transmitted to the game. The .30/06, to cite an example, used to be cataloged with two entirely different 180-grain bullets,

Several popular bullet styles. From left to right, a typical "full patch" military bullet with no lead exposed at the tip and a very poor game bullet; a typical soft-point with cannelures that lock core and jacket; a soft-point spitzer; a Remington Bronze Point; an open-point or hollow-point style; a Winchester-Western Silvertip; and a Nosler Partition Jacket.

an expanding bullet and a full-metal-jacketed bullet. They were both listed as having identical energy figures. The expanding bullet was intended for game shooting and the full-metal-jacketed bullet for target; but the uninitiated could easily scan the charts and think both bullets had the same energy. And they did! But one of them was not transferrable to the game it hit and would slip through, like a sword. It might kill, but it would kill so slowly that the deer would be lost. While target ammunition is still manufactured it is not listed in current general catalogs.

The problem facing manufacturers and their designers is a complicated one, for it will become obvious that a bullet which will expand satisfactorily out of a .30/30 at 100 yards (2390 fps) will behave altogether differently when fired out of a .300 Winchester Magnum at the muzzle (3290 fps). This is a difference of 900 fps (more than the 810 fps muzzle velocity of a .45 automatic pistol). That's why there are many and varied methods of controlling expansion. That bullet out of the .300 Magnum will be expected to kill at close range. It also will be expected to do its job neatly at long range. Shoot a deer close to the muzzle with that .300 Winchester Magnum and your bullet will be moving around 3200-3300 fps. Mark that distance off to 500 yards and the bullet has slowed to 1813 fps. And you'd be mad as hell at somebody if you banged a buck at 500 yards and it didn't drop like a stone.

One of the earliest solutions to this problem of expansion was the hollow-point. Its function is pretty evident; on impact, the cavity fills and forces the jacket open, thus expanding the slug. Hollow-points work well, although most qualified observers of bullet behavior do not think they work any better than the common soft-point. It should be mentioned here that there are really no final answers to these questions. If the hollow-point were the best shape you can bet all bullets made would be hollow-points. And the same is true for any other configuration. But it's not that simple. I, for one, prefer the soft-point to the hollow-point primarily because the latter loses more velocity over long distances. On the other hand, hollow-point bullets work well for me on woodchucks at reasonable ranges (which I define as 300-400 yards with a .22 caliber centerfire rifle).

This is a good time and place to wipe out a favorite word of many TV newscasters, newspaper writers, and certain novelists who have failed to do their homework. They like the "dum-dum." The real story about the "dum-dum" bullet goes back to the days when the British army patrolled the frontiers of India. Shortly after jacketed bullets began to be used in the .303 British service rifle (around 1890), it was noted that these jacketed, round-nosed bullets snicked right through the Dervishes and didn't stop them. A British army captain had the bright idea of snipping off the noses of these bullets to expose lead at the tip and so create an expanding bullet. Some of these bullets expanded, all right, and, for a brief time, I believe, they were actually manufactured. But since the bullet was made with a lead-exposed base, removing part of the tip produced a jacket tube with both ends opened. In a few cases the act of firing caused the lead core to be blown out of the jacket and left the latter in the bore. The next shot met the obstruction and the rifle blew up. The period of the dum-dum was cut very short.

The name? It came from the Dum-Dum arsenal in India. It's so nice-sounding that fiction writers (which includes many newspaper reporters) never forgot it. It all happened before 1899 and it's high time the whole thing was forgotten.

Expansion is also controlled by doing various things to the jacket material. For example, it may have its edges scalloped at the front or sometimes appears with tiny lines cut in them. These are mechanical methods of encouraging the jacket to peel back like a banana skin and allow the soft lead core to expand. Ideally, the bullet should expand to 2 to 2½ times its original size

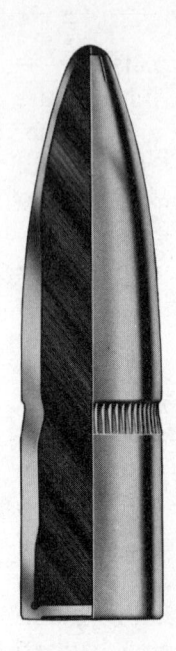

Typical of the modern expanding bullet is this Remington Core-Lokt. Note how the jacket material is thicker in some areas. Control of jacket thickness, and hardness, controls expansion. The Core-Lokt and Winchester's Silvertip are among the most popular of all expanding bullets.

without losing any weight. Jacket material can be hardened, and this is usually done by working it, just as you can make a piece of wire harder and harder until it ultimately breaks by bending it back and forth.

Jacket thickness is another mechanical way of controlling the expansion. In fact, most jackets are very thin at the nose, tapering gradually back to a point where they are quite heavy to resist further expansion. It's also very important that the cores remain in the jacket on impact. If the bullet flies apart, it can't penetrate deeply. Various means are used to keep the core where it belongs. One of the more common methods is to produce a jacket with a sort of inner belt that holds the base of the core locked in place. Remington uses this in the Core-Lokt bullet, which succeeded the famous Peters Belted bullet of a couple generations ago. The Peters Cartridge Co. was purchased by Remington, and Peters had developed an excellent bullet with an outer belt that was visible. Many proclaimed it one of the best bullets ever designed. When Remington took over the company the bullet was changed slightly because it was too costly to produce. The change was simply to put the belt inside and form it as part of the jacket. It works as well, though it isn't quite as handsome as the old Peters.

Another method of holding cores in place is practiced by

130 150	160 175	165 180
.270 CAL.	7 MM	.30 CAL.

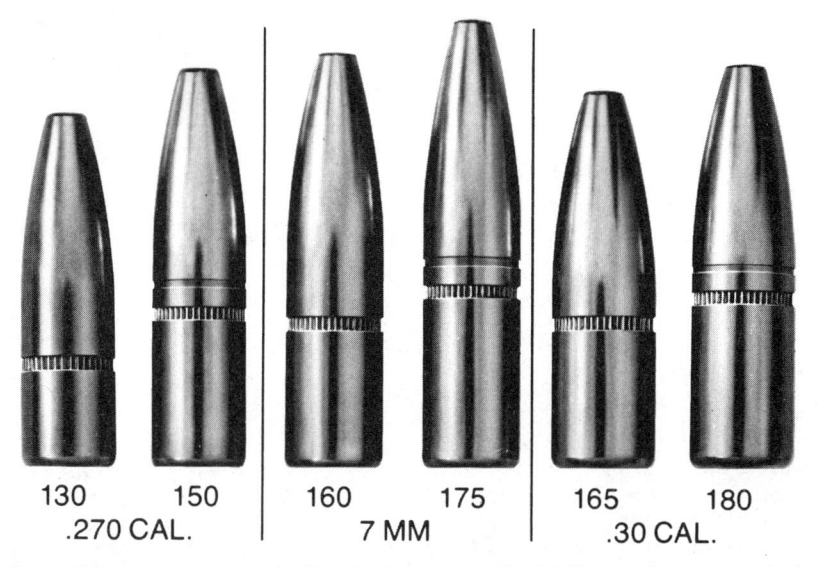

One of the newest game bullets is the Speer Grand Slam, shown here in its present available calibers and weights. This bullet has a double core with special attention given the jacket in manufacture. The jacket is said to positively control bullet expansion over the full range of speeds at which these bullets are likely to be employed. One distinguishing characteristic: the letters GS are imprinted on the base of each Grand Slam bullet.

Speer, a division of Omark Industries. Speer uses a method of hot-bonding the cores to the jacket which is known as the Hot-Cor process. The company also produces a premium-quality game bullet for handloaders called the Grand Slam which is made with a double core; the rear half of the core is harder than the front, and they are bonded together and both are bonded to the jacket. Additionally, the nose of the jacket has ten longitudinal flutes inside and it is annealed for softness. The result, according to the maker, is a game bullet that works properly at all ranges.

Yet another way to make a bullet that won't lose its core, ever, is seen in the Nosler Partition bullet. These bullets were originally made by boring out both ends of a short length of wire made from jacket material. The holes were not drilled completely through, so a web of jacket was left in the middle. A core was seated from each direction, so there was no way in the world that the rear part of the bullet could come apart, no matter what happened to the nose. Just how Nosler was able to accomplish this and still produce a concentric bullet that produced

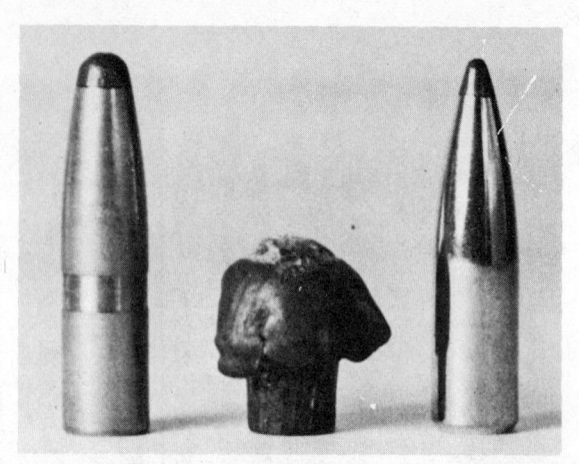

One of the finest of all game bullets is the Nosler Partition Jacket, so-called because the jacket is one piece while the cores are separate and fitted from each end. The result is a bullet which cannot separate no matter what it impacts. Shown is the original style at left, a fired bullet in the middle, and the new style at right. There is a solid web of jacket between front and rear cores.

good accuracy is beyond me, but he succeeded. I have used his bullets in .338 Winchester Magnum rifles and in .30/06s to take deer, caribou, wolves, and other game animals. And I have shot them on targets enough to believe what kind of accuracy they can deliver. It is quite astounding.

One of the best-known of all hunting bullets is the famous Winchester-Western Silvertip. An early problem to be overcome was that a sharp-pointed bullet became deformed in the magazine from recoil. A couple of shots and the cartridges in the magazine would be slammed against the front end of the magazine box, with the result that the soft nose of a bullet became battered.

That problem was solved by Winchester with its Pointed Expanding Bullet in which the tip was enclosed with a very thin covering of gilding metal that extended inside the jacket itself. This was a forerunner of the present Silvertip and should not be confused with it. The latter is an improvement on the original and has proved itself on the worlds game fields over many years. The present Silvertip has a thin cupronickel jacket that surrounds the entire core, extending down nearly to the bottom of the jacket. In effect, the bullet has a double jacket, and it works well at all distances.

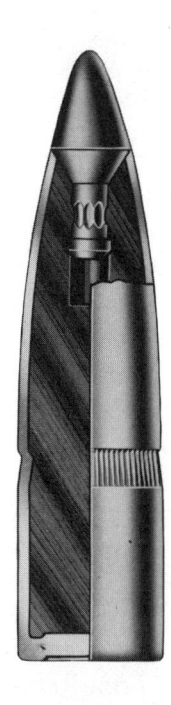

Details of the Remington Bronze Point bullet are shown in this cutaway. A hard bronze tip is simply inserted into a hollow-point bullet. The tip helps prevent damage to the bullet in the magazine and also helps the bullet expand on impact because the tip drives into the core.

Another solution to the problem of battered bullet noses was the Remington development of the Bronze Point bullet, which is simply a hollow-point bullet with a bronze tip stuck in the hole. The tip serves two purposes; it protects the point from battering in the magazine and it serves to help expansion on impact by driving into the bullet to help rupture the jacket.

Many bullets are made with a knurled ring (sometimes two) around their midsection. This serves several purposes. It is often used as a way to force a ring of jacket material into the lead core to help hold the core in place. It work-hardens the metal slightly and it provides a place for the cartridge-case mouth to be crimped and hold the bullet in place. Only bullets with this groove, called a cannelure, can be crimped. A cannelure is sometimes also used to identify a bullet. When two similar-appearing bullets of different weight are loaded you can't tell them apart when they are seated in cartridges. The addition of a cannelure can be used to identify one or the other. A case in point was the .350 Remington Magnum, available in two bullets weights, one of which was cannelured for identity.

There is a world of difference in bullets needed for big-bore shooting vs. small-bore high-velocity shooting. Even though it's the same bore size, a case in point is the .444 Marlin, which is discussed more completely in Chapter 12. Note here that the bullet used by Remington to load this cartridge is the same as used for the .44 Magnum revolver (and rifle) ammunition. In the .44 Magnum rifle the bullet develops 1760 fps (vs 1300 in a revolver; same ammunition). But in the .444 Marlin rifle with a bigger case and longer barrel, the bullet is driven at 2400 fps.

Anyone who has hunted extensively with these rifles knows that the .44 Magnum rifle is a dandy deer rifle. And they also know that the same bullet driven out of the .444 at greatly increased speed is not worth much at all. The bullet is constructed with a thin jacket; it expands rapidly out of a revolver and expands nicely out of the .44 Magnum rifle, but blows up too fast with the .444 load. The owners of .444 Marlin rifles should reload (Hornady makes a good bullet) to get the best performance from their rifles. This is not condemnation of the .444, but it is criticism of the load as issued by Remington.

Similarly, bullets driven at extreme speeds such as some of the hot magnums (examples are the .264 Winchester, 7mm Remington, and .300 Winchester) must use bullets which are made with jackets tough enough to hold together at their high speeds near the muzzle. Yet, the same bullet must be expected to perform correctly at long ranges when called upon.

One more example of bullet behavior is interesting. If you load a bullet designed for the .222 Remington (at about 3200 fps) in the .220 Swift and drive it at maximum velocity (about 3900 fps), the bullet will vaporize in the air. The increase in muzzle velocity with corresponding increase in rotational speed will simply cause the bullet to disintegrate shortly after leaving the muzzle even though it strikes nothing.

On the other hand, if you go the other way, use a Swift bullet in the .222, it will not expand properly on a woodchuck or other small game but will pass through like a sword.

The job to be performed by the modern expanding bullet, then, is to penetrate sufficiently to transmit its energy to vital areas and to expand to approximately 2 to 2½ times its original diameter. It must perform these functions at ranges commonly fired over, which means at a wide variety of speeds. That's a tall order and today's bullets do an extremely good job of it. You might also keep in mind that new bullet concepts are still being developed despite the fact that jacketed bullets have been in use for nearly a century.

THE BULLET'S FLIGHT INSIDE THE BARREL: INTERNAL BALLISTICS

A common misconception about rifles is that it's always the man behind the gun who's to blame if the shot misses the target. In fact, many rifles are not capable of hitting a pie plate at 100 yards, let alone a target the size of a deer's heart. Rifle accuracy is measured by "group size," a group being the cluster of shots fired into a target. The ideal rifle would deliver every one of its shots through the same hole. The hole would be exactly the diameter of the bullet. Such a rifle has yet to be made.

The modern rifle ought to be able to keep all its shots inside a 1-inch circle at 100 yards. There are some who would argue that point with me, but I'll stand on it. I have not yet seen any modern rifle design that cannot be made to shoot within that definition. Many of the actual rifle samples have had to be tuned to deliver that accuracy, but I contend that manufacturers ought to deliver a product that will perform to that standard.

Several things need clarification. When I say within a 1-inch circle, I'm talking about no more than three shots in a target, which are all that are practical or necessary in a hunting rifle. And I'm talking about eliminating the human error so the rifle can perform to its full potential. (That means firing the rifle with a scope sight from a steady bench rest, which is the most reliable way of squeezing the last ounce of accuracy out of a rifle; it's more accurate than a machine rest.)

I have had rifles that wouldn't shoot within these limits and have gotten rid of them. Every rifle in my rack will perform just that well. Often, a given model of a rifle won't shoot for sour apples. It can often be corrected by some judicious tuning, although there are times when such a rifle won't perk for you. I recently had a heavy-caliber rifle for testing and was somewhat startled to find it sprayed its shots competely over the target frame at 100 yards. Most of the bullets "keyholed" (went through the paper sideways). I sent the rifle back. They never did tell me what ailed it, but a visual check on my part couldn't detect any problems. It's likely the bore was off in one way or another. The replacement plunks its whopping .45 caliber slugs into just about an inch and that's close enough, especially when you consider that this rifle is painful to shoot from the bench.

Not too long ago it was acceptable practice to manufacture rifles and ammunition so the cartridge could be easily inserted into the chamber. This gave rise to serious errors and some damned poor shooting. But the condition would probably still prevail were it not for the efforts of a small number of dedicated riflemen. Probably the first such man was the late Dr. Franklin W. Mann, who published a book in 1909 that exposed most of the errors leading to poor accuracy. But Mann's work was largely forgotten until after World War II, when a group of shooters organized for the sole purpose of improving rifle accuracy. This group formed the Bench Rest Shooter's Association and, in a relatively short period of time, learned why rifles shot poorly, and they corrected it.

What bench-rest shooters learned was passed along via the gun magazines. The word was not wasted on the industry, and the result is that today you can buy a rifle that will shoot targets about four times as small as was possible in 1940. Credit those shooters who sit down at a bench to shoot a heavy rifle with making the rifle you buy a much better product. And don't think this kind of shooting is an old man's game; it's quite a challenge, and a lot of the challenge lies in knowing what makes the rifle shoot—or not shoot. (When a rifleman says a rifle shoots he means it shoots with gilt-edge accuracy. If he says it doesn't shoot he means it shoots lousy targets, not that it does not go boom!)

What goes on within the rifle barrel at the moment of firing has a great bearing on what happens to that bullet once it's delivered to the atmosphere, when you lose all control over its destiny. Some of the things we will discuss are lock time, ignition time, pressure, barrel time, ratio of bullet to bore, bullet's bearing area, twist of rifling, and efficiency of the load—quite a formidable number of things that have a bearing on where your bullet hits. You should know something about them.

Lock time. Lock time is defined as the amount of time it takes for the hammer or firing pin to fall and ignite the primer. This varies from about .002 to .0057 second. The former is an enormously quick lock time found in some modern rifles (the Remington Model 788 is among the fastest) and in many of the "best quality" English shotguns. The slower lock times are found in older military rifles, like the 1903 Springfield.

If you have ever fired a flintlock you know that you can distinctly notice the three separate phases of ignition: the click of the big hammer going down, the "p-f-f-f-t" of the powder in the pan and finally the boom of ignition itself. Click, pffft, boom. It takes about a second, or close to it. Plenty of time to swing your rifle and get off the target.

The faster the lock time the more accurate will be your shot. And the more the rifle moves when the lock is firing, the less accurate the rifle will be. This is not a factor with most modern rifles, but there have been rifles with such slow lock time that it is a factor. Of course, lock time occurs *before* the cartridge is fired, so while it's related, it is not strictly a part of internal ballistics.

Ignition time. Normal ignition takes place in about .0002 second. Ignition is when the primer ignites the propellant powder. A primer is an explosive which is fired by the blow of the firing pin. It takes only a tiny pinch of priming mix to ignite a powder charge, although there must be variations in primers. For example, black powder is much easier to ignite than smokeless, so stronger primers were demanded when the change to smokeless took place. A larger charge of slow-burning powder requires a hotter primer flame. For example, the big-cartridge, small-bore .264 Winchester Magnum employs a comparatively slow-burning powder to produce a high velocity. On the other hand, a small cartridge like the .22 Hornet uses much less powder of a fast-burning type. The ignition requirements of each are quite different and require different strengths of primer.

Pressure. When the powder is ignited it begins to burn, giving off gas which drives the bullet through the barrel. This gas develops enormous pressure inside the cartridge case, as you might expect. The time of maximum pressure is very fleeting, because it doesn't take much time to get the bullet out of the barrel. Chamber pressure is measured by complicated laboratory equipment. A hole is drilled in the test barrel chamber into which is fitted a steel plug. A copper disc is placed above the plug and the top is fastened. When a cartridge is fired, the pressure squeezes the copper disc, which is then measured and translated into a measurement of chamber pressure. This used to be expressed in psi or pounds per square inch, but it was no such thing. Today, we use the expression "cup" for copper units of pressure. This is more meaningful; it is interchangeable with the older psi figures and is suitable for comparison only. For example, a given rifle action may be made to safely handle a pressure of 50,000 cup. It follows that any cartridge developing more than that amount would be dangerous. Furthermore, a cartridge developing 25,000 cup develops just half of one that develops 50,000. That's all the figures mean and that's how they should be used. If DuPont lists a handload that develops a certain cup figure, you know at once whether or not that load may be used in your rifle.

There are other factors which can have a bearing on chamber pressure, and one of the most important is heat. Just hot weather can raise hob with pressures. This is one reason British sporting ammunition has always seemed to be underloaded by our standards. But British ammo is loaded for hunters who usually hunt the tropics, where steamy jungle heat can raise pressures. This is why, if you hunt any of the hot desert country of our Southwest, you should take pains to keep your ammunition out of the sun. Similarly, if you've fired a number of shots rapidly and your barrel has become hot, do not chamber another cartridge and let it sit in the rifle. This can become hot enough to fire itself! (This is called a "cooked-off" round in military parlance; it happens occasionally in machine guns.) A heated cartridge like this can cause seriously high pressure.

Barrel time. Since it takes time to get the bullet from chamber to the muzzle we have "barrel time," which varies from .0007 to .001 second. You can appreciate that it takes far less time for the .220 Swift bullet to make that short trip than the .458 Winchester Magnum. Now we can add up these three "times" and note that there can be a fairly significant difference between a slow rifle and a fast one—enough difference to matter.

For example:

Lock time	.002	to	.0057
Ignition time	.0002	to	.0002
Barrel time	.0007	to	.001
Total time	.0029	to	.0069

Pretty fast either way, yet the slowest total time is almost three times as slow as the quickest. Enough to miss a buck at long range!

Bullet-to-bore ratio. The inside of a rifle barrel has two dimensions, *bore* diameter and *groove* diameter. When a rifle barrel is manufactured the first operation is to drill a hole clear through the blank. Then that hole is slowly reamed up to bore diameter, which is exactly .300 inch in the case of a .30 caliber rifle. The barrel then is rifled, an operation that forms the spiral grooves in the barrel. In the case of a .30 caliber these grooves are .004 inch deep, giving us a groove diameter of .308 inch.

Bullets in .30 caliber are made to a diameter of .308 inch, the same as groove diameter. This is necessary in order for the bullet to cut into the rifling and accept the twist. In actual practice barrels are often cut a little bit larger than .308 inch, and sometimes bullets are made slightly off-size too. For example, bullets in .30 caliber used to be made in a die that measured .306 inch. After a few million bullets were made the die was worn to about .3085 inch, at which time it was retired. This might be called pretty sloppy manufacture but it was standard practice some years ago. Today, especially with the introduction of carbide bullet dies, that's a thing of the past.

It is also very important to realize that bullets, and ammunition, made anywhere in the world are supposed to fit your Winchester Model 70, or Remington Model 760, or Savage Model 99, or Marlin 336, or whatever. This cannot be accomplished if there are not tolerances. There is an organization known as the Sporting Arms & Ammunition Manufacturers Institute, or SAAMI (referred to as Sammy), which establishes standards. Most manufacturers in the United States belong to SAAMI, and all conform to its technical dictates.

When I say tolerances I mean that a maximum cartridge made by Norma or Federal must readily chamber in a minimum rifle made by Marlin or Savage or anybody. Chances are that you might be shooting a .307 inch bullet through a barrel measuring .309 inch. No problem; the bullet will "upset" or swell under the fierce hammer impact of the propellant and it will expand to fit the barrel.

Bearing area. Another factor that becomes important is the length of a bullet's bearing area—that part of the bullet that is full diameter. It isn't the same with all bullets. In fact, there are some bullets, called "two-diameter" bullets, which are manufactured with a short section made to groove diameter while a forward part is made to bore diameter. The theory is that the forward part of the bullet will ride on top of the lands, while the rear part will seal the bottoms of the grooves and accept the rifling twist. Sealing the bore is necessary to provide full thrust and it's known by a fifty-cent word—obturation. It will become obvious that the longer a bullet's bearing area the more resistance it will offer and the higher pressure it will develop.

An interesting example of bearing area is the large artillery shell (in artillery the projectile is called a shell). Artillery uses rifled barrels the same as any rifle and, for purposes of definition, the same things apply to the huge projectile thrown out of a 16-inch naval cannon that travels some 30 miles as to the .30/06 or .30/30 you shoot at a deer. In any event, artillery uses steel shells which are manufactured to bore diameter, and a copper band is added which surrounds the shell a little to the rear of center. This band is called the "rotating band"; its purpose is to accept the rifling twist and seal the bore while the projectile itself rides on top of the lands.

With further respect to bearing area, the upsetting of the bullet has an effect on that area. It has been proved that all bullets actually upset *before* they are in motion. That is because the slamming, piledriving thrust of the gas is so fast and so heavy that it smashes the bullet's base before the inertia of the bullet has been overcome. The actual amount of upset depends on many factors, including thickness and hardness of the bullet-jacket material plus, of course, the actual length of bearing area which resists the thrust of the gas.

Rifling. It is the twist of rifling that gives the bullet its spinning motion to keep it flying point-on. No bullet that is unstabilized in flight can possibly fly true. You can compare this flight to a football forward pass; you know that the ball will not fly far unless it spins. Toss a blooper and it will tumble end over end and have a short and slow flight, easily picked off by an opposing linebacker. On the other hand, a properly thrown pass with sufficient spin can be sneaked between defenders to its target because it is thrown fast and flies far and true.

The longer the bullet, the faster must be the rate of twist, which is expressed as so many complete turns in so many inches of barrel length. A twist rate of 1-10 means one complete turn in 10 inches of barrel length. Barrels must be made with a twist that will stabilize the longest and heaviest bullet used. For example, a 14-inch twist will stabilize the very light bullets in a .30/06, but a 10-inch twist is needed for 220-grain and long 180-grain bullets. So rifles in .30/06 caliber are made with a 1-10 twist. Some have theorized that a twist faster than necessary is harmful. This is nonsense. You can't twist a bullet too fast.

Some rather bizarre stories came out of Vietnam with regard to twist. It was claimed that the little U.S. rifle used in that war, the 5.56mm (which in civilian form is the .223 Remington), didn't stabilize its bullets—that they were deliberately understabilized to make the bullets tear through flesh like a saw. Not so. Not only did newspapers and others among the innocent media pick up these stories, but even a few of the gun magazines printed them. The truth is that every bullet must be stabilized if its flight is to be true. Any bullet that tumbles end over end has a very short flight—an erratic, inaccurate, and undependable flight—and don't you ever believe anything to the contrary.

Efficiency. Any firearm is a very inefficient engine (you can compare the firing sequence of a firearm with an internal combustion engine; simply exchange the engine's piston for a bullet or shot charge). You can use caliber as a rule of thumb for efficiency; in other words, the .22 caliber is about 22 percent efficient while the .45 caliber is about 45 percent. Efficiency rises as caliber gets larger because the projectile's base area increases with the square of the caliber.

Another insight into efficiency is gained when you compare powder charges in small cartridges to those in larger cartridges. The .30/30 drives a 150-grain bullet about 2250 fps with a handload of 28.5 grains of DuPont 3031 powder. The .300 Weatherby Magnum, using the same bullet but with a charge of 65 grains of the same powder, achieves a velocity of 3300 fps—more than twice the charge of powder but a velocity increase of only 1050 fps (data from Speer reloading manual; 3031 is not the most efficient powder for the .300 Weatherby). You do not always increase the velocity by simply boosting the powder charge. Generally speaking, the smaller the cartridge case, the greater the efficiency.

Muzzle blast is an annoying noise that heralds the waste of a vast amount of propellant force. Once the bullet is gone the gas has nothing more to do but whap itself on the atmosphere, causing a loud noise that will ruin your hearing if you don't use ear protection. Blast has little effect on the flight of a bullet, unless the bullet has a squeehawed (uneven) base. Blast can be silenced by installing a muffler to soak up the sound waves, except that while you can silence the report, you cannot silence anything that moves faster than the speed of sound (about 1100 fps at sea level), newspaper stories and TV newscasters notwithstanding. Almost all bullets fly faster than that, so any truly "silenced" gunshot must come from a small-caliber pistol or rifle (you cannot silence *any* revolver because of the gap between cylinder and barrel).

EXTERNAL BALLISTICS
Once the bullet leaves the muzzle its flight is in the lap of the

gods, as they say. You have relinquished all control at this point, although there are still a vast number of other factors affecting its flight.

A bullet's flight is known as its trajectory. It is a parabolic curve, which simply means that the curve is straighter at the beginning and more apparent at the end of its flight. Compare this to the throw to home plate by an outfielder trying to cut down a run to the plate. The ball starts fast and flat, then gradually slows and falls in a steeper curve than its ascension at the start of flight. A golf ball does the same thing.

No bullet goes in a straight line. That's impossible, because the force of gravity works on the bullet the moment it clears the muzzle. It makes the downward curve of the bullet greater at the latter part of the flight because the bullet is going slower; gravity has more time to work. Gravity is one of the major factors that affect the bullet's flight. Air resistance is the other. It is claimed that if you fired a bullet in a vacuum, it would travel at the same velocity until gravity pulled it to the earth. You may recall that a moon-walking astronaut whacked a golf ball on the moon, where there is no air and where the pull of gravity is less than it is here on earth. The golf ball went a long way. Had he fired a rifle on the moon, the bullet would have kept on flying at muzzle velocity until the moon's gravity pulled it to the surface.

Before the U.S. space program the average person knew little about supersonic flight and air resistance at high speeds in general. But now everybody knows that a returning space vehicle gets red hot high in the upper atmosphere and will burn to a cinder unless certain precautions are taken. That happens at an altitude of many miles where the air is far too thin to breathe. This is the same kind of air resistance that a bullet meets when it exits the muzzle of a rifle.

It has been estimated that a .30/06 bullet at 2700 fps meets the air with the exact same impact as a wind striking it at 1841 miles per hour! Think about that for a moment. A hurricane wind is any wind in excess of 75 miles per hour, and you hear what damage hurricane winds do every year around early fall. Winds that can blow a straw into the side of a frame house. Winds that can blow a barn right off its foundation. And those are gentle puffs compared to the wind a bullet faces when it exits the muzzle.

That .30/06 bullet we just mentioned at 2700 fps of muzzle velocity has slowed to 2460 at 100 yards and to 1068 at 1000 yards. Air resistance is a very difficult thing to penetrate.

Bullets travel through the air with varying degrees of efficiency. You can imagine with no great mental stress that a .45/70 bullet pushes a lot of air in front with its flat-as-a-barn-door nose. On the other hand, a slim boattail bullet slips through the air with a minimum of fuss. Compare this to a racing sailboat and a garbage scow. The former cuts through the water and, if you remove the source of power, will glide a long distance. Remove the power source from a flat-ended barge and it soon stops. Water and air are very different things, but the ability of an object to penetrate either one can be compared.

A round projectile is the worst ballistic shape of all. A slightly elongated slug (like most pistol and revolver bullets) is only slightly better. The typical round-nose bullet is better, but a pointed shape is better still, and the boattail spitzer is the best of all in terms of air resistance.

Weight also has a great bearing on the flight of a bullet. You can visualize instantly the difference in flight characteristics between a golf ball and a Ping-Pong ball. They are of similar size but one outweighs the other substantially. You can drive, push, or whack a golf ball much farther than a Ping-Pong ball. Similarly, lead is used for bullet core material because it has the desired weight to achieve decent ballistics. Substitute a lighter metal and the bullet will not perform as well.

By taking a bullet's weight, diameter, shape, and material into consideration we can establish an index which ballisticians call the "ballistic coefficient," defined as the bullet's ability to overcome resistance relative to the performance of a known standard used to compute ballistic tables.

If you were to hold a rifle perfectly level and fire it, and at the same instant drop an identical bullet from the same height, both bullets would strike the earth exactly at the same time. One would be a long way off, but the pull of gravity is the same on each. Forward momentum has no effect on the pull of gravity. Gravity accelerates a falling object at an increasing rate until air resistance balances the force of gravity so the falling body does not increase speed beyond that point. In the first second of a bullet's flight, it will fall 16.1 feet below the line of departure. A 150-grain bullet from the .30/06 leaving the muzzle at 2700 fps takes .116 second to travel the first 100 yards. In that length of time the bullet drops 2.4 inches; if aimed perfectly horizontally, the bullet would hit the target exactly 2.4 inches low at 100 yards.

One of the most important factors involved in the accuracy of a rifle is the bullet's balance. This can best be expressed by saying that its center of gravity must coincide with its center of form. Bullet balance is easily understood when you think back to the days when you might have played with a toy top. These were wound with a string and spun at high speed while being delivered to the floor, whereupon they spun on their point until spinning slowed enough to make them start to wobble and finally flop about on the floor. A spinning top can be compared to the spinning bullet in flight.

The toy top is a cheap affair and it won't spin long because it is not balanced. What you may not know is that precision tops have been made and spun for hours in the laboratory. Ideally, a top ought to spin on its point until spinning finally stops, at which time it should remain standing on its point. But that won't happen, though a precision top will spin a good deal longer than is generally imagined. The bullet is no different; if it is unbalanced, it will have an erratic flight. When you consider that perfection is for every bullet to pass through the same hole at the target, you can appreciate that a little unbalancing can cause the bullet to print away from the aiming point.

When a bullet has its center of balance away from the center of form an interesting flight characteristic is set up. The bullet will be forced to rotate around its center of form while in the rifle barrel, because it is held in place by the barrel. But once the bullet leaves the barrel, it tends to want to rotate around the center of balance, and the result is that the direction of flight takes off in a tangent to the spiral described by one center rotating around the other. The flight will not print where expected and you will not be able to determine the point of impact.

A bullet can be unbalanced when the jacket is thicker on one side than the other. That means the lead core will be centered toward the thin side. Sometimes, though not often, an air pocket may be present between core and jacket. Any of these things can cause an unbalanced bullet that won't fly true. While we are talking about very minor imperfections, they cause inaccurate shooting. And they belie the claim that it's always the man behind the gun that misses.

Balanced bullets have only become a reality in the years since the last war. Before that war, rifle accuracy was a good deal less than it is today. The improvement is thanks to a group of bench-rest shooters who banded together in 1947 at Johnstown, N.Y. I was a part of that group during its initial stages. The benchresters sought pure rifle accuracy, and they soon discovered that the "missing link" was bullet construction. Once they had isolated this as the major problem (it was far from the only problem) it was simply a matter of making balanced bullets. This they did, and today just about everybody makes good-shooting bullets.

You've spotted a nice buck that's an estimated 300 yards away. He's standing there in the early morning sunshine, slowly feeding as he drifts toward his bedding area. Your rifle is a good one, and you know you can hit the mark at 300 yards. But there's a stiff wind blowing, and that can raise hell with your bullet as it travels cross-canyon toward the deer. Riflemen have to "dope" the wind—predict how far their bullets will be blown off course by a crosswind. The wind does not always blow predictably, either; sometimes it shifts around, sometimes it blows one way where you are and from the opposite direction where the game is, or at some point between. Nor does it always blow exactly at 90 degrees. A tail wind will push your bullet a little faster, while a headwind will slow it slightly (neither effect amounts to much). However, a common question is, what about bullets shot from aircraft? The answer is that you add the speed of the plane to the velocity of a bullet fired in a forward direction while you subtract it from the velocity of a bullet fired toward the rear. A plane whose speed exactly matched the velocity of a bullet would allow that bullet to be delivered to the air with zero velocity if fired toward the rear.

Think a big, heavy .45/70 slug is windproof? Wrong! It will be pushed 2 inches off the mark at 300 yards by only a 15-mph breeze, and that's a trifling puff of gentle air. A 10-mph breeze will push a 150-grain .30/06 aside 1 inch at 100 yards. So you see wind is quite a factor indeed, hard to dope and hard to provide for. There are scopes available (which I'll discuss in the following chapter) which can compute range and trajectory for you. But there's nothing any optical arrangement can do about doping the wind.

Then there is "drift," which I prefer to call "crawl." It's defined as the sideways crawling of a bullet due to its spin. You might compare this to dropping a baseball bat in the water and giving it a spinning motion as you drop it. As soon as the splash and waves subside, the bat will crawl to one side ever so slightly. So will a bullet in the air, to the right from a right-hand rotation. But only 13 inches at 1000 yards from a 150-grain .30/06 so it's not a big deal.

Altitude and temperature also make a difference in your shooting, and if you've sighted in somewhere at or close to sea level, you'll find it quite different at high elevations. You'll also find a difference in the heat of the desert. The effect of rarefied air is lower air resistance, and high temperatures build not only higher pressures but also higher velocities. They can sometimes make a difference.

It's an old rule of thumb that you shoot higher when you shoot at extreme angles, either up or down. This isn't a factor at less than 200 yards but is indeed a big factor if the range is great. To illustrate, if you shoot at a 45° angle (up or down) you are forming an equilateral triangle. Say the actual distance from muzzle to target is 150 yards—the hypotenuse. But the base is only 100 yards. Gravity only affects the bullet over the level distance of 100 yards. Extend this to a 300-yard shot and you'll see how simple it is to miss. Shoot at a deer almost straight down at the bottom of a canyon and, no matter how deep the canyon, you must hold for zero elevation or you'll shoot way over its back.

Velocity is measured by instruments called chronographs. Two screens are set up at prescribed distances and the rifle is fired so that the bullet passes through both screens. The first starts an electrical circuit; the second stops it. The time is recorded in milliseconds and translated into feet per second. The usual rule is to fire ten shots and average them, because there is a variation between shots. Since the screens are located a small distance from the muzzle, a factor is added to give true "muzzle velocity."

Energy is a unit of work expressed in foot-pounds—the amount of energy required to lift 1 pound a distance of 1 foot. These figures, both velocity and energy, are produced in chart form by the ammunition-loading companies at many distances. The important thing to keep in mind when reading these charts is that the important thing is what happens out where the deer stands and not at the muzzle. Moreover, it's the bullet that *transmits* its energy that will do the job.

AMMUNITION BRANDS
Everyone is familiar with ammunition made by the two big giants, Winchester and Remington, and knows that both companies have two labels: Winchester and Western, Remington and Peters. But not everybody is familiar with many of the other brands of ammunition available.

The third major American ammunition company is Federal. Located in Minnesota, the company has long been a major source in the Midwest and has also long been a supplier to other companies, manufacturing ammunition to their brand names, (such as Sears, for example). During recent years, Federal has expanded its marketing base and this excellent ammunition is available over a wide section of the country.

Norma is a Swedish company which makes ammunition as well as powder, primers, cartridge cases, and bullets for reloaders. Norma also manufactures ammunition for other companies using their brand names. The firm is one of the oldest and most respected ammunition makers in the world. It is an excellent source for a large number of foreign cartridges which are not available in American brands.

A relatively new name in loaded ammunition is Frontier division of the Hornady Manufacturing Company. Frontier-brand ammunition is loaded with Hornady bullets. It is available in an ever-widening list of available calibers.

Omark Industries has produced ammunition for some time in Speer and CCI brands. Speer (the bullet maker) ammunition at one time was known as Speer-DWM—DWM being a widely known German ammunition producer for many years. The ammunition was loaded to Speer's specifications by the West German company but has been discontinued. CCI is presently supplying a long line of excellent rimfire ammunition. It is quite possible the Omark people may get back in rifle ammunition, and, if so, it will be a high-quality product.

From time to time over the years, ammunition has been available in Savage brand, but none is listed as this book is being prepared. Savage does import excellent British Eley ammunition for .22 match rifle shooting.

Weatherby ammunition, available only for the company's magnum cartridges, is manufactured by Norma and branded Weatherby. The ammunition is loaded to Weatherby specifications. The well-known British Kynoch ammunition is also available in America, and it's best known for use in double rifles. Interarms, with U.S. offices in Alexandria, Va., also imports ammunition, chiefly in some of the hard-to-find foreign calibers. This is a line which could be expanded to embrace more cartridges as time goes by.

From time to time there will be other brands of ammunition available here. Suffice to say that all of the above brand names are well known to me as well as to most serious riflemen. Most of the people involved in their operation are known to me personally, and I have no reluctance whatever in recommending these brands. Maybe *you* haven't heard of them, but I've known them for years. I can't speak for new names and brands that may come along, but it's safe to say they will comply with the technical specifications set forth by the Sporting Arms and Ammunition Manufacturers Institute.

BALLISTICS CHART (pages 165-166)
(Courtesy Winchester-Western)
Ballistics charts are useful but they can be misleading, because they do not include any factor for bullet design or construction. A .270 Winchester 130-grain open-point expanding bullet will *deliver* more energy to a deer than the .458 Winchester Magnum with 500-grain full-metal-case bullet, even though the .458 has nearly twice the energy of the .270. The .458 is meant to penetrate an African elephant's skull to reach the brain; it would go through a deer like a sword. When you study charts you must consider what the bullet will do when it hits.

Velocity is simply a measurement of speed; energy is a function of speed plus weight. The figures are interesting, and you should note that some states limit deer hunting to rifles of a certain caliber, others by muzzle-energy figures, and others by specific calibers.

Ammunition is available from other manufacturers, often in calibers not shown on this list. You should obtain catalogs from both Winchester-Western and Remington, and also from Federal, Norma, Frontier, and Weatherby.

TRAJECTORY CHART (pages 167-169)
(Courtesy Winchester-Western)
These chart figures will be helpful in choosing a cartridge when you consider the type of shooting you will do. They show the bullet's flight above and below the line of sight for "short-range" shooting and for "long-range" shooting. Note that the chart suggests sighting some rifles to hit point of aim at 100, 150, 200, and 250 yards. The distance at which you sight in is something you must judge for yourself. It depends on the cartridge's trajectory, its retained energy, the country over which you will hunt, and your ability as a marksman. I have eliminated loads that are not considered suitable for deer hunting.

BALLISTICS CHART

CARTRIDGE	BULLET WT. GRS	VELOCITY IN FEET PER SECOND							ENERGY IN FOOT POUNDS					
		MUZZLE	100	200 YARDS	300	400	500	MUZZLE	100	200	300 YARDS	400	500
.243 Winchester Super-X	100	2960	2697	2449	2215	1993	1786	1945	1615	1332	1089	882	708
6mm Remington Super-X	100	3130	2857	2600	2357	2127	1911	2175	1812	1501	1233	1004	811
.25/06 Remington Super-X	120	3050	2786	2538	2302	2080	1870	2478	2068	1716	1412	1153	932
.25-35 Winchester Super-X	117	2270	1902	1576	1306	1112	994	1338	940	645	443	321	257
.250 Savage Super-X	100	2820	2467	2140	1839	1569	1339	1765	1351	1017	751	547	398
.257 Roberts Super-X	100	2900	2541	2210	1904	1627	1387	1867	1433	1084	805	588	427
.257 Roberts Super-X	117	2650	2291	1961	1663	1404	1199	1824	1363	999	718	512	373
.264 Winchester Mag. Super-X	100	3620	3198	2814	2462	2136	1836	2909	2271	1758	1346	1013	748
.264 Winchester Mag. Super-X	140	3140	2886	2646	2419	2203	1998	3064	2589	2176	1819	1508	1241
.270 Winchester Super-X	130	3110	2849	2604	2371	2150	1941	2791	2343	1957	1622	1334	1087
.270 Winchester Super-X	130	3110	2823	2554	2300	2061	1837	2791	2300	1883	1527	1226	974
.270 Winchester Super-X	150	2900	2632	2380	2142	1918	1709	2801	2307	1886	1528	1225	973
.284 Winchester Super-X	150	2860	2595	2344	2108	1886	1680	2724	2243	1830	1480	1185	940
7mm Mauser (7 × 57) Super-X	175	2470	2165	1883	1626	1402	1219	2370	1821	1378	1027	764	577
7mm Remington Mag. Super-X	150	3110	2830	2568	2320	2085	1866	3221	2667	2196	1792	1448	1160
7mm Remington Mag. Super-X	175	2860	2645	2440	2244	2057	1879	3178	2718	2313	1956	1644	1372
.30/30 Winchester Super-X	150	2390	2018	1684	1398	1177	1036	1902	1256	944	651	461	357
.30/30 Winchester Super-X	150	2390	2018	1684	1398	1177	1036	1902	1356	944	651	461	357
.30/30 Winchester Super-X	150	2390	2018	1684	1398	1177	1036	1902	1356	944	651	461	357
.30/30 Winchester Super-X	170	2200	1895	1619	1381	1191	1061	1827	1355	989	720	535	425
.30/30 Winchester Super-X	170	2200	1895	1619	1381	1191	1061	1827	1355	989	720	535	425
.30 Remington Super-X	170	2120	1822	1555	1328	1153	1036	1696	1253	913	666	502	405
.30/06 Springfield Super-X	125	3140	2780	2447	2138	1853	1595	2736	2145	1662	1269	953	706
.30/06 Springfield Super-X	150	2920	2580	2265	1972	1704	1466	2839	2217	1708	1295	967	716
.30/06 Springfield Super-X	150	2910	2617	2342	2083	1843	1622	2820	2281	1827	1445	1131	876
.30/06 Springfield Super-X	180	2700	2348	2023	1727	1466	1251	2913	2203	1635	1192	859	625
.30/06 Springfield Super-X	180	2700	2469	2250	2042	1846	1663	2913	2436	2023	1666	1362	1105
.30/06 Springfield Super-X	220	2410	2130	1870	1632	1422	1246	2837	2216	1708	1301	988	758
.30/06 Springfield Super-X	220	2410	2192	1985	1791	1611	1448	2837	2347	1924	1567	1268	1024
.30/40 Krag Super-X	180	2430	2099	1795	1525	1298	1128	2360	1761	1288	929	673	508
.30/40 Krag Super-X	180	2430	2213	2007	1813	1632	1468	2360	1957	1610	1314	1064	861
.30/40 Krag Super-X	220	2160	1956	1765	1587	1427	1287	2279	1869	1522	1230	995	809
.300 Winchester Mag. Super-X	150	3290	2951	2636	2342	2068	1813	3605	2900	2314	1827	1424	1095
.300 Winchester Mag. Super-X	180	3000	2783	2577	2379	2190	2010	3597	3095	2654	2262	1917	1614

BALLISTICS CHART

| CARTRIDGE | BULLET WT. GRS | VELOCITY IN FEET PER SECOND ||||||| ENERGY IN FOOT POUNDS |||||||
		MUZZLE	100	200	300 YARDS	400	500	MUZZLE	100	200	300 YARDS	400	500
.300 Winchester Mag. Super-X	220	2680	2448	2228	2020	1823	1640	3508	2927	2424	1993	1623	1314
.300 H.&H. Magnum Super-X	150	3130	2822	2534	2264	2011	1776	3262	2652	2138	1707	1347	1050
.300 H.&H. Magnum Super-X	180	2880	2640	2412	2196	1991	1798	3315	2785	2325	1927	1584	1292
.300 H.&H. Magnum Super-X	220	2580	2341	2114	1901	1702	1520	3251	2677	2183	1765	1415	1128
.300 Savage Super-X	150	2630	2311	2015	1743	1500	1295	2303	1779	1352	1012	749	558
.300 Savage Super-X	150	2630	2354	2095	1853	1632	1434	2303	1845	1462	1143	887	685
.300 Savage Super-X	180	2350	2025	1728	1467	1252	1098	2207	1639	1193	860	626	482
.300 Savage Super-X	180	2350	2137	1935	1745	1571	1413	2207	1825	1496	1217	986	798
.303 Savage Super-X	190	1940	1657	1410	1211	1073	982	1588	1158	839	619	486	407
.303 British Super-X	180	2520	2290	2072	1867	1675	1501	2538	2096	1716	1393	1121	900
.308 Winchester Super-X	125	3100	2743	2413	2107	1824	1569	2667	2088	1616	1232	923	683
.308 Winchester Super-X	150	2820	2488	2179	1893	1633	1405	2648	2061	1581	1193	888	657
.308 Winchester Super-X	150	2820	2533	2263	2009	1774	1560	2648	2137	1705	1344	1048	810
.308 Winchester Super-X	180	2620	2274	1955	1666	1414	1212	2743	2066	1527	1109	799	587
.308 Winchester Super-X	180	2620	2393	2178	1974	1782	1604	2743	2288	1896	1557	1269	1028
.308 Winchester Super-X	200	2450	2208	1980	1767	1572	1397	2665	2165	1741	1386	1097	867
.32 Win. Special Super-X	170	2250	1870	1537	1267	1082	972	1911	1320	892	606	442	357
.32 Win. Special Super-X	170	2250	1870	1537	1267	1082	972	1911	1320	892	606	442	357
.32 Remington Super-X	170	2140	1785	1475	1228	1064	963	1728	1203	821	569	427	350
8mm Mauser (8 × 57) Super-X	170	2510	2105	1741	1429	1188	1035	2378	1672	1144	771	533	404
.338 Winchester Mag. Super-X	200	2960	2658	2375	2110	1862	1635	3890	3137	2505	1977	1539	1187
.338 Winchester Mag. Super-X	250	2660	2395	2145	1910	1693	1497	3927	3184	2554	2025	1591	1244
.348 Winchester Super-X	200	2520	2215	1931	1672	1443	1253	2820	2178	1656	1241	925	697
.35 Remington Super-X	200	2080	1698	1376	1140	1001	912	1921	1280	841	577	445	369
.35 Remington Super-X	200	2080	1698	1376	1140	1001	912	1921	1280	841	577	445	369
.351 Winchester S.L.	180	1850	1556	1310	1128	1012	934	1368	968	686	508	409	349
.358 Winchester Super-X	200	2490	2171	1876	1610	1379	1194	2753	2093	1563	1151	844	633
.358 Winchester Super-X	250	2230	1988	1763	1557	1375	1224	2760	2194	1725	1346	1049	832
.375 H.&H. Magnum Super-X	270	2690	2420	2166	1928	1707	1507	4337	3510	2812	2228	1747	1361
.375 H.&H. Magnum Super-X	300	2530	2268	2022	1793	1584	1397	4263	3426	2723	2141	1671	1300
.44 Remington Magnum Super-X	240	1760	1362	1094	953	861	789	1650	988	638	484	395	332
45/70 Government	405	1330	1168	1055	977	918	869	1590	1227	1001	858	758	679
.458 Winchester Mag. Super-X	510	2110	1834	1583	1366	1192	1070	5041	3808	2837	2113	1609	1296

TRAJECTORY CHART

TRAJECTORY

Inches above (+) or below (−) line of sight
0 = Indicates yardage at which rifle is sighted in.

CARTRIDGE	BULLET WT. GRS.	SHORT RANGE YARDS							LONG RANGE YARDS				
		50	100	150	200	250	300	100	150	200	250	300	400	500
.243 Winchester Super-X	100	0.5	0.9	0	−2.2	−5.8	−11.0	1.9	1.6	0	−3.1	−7.8	−22.6	−46.3
6mm Remington Super-X	100	0.4	0.7	0	−1.9	−5.1	−9.7	1.7	1.4	0	−2.7	−6.8	−20.0	−40.8
.25/06 Remington Super-X	120	0.5	0.8	0	−2.0	−5.4	−10.2	1.8	1.5	0	−2.9	−7.2	−21.0	−42.9
.25/35 Winchester Super-X	117	0.6	0	−3.0	−8.8	−18.2	−31.8	2.0	0	−4.9	−13.3	−25.9	−67.4	−136.9
.250 Savage Super-X	100	0.2	0	−1.6	−4.9	−10.0	−17.4	2.4	2.0	0	−3.9	−10.1	−30.5	−65.2
.257 Roberts Super-X	100	0.6	1.0	0	−2.5	−6.9	−13.2	2.3	1.9	0	−3.7	−9.4	−28.6	−60.9
.257 Roberts Super-X	117	0.3	0	−1.9	−5.8	−11.9	−20.7	2.9	2.4	0	−4.7	−12.0	−36.7	−79.2
.264 Winchester Mag. Super-X	100	0.2	0.5	0	−1.5	−4.1	−7.9	2.1	2.4	1.8	0	−3.0	−13.6	−31.9
.264 Winchester Mag. Super-X	140	0.4	0.7	0	−1.9	−4.9	−9.4	2.7	3.0	2.1	0	−3.5	−15.0	−33.7
.270 Winchester Super-X	130	0.4	0.7	0	−1.9	−5.1	−9.7	1.7	1.4	0	−2.7	−6.8	−19.9	−40.5
.270 Winchester Super-X	130	0.4	0.8	0	−2.0	−5.3	−10.0	1.7	1.5	0	−2.8	−7.1	−20.8	−42.7
.270 Winchester Super-X	150	0.6	0.9	0	−2.3	−6.1	−11.7	2.1	1.7	0	−3.3	−8.2	−24.1	−49.4
.284 Winchester Super-X	150	0.6	1.0	0	−2.4	−6.3	−12.1	2.1	1.8	0	−3.4	−8.5	−24.8	−51.0
7mm Mauser (7 × 57) Super-X	175	0.4	0	−2.2	−6.6	−13.4	−23.0	1.5	0	−3.6	−9.7	−18.6	−46.8	−92.8
7mm Remington Mag. Super-X	150	0.4	0.8	0	−1.9	−5.2	−9.9	1.7	1.5	0	−2.8	−7.0	−20.5	−42.1
7mm Remington Mag. Super-X	175	0.6	0.9	0	−2.3	−6.0	−11.3	2.0	1.7	0	−3.2	−7.9	−22.7	−45.8
.30/30 Winchester Super-X	150	0.5	0	−2.6	−7.7	−16.0	−27.9	1.7	0	−4.3	−11.6	−22.7	−59.1	−120.5
.30/30 Winchester Super-X	150	0.5	0	−2.6	−7.7	−16.0	−27.9	1.7	0	−4.3	−11.6	−22.7	−59.1	−120.5
.30/30 Winchester Super-X	150	0.5	0	−2.6	−7.7	−16.0	−27.9	1.7	0	−4.3	−11.6	−22.7	−59.1	−120.5
.30/30 Winchester Super-X	170	0.6	0	−3.0	−8.9	−18.0	−31.1	2.0	0	−4.8	−13.0	−25.1	−63.6	−126.7
.30/30 Winchester Super-X	170	0.6	0	−3.0	−8.9	−18.0	−31.1	2.0	0	−4.8	−13.0	−25.1	−63.6	−126.7
.30 Remington Super-X	170	0.7	0	−3.3	−9.7	−19.6	−33.8	2.2	0	−5.3	−14.1	−27.2	−69.0	−136.9
.30/06 Springfield Super-X	125	0.4	0.8	0	−2.1	−5.6	−10.7	1.8	1.5	0	−3.0	−7.7	−23.0	−48.5
.30/06 Springfield Super-X	150	0.6	1.0	0	−2.4	−6.6	−12.7	2.2	1.8	0	−3.5	−9.0	−27.0	−57.1
.30/06 Springfield Super-X	150	0.6	0.9	0	−2.3	−6.3	−12.0	2.1	1.8	0	−3.3	−8.5	−25.0	−51.8
.30/06 Springfield Super-X	180	0.2	0	−1.8	−5.5	−11.2	−19.5	2.7	2.3	0	−4.4	−11.3	−34.4	−73.7
.30/06 Springfield Super-X	180	0.2	0	−1.6	−4.8	−9.7	−16.5	2.4	2.0	0	−3.7	−9.3	−27.0	−54.9
.30/06 Springfield Super-X	220	0.4	0	−2.3	−6.8	−13.8	−23.6	1.5	0	−3.7	−9.9	−19.0	−47.4	−93.1
.30/06 Springfield Super-X	220	9.4	0	−2.2	−6.4	−12.7	−21.6	1.5	0	−3.5	−9.1	−17.2	−41.8	−79.9

TRAJECTORY CHART

TRAJECTORY

Inches above (+) or below (−) line of sight
0 = Indicates yardage at which rifle is sighted in.

CARTRIDGE	BULLET WT. GRS.	SHORT RANGE YARDS 50	100	150	200	250	300	TRAJECTORY 100	150	200	LONG RANGE YARDS 250	300	400	500
.30/40 Krag Super-X	180	0.4	0	−2.4	−7.1	−14.5	−25.0	1.6	0	−3.9	−10.5	−20.3	−51.7	−103.9
.30/40 Krag Super-X	180	0.4	0	−2.1	−6.2	−12.5	−21.1	1.4	0	−3.4	−8.9	−16.8	−40.9	−78.1
.30/40 Krag Super-X	220	0.6	0	−2.9	−8.2	−16.4	−27.6	1.9	0	−4.4	−11.6	−21.9	−53.3	−101.8
.300 Winchester Mag. Super-X	150	0.3	0.7	0	−1.8	−4.8	−9.3	2.6	2.9	2.1	−2.8	−3.5	−15.4	−35.5
.300 Winchester Mag. Super-X	180	0.5	0.8	0	−2.0	−5.3	−10.1	1.8	1.5	0	−3.8	−7.0	−20.2	−40.7
.300 Winchester Mag. Super-X	220	0.2	0	−1.7	−4.9	−9.9	−16.9	2.5	2.0	0	−2.8	−9.5	−27.5	−56.1
.300 H.&H. Magnum Super-X	150	0.4	0.8	0	−2.0	−5.3	−10.1	1.7	1.5	0	−3.2	−7.2	−21.2	−43.8
.300 H.&H. Magnum Super-X	180	0.6	0.9	0	−2.3	−6.0	−11.5	2.1	1.7	0	−4.2	−8.0	−23.3	−47.4
.300 H.&H. Magnum Super-X	220	0.3	0	−1.9	−5.5	−11.0	−18.7	2.7	2.2	0	−4.5	−10.5	−30.7	−63.0
.300 Savage Super-X	150	0.3	0	−1.9	−5.7	−11.6	−19.9	2.8	2.3	0	−4.2	−11.5	−34.4	−73.0
.300 Savage Super-X	150	0.3	0	−1.8	−5.4	−11.0	−18.8	2.7	2.2	0	−4.2	−10.7	−31.5	−65.5
.300 Savage Super-X	180	0.5	0	−2.6	−7.7	−15.6	−27.1	1.7	0	−4.2	−11.3	−21.9	−55.8	−112.0
.300 Savage Super-X	180	0.4	0	−2.3	−6.7	−13.5	−22.8	1.5	0	−3.6	−9.6	−18.2	−44.1	−84.2
.303 Savage Super-X	190	0.9	0	−4.1	−11.9	−24.1	−41.4	2.7	0	−6.4	−17.3	−33.2	−83.7	−164.3
.303 British Super-X	180	0.3	0	−2.0	−5.8	−11.6	−19.6	2.9	2.4	0	−4.4	−11.0	−32.0	−65.5
.308 Winchester Super-X	125	0.5	0.8	0	−2.1	−5.7	−11.1	1.9	1.6	0	−3.1	−7.9	−23.7	−50.0
.308 Winchester Super-X	150	0.2	0	−1.6	−4.8	−9.8	−16.9	2.4	2.0	0	−3.8	−9.8	−29.3	−62.0
.308 Winchester Super-X	150	0.2	0	−1.5	−4.5	−9.3	−15.9	2.3	1.9	0	−3.6	−9.1	−26.9	−55.7
.308 Winchester Super-X	180	0.3	0	−2.0	−5.9	−12.1	−20.9	2.9	2.4	0	−4.7	−12.1	−36.9	−79.1
.308 Winchester Super-X	180	0.2	0	−1.8	−5.2	−10.4	−17.7	2.6	2.1	0	−4.0	−9.9	−28.9	−59.8
.308 Winchester Super-X	200	0.4	0	−2.1	−6.3	−12.6	−21.4	1.4	0	−3.4	−9.0	−17.2	−41.1	−81.1
.32 Win. Special Super-X	170	0.6	0	−3.1	−9.2	−19.0	−33.2	2.0	0	−5.1	−13.8	−27.1	−70.9	−144.3
.32Win. Special Super-X	170	0.6	0	−3.1	−9.2	−19.0	−33.2	2.0	0	−5.1	−13.8	−27.1	−70.9	−144.3
.32 Remington Super-X	170	0.7	0	−3.4	−10.2	−20.9	−36.5	2.3	0	−5.6	−15.2	−29.6	−76.7	−4.5
8mm Mauser (8 × 57) Super-X	170	0.4	0	−2.3	−7.0	−14.6	−25.7	−1.6	0	−3.9	−10.7	−21.0	−55.4	−114.3
.338 Winchester Mag. Super-X	200	0.5	0.9	0	−2.3	−6.1	−11.6	2.0	1.7	0	−3.2	−8.2	−24.3	−50.4
.338 Winchester Mag. Super-X	250	0.2	0	−1.7	−5.2	−10.5	−18.0	2.6	2.1	0	−4.0	−10.2	−30.0	−61.9
.348 Winchester Super-X	200	0.3	0	−2.1	−6.2	−12.7	−21.9	1.4	0	−3.4	−9.2	−17.7	−44.4	−87.9
.35 Remington Super-X	200	0.8	0	−3.8	−11.3	−33.5	−41.2	2.5	0	−6.3	−17.1	−33.6	−87.7	−176.3
.35 Remington Super-X	200	0.8	0	−3.8	−11.3	−23.5	−41.2	0	0	−6.3	−17.1	−33.6	−87.7	−176.3

168

Cartridge	Weight									
.351 Winchester S.L.	180	0	−2.1	−7.8	−17.8	−32.9	−53.9	1.5	−4.7	−13.6	−27.6	−47.5	−108.8	−203.9
.358 Winchester Super-X	200	0.4	0	−2.2	−6.5	−13.3	−23.0	1.5	0	−3.6	−9.7	−18.6	−47.2	−94.1
.358 Winchester Super-X	250	0.5	0	−2.7	−7.9	−16.0	−27.1	1.8	0	−4.3	−11.4	−21.7	−53.5	−103.7
.375 H.&H. Magnum Super-X	270	0.2	0	−1.7	−5.1	−10.3	−17.6	2.5	2.1	0	−3.9	−10.0	−29.4	−60.7
.375 H.&H. Magnum Super-X	300	0.3	0	−2.0	−5.9	−11.9	−20.3	2.9	2.4	0	−4.5	−11.5	−33.8	−70.1
.44 Remington Magnum Super-X	240	0	−2.7	−10.2	−23.6	−44.2	−73.3	0	−6.1	−18.1	−37.4	−65.1	−150.3	−282.5
.45/70 Government	405	0	−4.7	−15.8	−34.0	−60.0	−94.5	0	−8.7	−24.6	−48.2	−80.3	−172.4	−305.9
.458 Winchester Mag. Super-X	510	0.7	0	−3.3	−9.5	−19.2	−33.0	2.2	0	−5.2	−13.8	−26.5	−66.5	−131.0

169

14

Sights, Scopes, and Mounts

You can hit an object with a rifle if you point it in the general direction of the target, as long as the target is close enough and large enough. To make a hit on an object farther away you have to squint down the barrel. Long ago it was learned that you could improve on that by putting "sights" on the barrel.

At first these were a post of some sort at the muzzle and a notch at the breech. Today's open sights, with which most rifles come equipped when you open the box, are not much better that that. We call such sights open sights to distinguish them from a peep sight or a scope. The latter has optics.

There are several reasons why rifles are equipped with plain open sights instead of something better. First, and most valid, is that most buyers will purchase their own scope and mount anyway, so there is no earthly point in furnishing expensive sights that won't be used. But I suspect another reason is that better sights cost money and the higher the price the less competitive. So it's going to mean more sales if cheap sights are supplied. It also reduces the total that is taxed—the 11 percent excise tax. (This tax is paid by the manufacturer, based on the wholesale price. The money goes into special funds and is returned to the states in direct relation to the hunting-license sales in each state. Over the years many hundreds of millions of dollars have been paid the states, money earmarked for wildlife and habitat improvement. The tax is collected on sales of all arms and ammunition.)

The open rear sight on a Model 70 Winchester .458 Magnum. This sort of sight, with wide, shallow V, is meant to be picked up quickly when chasing a wounded, savage beast in thick cover. It hasn't any other purpose.

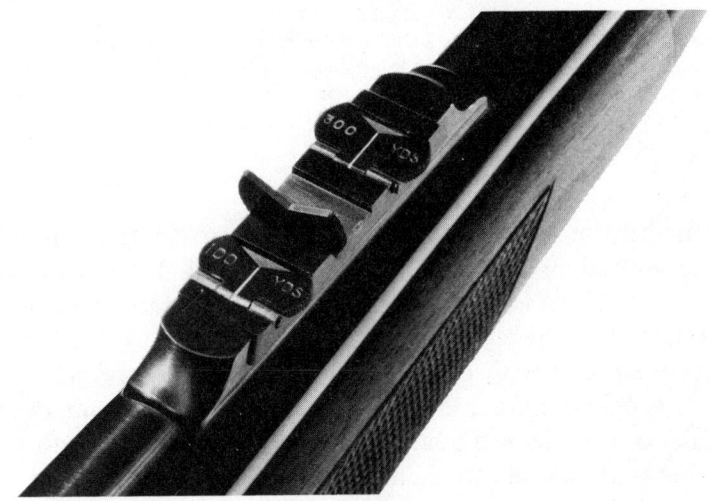

This British line of sights appears here on a Whitworth rifle imported by Interarms. Such sights are, frankly, more expressive of the gunmaker's art than useful. Still, the English like them and often extend them to prohibitive ranges. Such a sight is only useful at ranges of 100 yards or less under most circumstances.

    Generally speaking, the open sights found on a rifle when you buy it are next to useless. The best bet is to replace them, as the factory expects you to. These open sights often lack any windage adjustment, so the owner must bang them back and forth in their slots. This is a pretty antique way to have to adjust the sights on any modern firearm. Many rear sights obscure too much of the target; this is a particular fault of the so-called "buckhorn," which has ears on either side of the notch.

    But the most serious objection to any kind of open sight is that

Conventional rear sights are mounted in dovetail slots and the usual way to adjust them for windage is to whack them back and forth as shown, with a brass drift and a hammer. For the record, these slots are tapered and the sight is driven out from left to right as shown. Driving the opposite way tightens the combination.

it forces the shooter to focus on three objects at once, all at widely varying distances: the rear sight, the front sight, and the target. The eye is a wonderful organ, but it's an impossibility for it to focus on these three objects all at once. So you cannot shoot nearly as well with open sights as with a peep (aperture) sight or a scope. There are many old-timers who claim otherwise. Many of them won't even try a scope, or when they do shoulder a rifle with scope attached, they get their eye right up close to the lens and complain that they can't shoot that way. You bet they can't. They'd get a badly blackened eye if they did.

The subject of rifle accuracy has many facets. There is the inherent error in the rifle and some error in the ammunition. You can determine this error in most cases by attaching a good scope that reduces your aiming error and shooting from a bench. But you cannot do much about aiming error built in with open sights. This varies all over the lot depending on eyesight (which depends on age to a degree), the range over which you're shooting, the target, the light, and, finally, the sights themselves, since some types are more suitable than others.

A good man, and I mean a real good one who shoots a great deal, can shoot into perhaps 2 inches at 100 yards. Marlin used to have a foreman at its range, where every rifle is targeted, who could get 100-yard groups of between 1 and 2 inches with Model

336 rifles and factory ammunition. I've seen him do it. But that's an exception. Most shooters will do well to have an *aiming error* that's no greater than 5 or 6 inches at 100 yards.

There are some rifles which are difficult to scope because they eject at the top. It's necessary either to use a peep sight on these rifles, which is the smart thing to do, or to use the open sights with which they come out of the box. Probably the most visible of these rifles is the greatest deer rifle of them all, the Winchester Model 94. Great as this rifle is, a scope for it either has to be mounted offset (which prevents snugging the cheek down on the stock for a steady position) or has to be one of those long-eye-relief models which can be mounted forward of the action. Aside from looking a bit peculiar this is a sensible solution.

PEEP SIGHTS
The next step up from an open sight is the peep. It is a rather surprising thing that peep sights are not more popular. The peep sight was invented, or discovered, by the Lyman family many years ago. Its principle of operation is similar to that of a camera. The peep hole determines the amount of light that reaches the eye (film in a camera). Close down the hole size and the sight picture becomes sharper.

Peep sights must be mounted close to the eye if they are to be useful. The early Lyman sights were known as "tang" sights; they were mounted on the tang, the strap behind the hammer of a rifle like the Model 94 Winchester. They used the stock screw for the rear of the sight base, and a new hole had to be drilled and tapped for the front. This placed the peep hole exactly where it ought to be. The bolt would hit most of these sights in its operation, so they were made to flop down and up as the action was stroked.

For some reason which defies logic those who designed the Model 1903 Springfield rifle placed the rear peep sight on the barrel forward of the receiver and about 7 inches ahead of where it should have been. This was so far from the eye that the sight's value was questionable. This was corrected in 1936 when the Garand M1 rifle was adopted. Today just about every rifle worthy of the name is drilled and tapped for a receiver or peep sight, located close to the eye where it should be.

Peep sights have never become as popular as I think they should have. Most older shooters clung to open sights and wouldn't change. Peep sights are supplied with a "target disc" which has never been popular. But because the sights come that way, most shooters leave them that way. The right way to use a sight, especially for hunting, is to unscrew that disc and throw it as far as you can. That's right—discard it entirely. Use the big hole the disc screws into for your sight picture. That's the way to use a peep sight.

Strange as this may sound to the uninitiated, you can hold every bit as close with the big hole, and it allows you to see a lot more of the area around the target. You see, your eye will automatically center itself in the big hole. And that's the secret of a peep sight's usefulness—you do not need to concentrate on centering your eye. You need only place the front sight on the target without paying any attention to the rear sight. Most shooters and hunters don't understand that, and this is why they don't like and won't buy peep sights.

At one time Lyman made a splendid peep sight, the famous Lyman 48. It was a crackerjack and usually adorned every fine rifle made. Then Lyman made a cheaper version, the Lyman 57, and Redfield and Williams also made peep sights; quite a few were sold during the years just after World War II. Then the scope became popular and pushed all iron sights virtually out of the picture.

SCOPE DEVELOPMENT
There's nothing very new about scope sights. They were used in the Civil War on many of the huge rifles employed by sharpshooters. These older scopes were nearly as long as the rifle barrels themselves—and those were pretty long. Scopes were also used by buffalo hunters, but there was little interest in hunting rifles with scopes in this country until after World War I.

Before that war, most scopes were of the target variety and were used by Schuetzen shooters (who fired from the standing position) and experimental riflemen (who were the bench-rest shooters of their day). Brand names of these early scopes were Winchester, Malcolm, Stevens, and Seidel.

After World War I some publicity was given scopes by such writers as Townsend Whelen in *Outdoor Life*, Paul Curtis in *Field & Stream*, and Captain E. C. Crossman in a variety of magazines. The first hunting scopes were imported from Germany in Zeiss and Hensoldt brands. Target scopes were made by J. W. Fecker in Pittsburgh; later a man named Wray Hage-

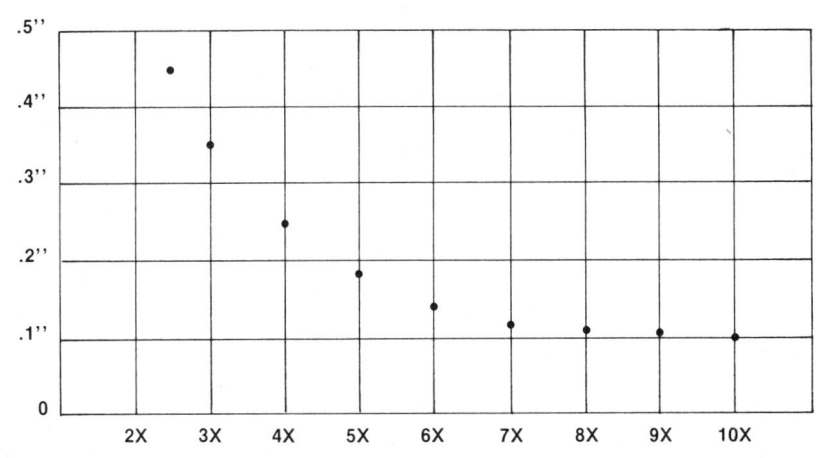

A quality scope, properly focused, vastly reduces aiming error. This chart indicates approximate aiming error with a scope as it relates to magnification at 100 yards. Read the power of your scope across the bottom, then read up the side to find the average aiming error. A 4× scope shows an average error of .25 inch. You will find that with a little practice, you will be able to reduce your aiming error to the above limits—from a steady rest, of course.

man left Fecker and went to Lyman and set up their scope business. John Unertl also left Fecker and set up his own business.

In the 1920s, R. Noske of California developed a side scope mount which attached to the side of the receiver; scopes were almost exclusively attached to bolt-action rifles in those days. The Noske mount was similar to those later made by Griffin & Howe of New York City and Paul Jaeger of Jenkintown, Pa. Griffin & Howe's mount uses two levers to secure the mount top to the base, while the Jaeger uses a single lever. Either style is quickly removable leaving only the base attached.

A few years later, Rudolph Noske made a 2½× scope with a ⅞-inch-diameter tube with lenses ground to give long eye relief so the scope could be mounted forward of the unaltered bolt handles on Mauser, Springfield, and Winchester Model 54 rifles. This early Noske scope had another interesting feature: adjustments were in the scope tube itself. Earlier scopes provided no windage adjustment (it was provided in the Noske side mount). As a matter of fact, Griffin & Howe and Jaeger supplied their mounts with or without windage adjustment for years.

Bill Weaver followed the Noske with his 330 scope, which had a small tube, was actually about 2× (although advertised as 2½×), and was sold complete with a satisfactory though homely mount at $27.50. Lyman followed with a scope called the Stag which was a flop but later produced the Alaskan, probably one of the finest scopes in its day.

During World War II, Remington manufactured 1903 Springfield rifles (as did Smith Corona) with specially shaped bolt handles to accommodate a scope. These were designated Model 1903A4 and saw wide service as sniper rifles. Most of them used Weaver 330 scopes, but a very few wore Lyman Alaskans. There was a vast difference in these two scopes and I've always felt Lyman missed the boat when they dropped the Alaskan and its name shortly after World War II. The company had the top-quality-scope market in its hands when World War II ended, but allowed others to take it away. Weaver's 330 was followed by a 440, which was short-lived, and both were succeeded by the K2.5, which is still around and is an excellent scope. The K2.5 Weaver (2½×) had a 1-inch tube which soon became the standard. Prior to that scope, tubes came in various diameters, which raised hell with mounts, as you can imagine. Most scopes were available in ¾-inch, ⅞-inch, 1-inch, and 26mm (1.23-inch). I think it was probably Weaver's influence that made 1 inch the standard, simply because he had more scopes in the marketplace than anybody else.

One of the most important advances in optics came about during World War II: coated lenses. Many of today's shooters don't know anything else, since they were brought up with coated lenses. Coating, which is a treatment of the surfaces applied not only to scopes but to cameras and binoculars too, cuts reflected-light loss to almost zero. The result is an increase in efficiency of *30 percent*. I certainly can remember prewar scopes and binoculars when quite a bit of performance was lost. Looking at an object with the two was quite an experience—coated lenses were like turning on a light. I still have one prewar scope on a rifle, the Lyman 438 Field telescope, which is a target-type scope of 4× that I have mounted on a Savage .22 Model 23A sporter. It was a good scope in its day and I used to use it for varmint shooting. To look into that scope today is like looking into a dark room through a spidery keyhole. The scope has come a long way.

Scopes used to fog up like blazes with rapid changes in temperature due to condensation. When the moisture inside a scope was subjected to fluctuations in temperature, it condensed on the lenses. You couldn't see and the scope was useless. This happened if you brought a cold rifle into a warm room, or vice versa, and it happened when the weather got steamy and wet as it often does in parts of coastal Alaska.

Hunters were cautioned to leave their scoped rifles outside each night and not to bring them into a warm cabin or tent. It wasn't so bad to bring them inside at night, because you were not hunting at night. But the next morning the same thing would happen and your rifle was useless until it cooled to the outside air temperature and the fog disappeared. You also learned to keep scopes dry in the rain; the high humidity that often accompanied a shower would fog the scope.

Then scope makers learned to prevent fogging by sealing scope tubes with nitrogen gas under a little pressure. In the early days of sealed scopes many of them leaked, and many owners made their own immersion test, which often prompted leaking. In manufacture, scopes are subjected to a bath in warm water for a short period of time to make certain they are sealed. It should also be mentioned that some of the early scope mounts had rings that could only be opened on one side, which necessitated removal of the turret (where the adjustment knobs are) to slide the rings over the scope tube. Naturally this would remove any seal. Scope mounts had to be changed to the present split rings. Today's scope doesn't leak and doesn't fog. You can move it in and out of a cold/warm room regardless of the outside temperature, and it will survive an overnight bath in a pond.

It's also tough as hell. Bausch & Lomb has just about gone out of the scope business (except that the company owns Bushnell, which does a land-office business), but in the late 1940s and early 1950s the B&L scope was promoted widely. One of the gimmicks they used was to drive a nail into a piece of wood, using the scope as a hammer, at the various exhibitions catering to gun and hunting equipment manufacturers. Then, when a sufficiently large crowd was on hand, they'd toss the scope on the floor. It wasn't hurt.

You used to have to baby a scope—protect it with loving care, hide it under your jacket if it began to rain, and never, never, never let it get bumped. You can give today's scope a pretty good whupping, though it's not to be recommended.

The fragility of earlier scopes made the alternative of iron sights a pretty sensible proposition. That's why side mounts were so popular, since the scope could be whipped off the rifle and iron sights used. Some scopes were mounted high enough to allow you to look under the scope and use the iron sights. But this defeated the proper use of a scope; you should be able to get your head down low and squeeze it against the stock so you're good and steady. You can't do that with a too-high, or an offset, mount.

Then there were so-called swing mounts, held in place by a clip spring so you could push the scope aside to use iron sights if necessary. They always claimed a swing mount would return to zero time after time, but I never had any faith in their ability to do that. Even today, there are mounts available that place the scope high enough to see sights beneath the scope. There is no earthly use for them today and such a provision is silly. I have always believed a rifle looks best with a front sight, and if I ever had to spend a winter in the bush or was otherwise isolated for a long period of time, I would want to provide an alternate sighting system. But in ordinary use there is no reason for that.

In the 1950s, when I was gunsmithing in upper New York State, Bob Sears, who then worked for Kollmorgen (now the Redfield scope) and now is a technical editor of *The American Rifleman* magazine, dropped into my shop with the first sample of a scope with the new "Tuff Coat" finish. Scope tubes are made of aluminum in nearly all cases today. Aluminum is a relatively soft metal, but it does not rust like steel. Its light weight is an advantage in aircraft, automobiles, and rifle scopes. Aluminum requires a finish for protection, for though it doesn't rust, it does tarnish. The finish is called anodizing, and it's done by an electrolytic process. What Kollmorgen had done was to borrow a hard-anodizing treatment from the aircraft industry, and it worked slick as silk on a scope tube. Bob Sears told me to lay a file on the scope and push it across the surface. File a brand-new scope tube? "Sure," he said, "go ahead and try it." It didn't touch the scope tube, but it did turn the file's edges!

Ever since, everybody has used hard-coated aluminum scope tubes, and they are extraordinarily abrasion-resistant. I still have that first Kollmorgen that Bob Sears left with me that day, and it's seen a lot of service but still looks like new.

Back in my early gunsmithing days, mounting a scope was sometimes a difficult proposition, especially with a side mount. To mount a side mount you had to drill three holes in the side of the receiver for screws and two more for taper pins. The first hole had to be located with enormous precision, because all the remaining holes' locations were based on the first. And when you were finished, you wanted the rifle to be sighted in with the reticle in the middle of the field.

That often took some fiddling, and I always felt I earned my fee for this job. You had to clamp the mount base in place, then align the mount, scope, and rifle bore by bore-sighting, and mark the hole's location. Then, with fingers crossed, you drilled and tapped that first hole. Once that hurdle was passed, you fastened the base and checked your hole, still using only the first hole. If all was OK, you marked and drilled the remaining holes. But you were never done until you had the mount fully installed and shot the rifle. If the reticle was up in one corner of the field, you had to shim until it was corrected.

All that was changed when the first self-centering reticle was invented. This was quite a boon to everybody—gunsmiths who mounted scopes, mount manufacturers, and rifle makers too—for it wasn't quite so important to get everything to perfect specifications. You could allow a little sloppiness and the reticle would compensate.

The self-centering reticle is accomplished rather simply. In earlier scopes, the reticle alone was moved when you made adjustments. That's why it moved across the field of view. But in the self-centered reticle the reticle moves across the target but not across the field. This was quite startling when the feature was new. What is done now is to move the entire "erector lens system" which contains the reticle.

It is important to understand that you *look into* a scope. You do not look through it. What you see is an image of the target and not the target itself. As in a camera, the image as presented by the front lens of the scope is upside down and must be inverted optically. This is performed by a system of lenses in the middle of the scope which are called the erector lenses. The entire erector system, as it is called, is mounted in a small tube inside the scope which is spring-loaded against the adjustment screws. When you make an adjustment you move the whole erector system so the reticle moves with respect to the target but it stays in the center of the field of view. Quite clever and a very real improvement.

In the mid-70s, Redfield—which has pioneered a great many scope improvements—developed its Widefield, a means of flattening the picture seen in a scope by widening the field of view but also lowering it to more nearly resemble a TV screen. The intent was to provide more useful field at the sides by eliminating some of the useless field at top and bottom.

The idea has a lot of merit, but it's not really all that important, and, while it's a boon for many hunters, it doesn't help everyone because some prefer to see the "whole field." If a deer is running from one side to another it's an obvious advantage; otherwise, its value would seem to be rather slight.

SCOPE POWERS

Scope magnification is expressed as "power" and designated as "×." Thus a 2½× scope is one that magnifies 2½ times. The average person who is not a shooter thinks magnification is a mysterious advantage that makes hitting the target simple. But that's newspaper talk and is wrong and meaningless. The hunter is usually better off with a low-power scope because more power magnifies aiming errors. You will be driven nutty by your wobbles as seen in a 10× scope which you wouldn't even see in one of 2½×. Moreover, a low-power scope gathers more light and has a larger field of view.

Most hunters completely miss the point of scope power. You are far better off with a scope of about 2½× for most of your hunting than with any scope of higher magnification. Since most deer are shot at less than 50 yards you have no need for anything more than 2½×. A scope of this power offers the most light gathering, which is a whopping advantage in poor light during dawn and dusk. Since these are the best hours of the day, it adds up to a big plus for the hunter. Also, the field of view is largest with low power. Think about it a moment. There is no reason for most hunters to go any higher in scope power.

If you plan to use the same rifle for other hunting which might be at longer range, then it would be wise to move up to 4× or to buy one of those great variables from 1½ to 5× (several makes vary within those ranges), which are very useful. But for most deer hunters, regardless of what part of the country you hunt, the 2½× scope is all you need.

Should your deer hunting be long-range sniping at up to 500 yards, then I don't think you can get too much power in a scope. You'll be shooting at a standing animal, so you'll have time. You will need a spotting scope to determine if the deer meets your specifications (assuming you're a trophy hunter), and there's no substitute for a spotting scope for this purpose. You can use your regular target spotter if it's at least 20× or something like the big Bausch & Lomb Zoom 60 which I've used on many trips or a Bushnell.

You also can use your scope for spotting if it's 20× or bigger. A 20× scope for deer hunting? Only if you're one of those real long-range hunters and you shoot from a steady rest. This sort of deer hunting is like woodchuck shooting; the game is the same except you shoot a heavier rifle and the target is a deer, not a chuck.

The variable-power scope is quite an interesting development. So far as I recall, the first were produced by Bausch & Lomb back about 1949 or 1950. And they were quite sensational when first produced. They offer the choice of low power with all its attendant advantages or the switch to higher power when that is called for. Or you can shoot with the adjustment anywhere in between the extremes. Today's variables have extremes of about 1½-5× at the low-power end and 6-18× at the high end, and there are other combinations in between. The higher-power variables are for the skilled rifleman, no others will find them either needed or useful. They are of little use to the deer hunter but are superb for varmint shooting.

You have to get used to a variable scope. It's all too easy just to set them on one power and leave the setting alone. This is the thing to do under certain circumstances, but there are times when you should crank up the power. You will find it hard to remember to do so under the excitement of sighting game. I can illustrate that point by an incident that happened to me in Quebec on a caribou hunt in the vicinity of Schefferville. I had been sitting in one location for several hours with no sign of caribou, and it was cold! The snow was blowing and it had the appearance of making weather. Snuggled down in the foul-weather parka hood, I looked around behind me to see five bulls feeding along in a way that suggested they would pass me about 100 yards away. They were moving pretty fast, although feeding, and I had to pick one and shoot quickly. My rifle was a .30/06 with a Redfield variable 2-7× scope. I had to decide, and decide quickly, which bull to shoot. They were all whoppers, all with impressive heads, and the choice was difficult. I finally chose one and dropped him, but it didn't occur to me until later that I had left the scope at 2× the whole time. If I had turned it to 7× I might have discovered that another animal was a better trophy, but I'll never know. To put that experience another way,

I completely blew a perfect opportunity to use a variable scope as they ought to be used—by cranking up the power when you need it.

I'm far from alone. Most shooters do not use variables correctly at all. In fact, most shooters set them at highest power and leave them alone. This is not the way to use a variable—you might as well use a fixed-power scope and save some money. There is a use for variables; they aren't as useful as you might think but they are a perfect solution for the guy who might hunt the deep woods today, more open places next week. They afford versatility.

RANGEFINDERS AND DROP COMPENSATORS
Over the years a number of systems have been developed to help estimate the range to an object. Some of these are for golfers, more of them are for hunters. One has been developed by Redfield and is available in some models of its variable scopes. To use one of these devices, which Redfield calls Accu-Range, you "bracket" the deer with two wires in the upper part of the field of view. These wires move closer together or farther apart as you change the power and, at the same time, a rod-shaped scale moves in and out of the lower-right-hand edge of the field. Figures are printed on the rod and you simply read off the range from these numbers.

By bracketing the deer's body you are supposed to get a good fix on its distance. Now, here's the catch. The wires are calibrated for an 18-inch object. This means you must bring them apart or together so that they will bracket an 18-inch object where the deer is standing. According to the Redfield catalog, 18 inches is the distance from "shoulder to brisket" of a common deer. I think this is pretty hard to swallow, because you might have a large deer or a small deer—not all deer come the same size—and it's been my experience that they vary quite a bit from beast to beast and from country to country. The size of a runty deer in the Adirondacks of New York where he has to scrabble for a living is far different from a sleek, fat buck in farm country where he grazes on alfalfa and other good feed. If you follow the Redfield advice you may or may not hit your deer. If you can find a better way of picking out a pretty exact 18 inches you'll find the AccuRange to be quite exact. It's determining the 18 inches that I think is just as hard as estimating the range in the first place.

Along the same line of thought there are now some scopes available that compensate for bullet drop. Bushnell calls its model the BDC, for bullet-drop compensator. This can become complicated, so let's take the steps slowly. You already know that a bullet flies in a parabolic curve and that its flight is not a straight line from sight to target. If you are to connect at long range you have to hold higher because the bullet will drop below the line of sight.

While not all bullets drop exactly the same, there are a large number that follow reasonably close trajectories. It is possible, for example, to use the same data for the .300 Winchester Magnum with 150-grain bullet and the 7mm Remington Magnum with 125-grain bullet. They drop 35.5 and 34.5 inches respectively at 500 yards (when sighted to hit point of aim at 200 yards). Similarly, the same cartridges produce similar results with 180-grain bullets in the .300, and 150-grain in the 7mm, where the respective drops are 40.7 and 42.1. And there are other examples too.

By introducing a cam in the elevation knob of a scope that is calibrated for the drops of a class of cartridges such as those mentioned above, the BDC becomes a reality. Here's how it works. You carefully sight in the rifle for 100 yards, to exactly hit the point of aim. Then you simply move the calibrated dial so it reads "100." You are now sighted for distances to 500 yards in increments of 50 yards. Let's say a target appears at 300 yards. You just turn the elevation dial until it reads 300 and shoot. Or 500, or 450, or whatever. That's because the cam inside moves the elevation to compensate for the drop.

Bushnell furnishes additional cams for a total of three groups of cartridges (all of which are listed in accompanying literature) and a blank dial which you can fill out yourself.

Of course there are some disadvantages to BDC (similar devices are available from others). For example, you still have to estimate range. You also have to hope your dial is as accurate as it's supposed to be. On the latter score, the man who takes to the field hoping to get some long-distance shooting without first knowing where his rifle shoots is a fool. But what is made much easier for you is the elimination of "holding over," which is a vertical way to apply "Kentucky windage." With holding over you have to estimate the range—let's say it's 400 yards. You are shooting a .300 Winchester Magnum with 180-grain bullets and you know they shoot about 20 inches low at that distance. You must hold 20 inches over the point you wish to hit.

But with a BDC scope you simply dial 400, hold on it, and shoot. The cam does the holding over and that's all it does.

There are no cure-alls, and scopes do not solve all the problems. Even if you had a precise rangefinder that would tell you exactly what the range was, you still have problems to contend with that can cause a wide miss. And that's good, because nobody really wants hunting to be so sure that you make an easy kill every time you go out. You must discipline yourself to shoot only when you know you can make a clean kill. That means you'll pass up a lot of shots others might take, but you'll feel a lot better about your hunting if you do.

Redfield is out with a scope they call Accu-Trac that combines its rangefinding system with a bullet-drop compensator. That ought to solve all your problems—but it won't!

One of the most sensible and useful gadgets to measure range with a high degree of accuracy is a rangefinder known as the Ranging 1000. A compact unit, it's less than 11 inches long and weighs 22 ounces, which isn't much to toss in the day pack. It will prove very handy when you spot a trophy animal across a canyon and when you have time to decide whether to try the shot and then how far it is and where you should hold. I only wish I'd had this gadget much earlier in my hunting career—it would have saved a lot of guesswork.

The Ranging 1000 operates on the triangulation method, the same as artillery rangefinders, and it has a capacity of 1,000 yards. I would not suggest using it beyond 500 yards, because that's a long enough shot under any circumstances and because the Ranging has an accuracy factor of 95 percent at 500 yards, which is plus or minus 25 yards. Beyond that, its accuracy suffers and is only 90 percent at 1,000 (plus or minus 100 yards), which is not sufficiently accurate for shooting.

I have found this device to be accurate enough to guarantee a shot up to 500 yards on an animal the size of a deer. This assumes you know where your rifle is shooting, and it also assumes you can properly dope the wind or that wind is not a factor. The Ranging's manufacturer (Ranging, Inc.) furnishes a number of stickers which can be pasted to the scale for a direct readout of your drops. You select the right sticker for the cartridge and bullet weight you are using.

The way I prefer to use the Ranging 1000 is to simply use it to measure distance. I prefer to figure out my own drops, but there are other reasons involved. I'm liable to be using many dif-

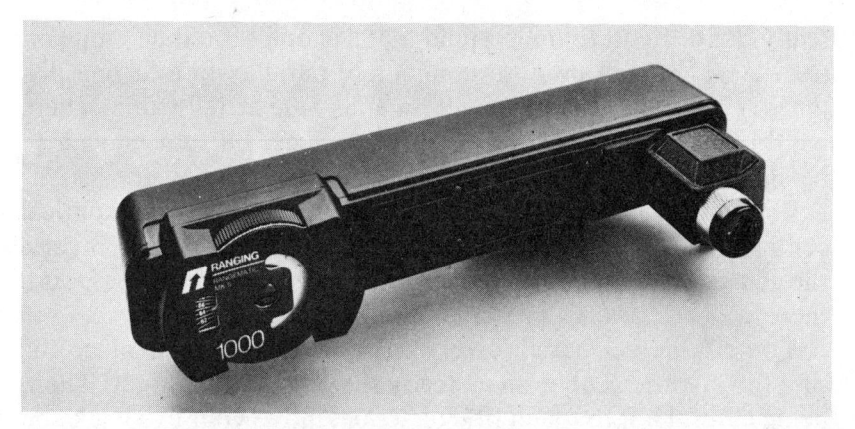

Estimating distance is a difficult job, particularly when you have no means of comparison, such as when you're estimating across a canyon or along a tidal flat. This little rangefinder by Ranging is very accurate to 500 yards, and that's about as far as you can shoot if you're a very skilled shooter with a gilt-edge rifle. This belongs in every mountain hunter's pack.

ferent rifles, so it's impractical for me to use a single sticker. Moreover, I think the hunter ought to have to figure out something for himself. This gadget does a fine job of measuring the range with a good degree of accuracy. You should know where the rifle is placing its bullet at whatever range is indicated.

FIELD OF VIEW
Field of view is a matter of concern to most hunters, or it ought to be. The term means the amount of area seen in the scope, and it is always expressed as so many feet at 100 yards. The greater the power the smaller the field. For example, a Redfield RM 6400 Model scope has a field of view in 24× of only 4.5 feet at 100 yards. That company's 2¾× scope has a field of 55.5 feet at 100 yards. Obviously, you wouldn't want a 24× scope for deer hunting under any circumstances (except a few long-range shooters), but the tiny 4½-foot field at 100 yards would exclude it from consideration in any event. Nor would you want the 10×'s 11½ foot field. You shouldn't go higher in power than about 4× for deer hunting (which has a 37½-foot field). Most scope brands have approximately the same fields as those listed by Redfield.

PARALLAX
"Parallax" is a word that tends to throw a lot of people. It is

really not difficult to understand that a scope should be parallax-free. A scope can only be completely parallax-free at one distance. Hunting scopes are built parallax-free at 100 yards. There will be some parallax at all other distances, but not enough to be significant in the usual hunting scope of low power.

What is parallax? It's simply placing the reticle in the optical center of the scope—exactly where the erecting system inverts the image. If the reticle is moved forward or aft of this point, there will be parallax present.

You can detect parallax very easily. The test is to place the rifle (or just the scope) on a steady rest aimed at a target. Then, being careful not to touch rifle or scope, move your eye back and forth, up and down. If the reticle moves across the target, parallax is present. You should make this test at 100 yards, and if the reticle moves, the scope should be returned. This is another way of saying that the scope is in focus. You will notice that higher-power scopes have an adjustment, usually provided in scopes from 8× up. This adjustment is provided by an adjustable objective (front) lens with graduations. The indicated marks will come close to the correct focus, but you must check for parallax as indicated before you are precisely in focus.

RETICLES
There is a rather wide variety of reticle styles available in today's scopes, and you should try them out before making a selection. It is hard to go wrong with standard crosshairs, which seem to suit everybody. For a hunting scope they should be relatively coarse so they can be picked up in poor light. For a target or varmint-shooting scope, the wires should be very fine. For many years a popular hunting reticle was the combination of a horizontal cross wire with a tapered post. Recently, a new reticle has become popular which is branded with various names like "4-plex" (Redfield), "Duplex" (Leupold), and "Dual-×" (Weaver). Basically, this type has heavy crosswires which have finer wires in the middle. I find it an excellent reticle and it has become very popular.

Some years back, the late exhibition shooter T. K. "Tackhole Dot" Lee developed a dot reticle. Lee made his for target rifles. They were tiny dots placed on tiny wires. Some Lee dots only covered ⅛ inch at 100 yards. For some reason Lee was able to make his dots round, while most of his competitors turned out dots that were more nearly square than round. The Lee dot was

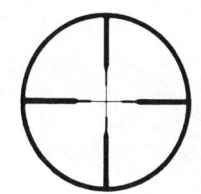

One of the more popular reticles in recent years is this general configuration, which most scope makers are using under different names. It features fine wires in the center, which is ideal for close holding, and coarser wires at the extremes that allow centering in poor light.

made by placing a small droplet of some kind of glue at the intersection of the cross hairs; Lee used spiderweb thread for his fine wires. Today every dot maker produces a round product and they are fairly popular.

EYE RELIEF
A scope must be mounted on the rifle so the eye relief is comfortable. Eye relief is that distance the eye ought to be away from the scope. It's common for someone unused to a scope to try to shoulder the rifle with his eye stuck into the eyepiece lens. Firing any centerfire rifle in such a position will severely whack the shooter in the eyebrow. Eye relief is intended to keep the shooter's eye out of trouble. That distance is generally around 3 to 4 inches in most scopes; you must slide the scope back and forth until shouldering the rifle positions the scope at some point within the eye relief. Your mount rings should not touch either the turret or the slope into the forward bell. Needless to add, the scope must be located to clear the mount fully, and it must also clear the open rear sight on the barrel. There are mounts that are correct for most all rifles made today and some which can handle special problems, such as may arise with a shooter with an abnormally long (or short) neck.

WHAT'S THE BEST SCOPE?
This is a frequent question and one which I always refuse to answer. There really is no "best scope," although there are many fine ones. I have rifles with scopes of the following makes, listed alphabetically: Bausch & Lomb, Bushnell, Leupold, Lyman, Marlin, Redfield, Swift, Tasco (same as Marlin), Unertl (target), Weatherby, and Weaver. These are all fine scopes and they all perform within their capability. But some are better than others. You needn't expect a scope that retails for half the cost of another to be of equal quality. Still, it's true that there is some variation even in scopes of the same make and model—from day

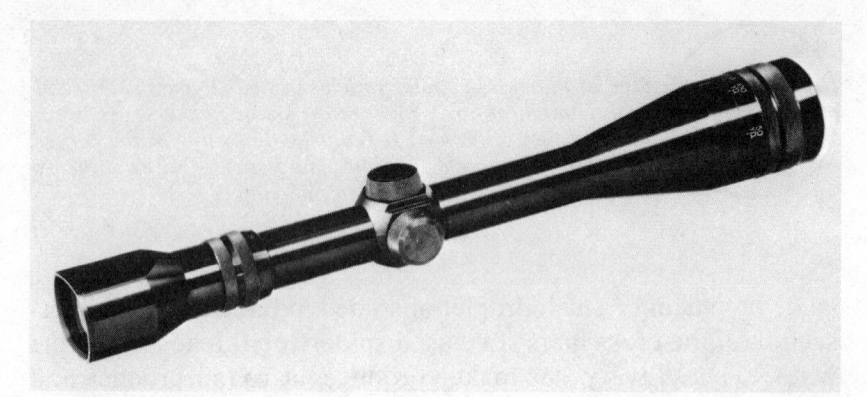

Ideal for almost any situation from reasonably short range to long range is a variable 3-9× scope such as this wide-range one by Weaver; this one has proved excellent.

A Swift 1.5-4.5× variable is an excellent scope for deep-woods or other short-range shooting. Yet at its higher settings, it can be used for most long-range shooting. Set at 1.5× it's an ideal scope for the deep brush at twilight.

to day and from month to month. The scope that might test out as No. 1 today might rate a different place on the pecking order next week.

We're talking about trivial differences that mean something to the precision rifleman or to the fussy types, but not to the ordinary deer hunter. In fact, there are differences that needn't matter to *any* deer hunter. Some of the scopes I've named are heavier than others, are more precise in their adjustments, have steel tubes (most have aluminum), or are available in wide-field style, and some brands have a broader variety of styles and reticle op-

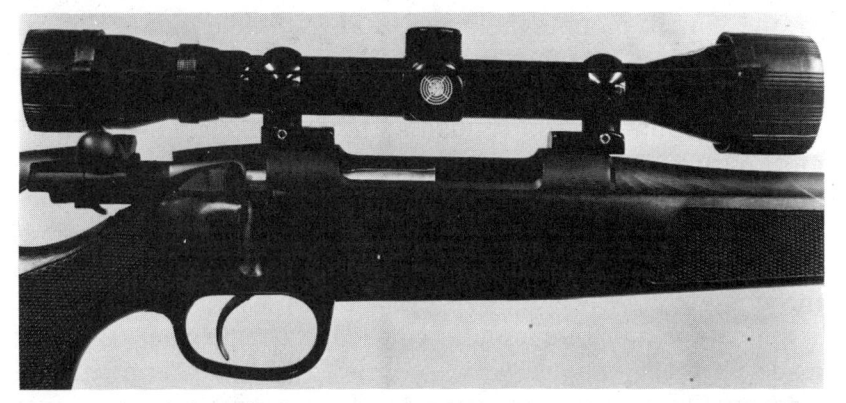

A Steyr-Mannlicher rifle from Austria with European scope and mounts. Generally speaking, most scopes imported from Europe are priced a lot higher than those made in the United States or Japan. Moreover, most European mounts are not the equal of American mounts such as Redfields or Weavers.

tions. You will have to make your own decision here. I will say that, in general, you get about what you pay for. The best route to follow, I think, is to get a copy of *Gun Digest*, because it lists all makes along with their specifications, and this will make you more familiar with what's on the market. Select a couple and send for their literature.

There are other excellent scopes on the market; I've listed only the brands I happen to have on hand at this moment. And there are also some imported scopes that carry list prices about an even $100 higher than scopes I consider top (and top-priced) American-made scopes. Offhand I can't see the value.

SCOPE MOUNTS
Until fairly recent years, rifles did not come with any suitable means of attaching scopes. Some of them simply were—and some still are—designed so that scope mounting is extremely difficult. A case in point is the popular Model 94 Winchester. This rifle has top ejection, which means you cannot mount a scope over the bore and down low; you are required to use an offset mount or mount a specially made scope with long eye relief forward of the receiver. An offset mount positions the head in midair, meaning that you cannot snug your face into the comb of the stock and get a solid position.

Early bolt-actions did not come with holes drilled and tapped for the kind of mounts that we consider suitable today. For example, the first Model 70 Winchester rifles in 1937 had two holes in the receiver ring (front) but none in the receiver bridge (rear). Military actions, of course, had no holes anywhere and furthermore required a bolt-handle alteration and a lower safety replacement. Because these early rifles were not made with scopes in mind, and scopes and mounts were not developed to their present state, there were quite a few rather odd lash-ups seen in those days.

One of the more commonly seen scope arrangements was that made by the Germans, which consisted of brackets fitted into a dovetail in the receiver ring and a clamp device on the receiver bridge. The mount itself was hooked into the front bracket and seated into the rear one. These were called "claw mounts" after the two hooks that were inserted into the front receiver base. You see, the Germans couldn't bring themselves to accept that the bolt handle ought to be lower, which would allow lower mounting of the scope. Another disadvantage of these mounts was that the dovetail cut weakened the receiver. The mounts also were not particularly likely to restore the scope to its former position with much regularity.

It's correct to say that there were probably as many scope mounts developed, invented, and made as there were custom gunsmiths plying the trade. And most companies that made scopes also offered mounts. Nearly all of them are now long gone and many should never have been made at all.

It is generally acknowledged that the first satisfactory scope mount was the one made by Noske. It was a side mount; the bottom portion consisted of a plate attached to the left side of the receiver with taper pins and screws and had a male dovetail along its upper edge. The top part of the mount had the female dovetail and a pair of rings that held the scope. The first Noske mounts contained a provision for windage adjustment, since the early scopes had only elevation adjustments. To remove a scope with the Noske mount, you turned two locking screws and slid the top off the base dovetail. A similar mount was later made by Griffin & Howe with two levers instead of screws and one with a single lever by Paul Jaeger.

One of the major problems with any of these side mounts was that they were difficult to install, since they required drilling five holes, three of which were tapped for screws and the remaining

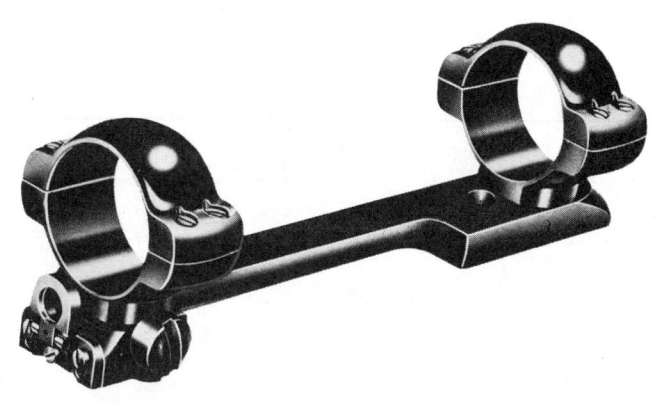

Quite possibly this Redfield JR mount is the best ever developed. It certainly is the most popular and among the simplest and most rugged. It is shown here in one of its many variations with built-in folding peep sight. Many mounts have come and gone over the years but this one and the Weaver are the two that have lasted.

two were reamed for taper pins. Getting these mounts properly installed was no simple job.

An early top mount that was quite popular was the Stith mount. (M.L. Stith also marketed the first scopes manufactured by Kollmorgen which were later branded Kollmorgen and then sold to Redfield. They also were known as "Bear Cubs.") A Stith mount for the early Model 70 Winchester had a front mount with a large ring into which the scope was slipped. The base was driven into the dovetail slot for the rear sight. The rear base of this mount was fastened to the receiver via the holes factory-drilled and tapped for a receiver sight.

About the same time, a top mount was introduced by the Redfield company, long a maker of fine iron sights. One of the Redfield mounts was known as the "Senior" mount; it consisted of two separate bases. Later came a "Junior" mount, essentially the same except it included a connecting bar between the front and rear parts. This system is still used by Redfield, only the names have changed to SR and JR. The front of the Redfield accepts a dovetail, which is inserted 90° to the base and then turned into locked position. The rear fits between two opposed screws and can be adjusted for windage. The Redfield mount continues to this day. It has, in fact, become one of the two most popular surviving mounts among all those invented through the years.

At one time Bausch & Lomb made a fine sight and a different kind of mount concept. The idea was to provide adjustments in the base, not the scope tube. Though a lot of time and money were spent promoting the idea it never went over well and is now abandoned. The photo shows a B&L 4× scope on a Remington Model 721 rifle in B&L mounts.

The other survivor is the Weaver. A low-priced mount consisting of aluminum bases which are available in heights to fit nearly all rifles made and rings of steel that surround the scope, the Weaver mount doesn't look like a lot of money has been invested, but you can rest assured it's been a winner and is just as satisfactory as the Redfield. And that's saying a lot.

These two mounting systems are so good that most other scope and mount makers have given up the ghost and are making copies of one or the other. In fact, the Leupold mount is interchangeable with Redfield. Leupold tried for years to market a variety of its own mounts, but none were successful.

Another concept that has finally died, although there was a vast effort behind it for many years, was the Bausch & Lomb idea of providing adjustments in the mount base rather than in the scope. An interesting idea with certain advantages—primarily that you could swap a single scope from rifle to rifle, because the mount bases contained the adjustments and they stayed on the rifles. This wasn't enough advantage, however, and the concept is gone now. B&L accomplished this with a set of cones in both front and rear mounts. One adjusted the elevation and the other the windage. The mounts were a bit cumbersome, although otherwise satisfactory. I still have them on a rifle or two and they give satisfactory service.

In the early days of scopes and mounts it was felt that you had to have a scope that could be removed fairly quickly in order to use the iron sights when and if the scope failed. The way they used to talk about it, it was a foregone conclusion that your scope was going to fail, break, fog, lose its adjustment, or otherwise be rendered useless. Today, that idea has been put to rest and you may as well anchor your scope as though it's going to stay on the rifle as long as you have the rifle. Chances are that it will do just that—in fact, I hate to remove a scope once I have a good combination perking.

An example of this is a .240 Weatherby Magnum rifle built on a Mauser action. Weatherby chambered the barrel for me; I made the stock and had Al Biesen alter the bolt handle in his usual excellent fashion. This rifle was last fired four years ago and at the time delivered ½-inch accuracy at 100 yards with 100-grain Nosler bullets and a load of 54 grains of Norma 205 powder. Today, Norma 205 is gone and has been replaced by Norma Magnum Rifle Powder (MRP). In checking out the new powder I fired some of the old loads and they repeated the older groups —½ inch. And the scope—JR mounts—was still sighted in!

Another older mount type that was once fairly popular was the so-called swing mount. This meant that you could flip the scope aside and use the iron sights fast if necessary. One of the more popular was the Pachmayr, which worked by allowing the scope to pivot on a couple of cones, a spring being employed to hold the scope down. If you wanted to use the iron sights in a hurry, you could punch or jab the scope with your thumb and kick it out of engagement so the spring would clear and it would swing aside. It would simply hang limply on the left side of the rifle. Most serious riflemen never gave these devices much room, because they had no faith in the mount's ability to return the scope to perfect zero. In those days, it was quite a test of scope and mount to produce a device that could be removed and replaced and maintain perfect zero. With the production of better scopes it was eventually seen that swing or other removable mounts were not necessary.

A long time ago it was thought that it would be an excellent plan to construct a scope as an integral unit with the receiver, and at least one custom rifle was made in this fashion. Obviously this left the owner in a hell of a fix if he ever decided to change scopes. But an owner of such a rifle would require so much money to build it in the first place that he wouldn't mind too much springing for a new rifle entirely.

A sort of offshoot from this concept is seen in the few rifles with integral scope bases. Samples of these are Sako, the fine Finnish rifle now imported by Stoeger (formerly by Garcia and Firearms International), and the Ruger Model 77. Both rifles are bolt-action. Ruger offers his Model 77 two ways—with his own scope mount or regular round receiver contour. The Ruger mount is an excellent one. The advantage to such a system is that there is no way the scope base can work loose. It eliminates one more possibility of error. For the record, both Sako and Ruger rifles with these mounts work very well and there is no reason to choose another mount for any reason that I can see.

The screws in any scope mount, including mount rings, should be treated with a drop of Loctite to hold them fast. Loctite is a liquid that, when sealed against the air, will harden and prevent a screw from loosening. Yet the screw can be removed if necessary. Some shooters place a drop of the goo under mount bases, and this is a good practice on any hard-recoiling rifle.

The proper way to mount any scope base is to start all screws, then tighten one screw. Make sure the base is tight by trying to move it with your fingers. Once you've proved it to be snug, loosen this screw and tighten another. Try to move the base again. Repeat this with each screw before you tighten any of them all the way. The reason for this caution is to make sure no screws are bottoming before they tighten the base. If a screw is a bit too long, or a hole a bit too shallow, it's easy to drive the screw home and find that it doesn't hold the base tightly. The remedy is to grind a bit off the tip of the screw.

At one time, the standard gun-sight screw was a rather small screw known as a 6-48, meaning that it was a number 6 (American Machine Screw basic size measuring .138 inch diameter) with 48 threads to the inch. There is now a move toward increasing the screw diameter to 8-40, which will provide a stronger assembly. This is a good move and should be encouraged.

There is no question in my mind that the best two scope-mounting systems today are the Redfield and Weaver. Redfield's was first used in 1938 and the Weaver a few years after World War II. Both survive with no major changes—all the improvements are primarily cosmetic. And both have been copied by a number of competitors. I have always found them to be thoroughly satisfactory, and they are simple to install.

SIGHTING IN

I have never understood why sighting a rifle in to hit the point of aim should be such a chore or such a mystery. It's easy; anyone can do it who has an ounce of brains and can read and follow instructions. A few tips may be useful.

I've found the little Bushnell TruScope to be one of the most useful gadgets ever invented. There are other similar devices in different brands. To use the TruScope, you slip the plug into the bore at the muzzle as instructed and tighten it. Then simply look into the scope and move the adjustments to coincide with the TruScope. This won't be your final adjustment—you'll have to verify it by shooting—but it should get you on the paper for your first shot. With today's cost of ammunition that's important, and a few sighting-in sessions will pay for the gadget.

Another useful way to use this TruScope is to take it along on a hunting trip, noting the reading on the TruScope after you have sighted in. You can verify before you hunt to make sure your scope wasn't damaged or jarred in travel.

If you do not have a TruScope, you'll need a large, clean piece of paper, and you should shoot at 100 yards (50 is a better place to start to get sighted to hit the paper). From the first shot that hits the paper, you just follow instructions that came with the sight. Most people have their problems when they can't hit the paper and have no idea where they are hitting. This means you should move up close, or have a friend watch the backstop as you shoot at a certain mark (such as a stone) within a large area of backstop. Then move the sights accordingly.

Scopes are plainly marked "up" and "right" (or "down" and "left"), so you can move the right way. Peep sights are usually marked; if not, the directions will tell you. Factory open sights are the hardest to adjust because most come with no windage adjustment. You have to bang the sight back and forth in the slot. That calls for a hammer and a drift pin, which is what you place against the sight and whack with the hammer. Your drift can be brass, aluminum, or steel. And that's the order in which I prefer to use them. Under no circumstances should you hit the sight directly with the hammer. A rear sight is moved in the direction in which you want the bullet to go. If a shot is low, you move the sight *up* (which lowers the butt or raises the muzzle).

You are interested in making two lines coincide. One is the line of sight, a straight line from eye to target and over or through the sights. The other line is the path the bullet takes and you want these lines to come together at a given distance.

The modern catalogs available from major ammunition makers offer excellent trajectory charts that are a valuable guide to sighting in. You can look these charts over with the thought in mind that you may want to sight in to hit point of aim at either 100 or 200 yards. The charts will tell you where your bullet will be at other distances. A .30/06, for instance, using a 180-grain load sighted at 200 yards, will be 2.4 inches high at 100 and 9.3 inches low at 300—but only 3.7 inches low at 250, so you know you could hold right on a deer at any distance up to 250 yards.

Federal's catalog also gives you a table showing wind drift from a 20-mph crosswind. It's quite interesting; the only hitch is that you have to guess the wind velocity! Of course, all the data in these tables is computed by feeding the various elements into a computer. None of it should be accepted as more than an approximation, because all rifles are a little different, all shooters hold their rifles differently, and wind velocity varies. If you expect to do any hunting where you might take a very long-range shot you *must* prepare by shooting over those distances so you know exactly where your rifle is printing under all situations.

15

Selecting *Your* Deer Rifle and Setting It Up

Many factors should be involved in your choice of a deer rifle. I'll try to outline them for you so you can make this selection intelligently. You must consider the country in which you hunt, because your rifle must be compatible with that, as explained in the early chapters of this book.

And the game hunted will be an important consideration. If you will hunt country where other species are shootable at the same time, you will want a rifle that's capable of handling them. For example, many Western states have concurrent elk and mule-deer seasons. If you have a tag for each it will behoove you to buy a rifle heavy enough for elk. Or if you will hunt in turkey country, you might want to plan on taking a few cartridges along "loaded for turkey"—and that will require a rifle with the necessary accuracy to handle turkeys.

Along with the terrain you hunt you will want to consider the weight of a rifle. A rifle can get very heavy after a long day's tramp in the woods. And your physical condition will have a lot to do with this. A heart patient, for example, ought to choose a lightweight rifle, and anyone who might be subject to heart attack also should consider this carefully. That includes the overweight, the deskbound worker who gets in the woods only on hunting trips, and the man who has been told to slow down. You can stand a lightweight hunting rifle because most deer rifles are shot only a few times a year. The added recoil isn't going to bother you for that little bit of shooting. And you may have a personal choice in action type. If so you can narrow your search right at the start. Men who hunt birds with a pump shotgun, for example, might elect to stick with that familiar type of action.

The recoil of a rifle should nevertheless be considered. A person who fears recoil or who is otherwise affected by it should choose a rifle he can shoot. It's far better to place a smaller bullet precisely than it is to miss or gut-shoot a deer with a heavy magnum. An outfitter friend of mine, now retired, used to make his clients target their rifles at the base camp before setting out. This was a sort of an excuse for him to observe the way they handled their rifles. If he noted a man with, say, a .300 Weatherby, he watched carefully and if the man flinched and couldn't hit the target satisfactorily, the outfitter gently suggested trying his .243 Winchester. It would usually come to pass that the man could shoot the .243 without flinching, so he was reintroduced to the .300. If the cure worked, all well and good. But if he went back to flinching, the outfitter insisted that the client hunt with the lighter .243—the theory being that it was better to have his man stick a .243 bullet into an elk's boiler room than to have a wounded elk to follow for hours.

I had an interesting experience on a Quebec moose hunt one year where specific management areas were allotted to each party. The provincial wardens had a target range set up, and each hunter was asked to shoot his rifle "to make sure it was sighted." That was only partly true. The real reason was so the warden could make sure the hunter was able to shoot. And, when I asked, the warden said he had full authority to refuse anyone permission to hunt. This, remember, after the hunter was there and had bought licenses, etc. It's a good idea and I wish every deer hunter had to pass such a test before he takes to the woods.

Recoil is a strange phenomenon indeed. It doesn't really hurt, and nobody really expects it to hurt, but shooters flinch badly anyway. Once they begin to flinch it is a very difficult habit to overcome. The best cure is to get started the right way, and it's often best to begin with a light-caliber rifle. If you can handle a .243 or .250/3000 with no trouble, there is no point in going to a heavier caliber. One of the biggest errors most hunters make is to buy a rifle that's overpowered. Whitetail and mule deer do not require a rifle capable of konking a grizzly. When you see a hunter on the rifle range with a heavy magnum rifle and he jumps a foot every time he fires the rifle, it makes you wonder what this guy is going to do in the woods.

That's why you ought to analyze your shooting requirements with care. If you elect to buy a light rifle, all well and good, as long as it is heavy enough for the game. And if you can handle a heavier rifle and want the added power or range, go ahead and buy it. But don't fall for that error of picking a rifle that's got the swat to decimate a Greyhound bus if you're going to hunt nothing bigger than deer or black bear.

If you shoot properly, very few rifles will really hurt you—certainly none that you are likely to choose. I must admit there are some rifles that I find punishing when shooting from the bench, but none are punishing when fired from the shoulder. And this is particularly true with shooting at game. You *never* feel recoil when you shoot at game.

While the only way to sight in is from a shooting bench, this is one of the more punishing ways to shoot. The recoil can really bother you then. Rifles I have that I find are no fun to shoot from the bench are the .338 Winchester Magnum Model 70 (a gas-operated Browning .338 is a pussycat), .340 Weatherby Magnum, .350 Remington Magnum, and .458 Winchester Magnum. The latter is meant for elephants and is hardly a deer rifle, but it does hurt when you shoot it from the bench.

Shooting any rifle like a .30/06 or smaller from the bench ought not to bother anyone. Certainly the rifle recoils, but just as certainly it isn't going to hurt if you hold the rifle correctly. Should you have any fears about it, use what is commonly called a "sissy bag." That's a small sandbag placed between your shoulder and the butt, and it soaks up and spreads out a great deal of recoil. I always use one of those when shooting a big rifle from the bench.

It would be well to spend a few moments on something which can be called the "myth of the magnums." The deer hunter would only be concerned with the .264, .300, and .338 Winchester Magnums and the 7mm and 8mm Remington Magnums plus certain of the Weatherby Magnums. You should not let the word "magnum" spook you into thinking these rifles will be punishing to fire. The .264 and 7mm are about on a par with the .30/06 in terms of recoil. The others are a bit more powerful, and there's no question that the .338 and 8mm can be called heavy-recoiling rifles. But so what. If you want added performance at the muzzle, you've got to expect some added ruckus at the butt. But it is common for persons to believe that just because of the word "magnum," a rifle is going to shoot faster, shoot harder, kick harder. It's not always true, and the best advice I can give you is to just ignore the word and concentrate on the size of the cartridges in question.

If you study ballistics a little bit you'll see that a cartridge like the .280 Remington is nearly as potent as the 7mm Remington Magnum anyway. It therefore will do just about what the Magnum will, and the .280 is pleasant to shoot. Nobody complains about its recoil. So why make a big flap about the Magnum? A lot of sophisticated shooters regard the 7mm Mauser very highly, and this is so much of a pussycat that it's often recommended for women. But, study the charts again (using reloaded ammunition) and note that the 7mm Mauser is also not that far behind the 7mm Magnum! By a similar reasoning the .30/06 is not far behind the .300 Winchester Magnum, and so on. Don't let yourself be snookered. The same thing happens in revolvers; the .357, .41, and .44 Magnums tend to scare people into thinking they're going to get hurt by firing them. And the same with shotguns.

TESTING YOUR NEW RIFLE

Once you have chosen your rifle and bought it, there are a number of things you should do. First, of course, is to mount the scope or sights you will use. And then you'll want to shoot it on the range. I've already commented on sighting in, but there are several other things that are important.

First, you should realize that the single most important thing is the first shot out of a cold, lightly oiled bore. Or perhaps a dry bore; that will depend on the way you prefer to leave your guns. For your interest, I prefer to hunt with a clean bore, not oiled but that has had a very slightly oily patch or a patch with a light application of Hoope's #9 run through it. However you leave your bore, you must check it out at the range, for very often a rifle will place that first shot out of the group. But that's the shot that is most important—which brings up the point that if you have fired the rifle on your trip, you should clean it and restore it to its original bore condition, unless your rifle delivers its succeeding shots into the same group.

The way to check all this out is first to get sighted in. Then let the barrel cool, clean it, and leave it dry or slightly oiled as you prefer. Making certain the barrel is thoroughly cooled, take another shot. No matter where this bullet prints, do not make any changes in your sight. Don't do a thing, in fact, except to cool and clean again. Cooling might take fifteen or twenty minutes, so don't get impatient. Then fire another shot. This will now indicate where the rifle is printing its first shot from a clean barrel. Your first shot of the hunt. If the two shots are nice and close, repeat the procedure for a third shot. If this prints the same, you have it made. You know right where your first shot will be.

Let the rifle cool again, but this time do not clean it. When it has cooled, fire a shot at a clean target. If this shot is where the first group printed, let the bore cool again and keep on until you have a three-shot group. That will prove to you that your rifle will deliver followup shots, from a cold and fouled bore, into the same point of impact as it did from a cold, clean bore. And you'll have a fine rifle that you won't have to baby and you won't have to clean it every time it's been fired.

But if that point of impact from a fouled bore is off the mark, then you'll have to clean the rifle after it has been fired. Unfortunately, there are more rifles like the latter than like the former.

These points cannot be overstressed. You spend a lot of time and money on a hunting trip. Once you get there and have a good buck in your sights, you don't want anything to go wrong. And that means your first shot is the most important one of all. The whole hunting trip is suddenly reduced to a single shot. In order to make it good you've got to know where the rifle is shooting. You must not depend on reserve shots in the magazine, because no followup shot is as good as that first one. It may take quite a bit of time to accomplish all this, but it will be well worth it.

Incidentally, this is part of the philosophy behind the popularity of single-shot rifles and of muzzleloading hunting seasons. When you are shooting a single-shot rifle you know darned well that you've got to make it good because there is no reserve. I have several great single-shots suitable for deer hunting, including a Ruger Number Three in .30/40 Krag, which is a fine little rifle and amply powerful for woods hunting, and a Browning .25/06, which is one of the finer cartridges for deer-sized game at long range. I also have an English Farquharson that I barreled a long time ago for a .25 caliber cartridge in the .30/40 Krag case. Its performance roughly parallels the .257 Roberts. Any rifle such as these is entirely suitable for deer hunting as long as its owner realizes he has but a single shot.

ACCURIZING
Many folks think a new rifle must be "broken in" before it settles down to good accuracy. This isn't necessarily true, although some are in that category. When a rifle is made properly it should arrive in its box in shooting condition and you should not have to break it in. But there are a lot of other things you can do to help it along.

Generally speaking, most pump, autoloading, and lever-action rifles will have to be fired as you receive them. There is little you can do in the way of improving their accuracy. About the only thing that you can work on is the trigger pull on hammer rifles. You do this by cocking the empty rifle, inserting a wide screwdriver blade under the hammer, and trying to force it forward as you pull the trigger. This treatment smooths the mating surfaces and will improve a creepy trigger pull. Use cardboard between the screwdriver blade and the metal surfaces.

The rifles that benefit most from a little "accurizing" are bolt-actions. It is widely held that a bolt-action is the most accurate of all rifles. And it is further claimed that this is so largely because the bolt has a one-piece stock. Neither claim is necessarily true. I find that many bolt rifles need some attention before they begin to shoot well, and I have developed the habit of performing certain treatments before I even fire them because there's no point in wasting ammunition.

Nearly all bolt rifles need some help in their barrel bedding. The front part of the stock in any bolt-action hunting rifle should exert heavy upward pressure against the barrel. The pressure point is at the front of the stock (but behind any tip if a tip is present). The easiest way to check this is to grasp the barrel forward of the stock with the right hand and try to pull the forend away. If it moves away freely you need more pressure.

How much is "freely"? Some folks say the pressure should be so many pounds, and I've never heard any explanation of that one—nor do I know how they "weigh" it. To explain further, loosen the guard screws but only enough to relieve the stress. Now, turning only the front screw, tighten until the forend tip just touches the barrel. There should be approximately another $1/32$ inch of screw takeup, which is measured by watching the receiver. In other words, take up the front screw as stated. Then continue tightening the screw, which should pull the receiver into the wood another $1/32$ inch.

Most rifles won't have this much pressure, so you loosen the screw again slightly and slip one thickness of a business card or a matchbook cover under the barrel at the front of the forearm. Retighten. If you still don't get the $1/32$ inch, you will need more cardboard. Once you have this pressure, simply tighten the screws as tight as you can get them, using a screwdriver that fits the slot.

Now you trim the cardboard with a razor blade to the top of the forend, touch its top edges with a pipe cleaner dipped in black shoe polish, and nobody but you will ever know it's there. If you want to be neater, trim the paper so it's below the stock edges before you tighten the guard screws. You'll be surprised how much better this will make any bolt-action sporter shoot.

I have found that some bolt-action rifles come out of the factory with tight bedding, some with no bedding, and others at various points in between. There is a school of thought that claims a barrel should "float"—that is, it should not touch the stock anywhere. This is often "proved" by sliding a piece of thin paper like a dollar bill back and forth in the channel. But what this doesn't tell you is that barrels vibrate when they are fired, like a piece of pipe held in a vise and struck with a hammer. This vibration will hit the stock and will ruin accuracy. Also, the mere weight of the barrel will often press into the stock when the forend is placed on a rest. The so-called free-floating barrel has worked in some bench-rest rifles but has no place on sporters. Moreover, it's a dandy place to catch leaves, pine needles, and other dirt as well as rain and snow. There is wide variation among rifles of same make and model.

Wood is usually very unstable, especially as compared to steel. It is much more difficult to hold dimensions when a wood stock is being shaped than it is to machine a piece of steel. The latter can be held to a tolerance of .001 inch, but you can't hold wood to that. Even if you could, the wood would change. If wood is fashioned in the hot, humid summer and then shipped to Arizona, for instance, it will shrink when it dries out. That explains part of the variations seen in gunstocks, but not all of them, because they are finished by men. You can set a machine tool to certain tolerances, and let it run by tape. It will produce many parts to the exact same size and shape out of metal. But let six men finish a stock and each one will be slightly different.

The uncertain nature of wood, and the men who work it, brings up another very important consideration which we call "metal-to-metal" contact. This occurs when the wood is too shallow, from top to bottom of the inletting, to allow the receiver and guard to be pulled tightly into the wood. Instead, it permits the top edge of the guard (in a Mauser or Springfield) to bear directly against the receiver bottom. In a rifle like the Model 70 Winchester or 700 Remington and others made along similar lines which have a separate magazine box, the box must not bear against receiver and guard. When it does, the receiver is not tightly bedded into the wood and will move around. The way you usually can tell this is when the guard screw or screws stop suddenly instead of coming to a gradual stop. In other rifles you will have to check by eye once the rifle is assembled but before the screws are tightened. This is not a factor, by the way, in any rifle without a floorplate, because the bottom of the magazine box rests against wood. But in any rifle where the magazine box rests against metal this problem can occur. The usual solution, with a rifle like the Model 70 Winchester, is to place a thin washer (which can be made of business card) under the floorplate hinge. If it's a Mauser or Mauser-type magazine you will have to file off the top of the entire magazine box. It is important to note that *no* bolt-action rifle will deliver its best accuracy with any metal-to-metal contact.

Many rifles today come with excellent adjustable triggers. These should be adjusted according to the instructions received with the gun. If you bought a used rifle and have no instruction sheet, a note to the manufacturer will bring one promptly. There are some triggers which are nonadjustable, like that on the Remington Model 788. But the trigger on this rifle is generally satisfactory for deer hunting. I have found that Remington 700 rifles generally come with an excellent trigger. Of the dozens of these models I have fired, I can recall only one with a slight amount of creep. And that was very slight indeed.

A trigger should ideally have no slack at the front of its movement before firing and should have no movement after firing; the latter is known as follow-through. To put it another way, the trigger should not move a detectable amount. The weight of pull should be between 3 and 4 pounds on a hunting rifle. These are relatively simple specifications and they allow sufficient room for precise adjustment. Yet, most bolt rifles come through with poorly adjusted triggers. And there is no excuse for it.

One of the finest triggers ever designed was the Model 70 Winchester. It's essentially the same today as when the rifle was first introduced in 1936. But despite more than forty years of manufacturing this rifle, Winchester still does not properly adjust these triggers when they leave the factory. The first thing I do with any Model 70 rifle I get my hands on is to adjust the trigger so all forward and rearward movement is eliminated, then set the pull to the desired weight (which can be as light as 1 pound with this trigger). Adjustment is easy in most cases, although sometimes the amount of contact has to be reduced by grinding. The whole job doesn't take even as much as five minutes and it could be done in final assembly at the plant much more quickly than that.

You can't shoot a rifle with any accuracy unless the trigger pull is good. That's basic. In my opinion, there is no reason today for any rifle to be delivered with a lousy trigger, but many of them are.

I cannot overemphasize the importance of sighting in, targeting, and making sure your rifle shoots to the utmost of its ability. For any hunter worth his salt, these things are an absolute must. Even if you expect to hit your deer within 50 yards, you'll do well to make sure the rifle hits where you aim at that distance. But it's the height of absurdity to travel a long way, spend a lot of time, and invest a lot of money on a deer hunt without knowing where your rifle shoots within an inch. The preferred time to do this is several months before you hunt (so you have time to make any necessary adjustments or repairs) and again just before you leave. Then check the rifle out once you arrive in game country.

AMMUNITION
Quite often a rifle will show a preference for one make of ammunition; at other times a certain bullet will shoot better than others. I have seen rifles that spread one brand into groups of 3 or 4 inches and then snuggled down to an inch when different ammo was tried. This happened with a friend's .30/06 before a hunt some years ago. Both Remington and Winchester would not have hit a saucer at 100 yards, but Federal tightened the groups right down to an inch. That's an extreme and sometimes

it works with the opposite brands, but it does happen and you should be aware that it may not be the fault of the rifle or the shooter.

It is a common misunderstanding that shooters reload their own ammunition to increase velocities. That's not so; you cannot and should not with most modern calibers. Those with which you can goose things up are only those of much older persuasion because there are older, weaker rifles still being used. Some examples are 7mm Mauser, 8mm Mauser, and .45/70. The .30/40 Krag in a strong, modern rifle like Ruger's Number Three single-shot can be boosted quite a lot.

The main reason people reload is to produce better ammunition and to produce it at far lower cost. The bullets available for reloading are superb, and they come in wide variations of weight, shape, and construction. There are many excellent powders from such as DuPont, Hercules, Hodgdon, Norma, and Winchester-Western, so you can tailor your loads to fit almost any possible requirement. And there are even variations in primers. Generally, a given rifle will perk a little better with one certain combination. But there are some rifles that are not at all fussy and will digest most any reasonable load. You'll never know this until you try the various combinations.

I cannot remember when last I hunted with a factory-loaded rifle cartridge. This is not to suggest that I don't rate factory ammo highly, since the main reason is that I do a vast amount of shooting and generally run through factory loads quickly and then reload. When it comes to hunting I usually have no choice anyway, since all the factory loads are gone. Some combinations of factory load and factory rifles are superb, some are not. I have a Remington Model 700 .25/06 rifle, for example, that shoots groups averaging ¾ inch at 100 yards with Winchester, Remington, and Federal ammunition. That's hard to beat, and it doesn't matter much if I use these or a handload for hunting, because that's one I can't much improve on.

I think the hunter who uses his rifle only a couple times a year would be foolish to reload—unless be began shooting more often, that is. Handloading requires an investment, the amount of which depends on many things. But even if you just count the components (primers, powder, and bullets), and get them in a reasonable variety, you'll spend the cost of several boxes of factory ammo. I would advise every hunter who fires a reasonable amount of ammunition during a year to reload. He will learn much more about his equipment, will have more fun, and will save money.

WILL ONE RIFLE DO IT ALL FOR YOU?
There are rifles on the market which are often called "combination rifles," meaning that they double as deer and varmint rifles. In earlier days, the .250/3000 Savage was one of the favorites, and it's still a fine choice. Then the .243 Winchester came along and the book was rewritten. This cartridge was conceived and marketed as a combination, and it turned out to be a superb one. If this kind of rifle is your choice, then the .243, 6mm Remington, and 25/06 are the top choices with the .250/3000 still in the running. The .264 Winchester magnum will fill the bill nicely for a long-range combination rifle; so will the 7mm Remington. But any bore larger than .25 caliber is getting a bit on the large size for such game as chucks and crows.

Many other rifles can be used for varmints as well as deer, but the above are the most popular and I think the most sensible choices. If I had to choose just one among them it would be the .243, but others will not necessarily agree.

There are also the excellent combination guns, the most visible of which is the Savage Model 2400, consisting of shotgun and rifle combination. These guns (it's always hard to know whether to call them guns or rifles) are useful in certain areas where you might be hunting both birds and deer at the same time. The seasons often overlap in the north, where the ruffed grouse is found. They also can be useful when you are hunting deer in an area where you're likely to run across a wild boar; a rifled slug may be useful in such a situation. This is the sort of gun where the hunter will have to make his own decision because only he knows what his style of hunting is.

Earlier I mentioned the possibility of a man who owned a pump shotgun opting for a pump deer rifle. There is another such situation with the lever-action family, and this is a very common and popular one that has been pushed hard by Winchester's promotional group. That is the Model 94 and 9422 Winchester combination, with the former being the .30/30 deer rifle and the latter being their .22 lever-action (which also comes in .22 WMR). Another lever pair is Marlin's 336 deer rifle in .30/30 or .35 Remington and that company's Model 39 .22 rifle.

This Marlin pair has been around the longest. The Model 39 rifle started in 1891 as the Model 1891 and was followed by the 1893, which is the direct ancestor of the present 336. These are the oldest and second-oldest shoulder arms in production. Winchester's Model 94 was originally the Model 1894 and is third-oldest. The Model 9422 Winchester was introduced in the 1970s. The idea makes a lot of sense, since one can become thoroughly familiar with the system by using the .22 during the off-season.

Should you own, or happen to acquire, a rifle that is graced by some engraving, you will probably be tempted not to use it for fear of marring its looks. That choice is up to you. I've always found that the main idea behind a gun or rifle was to use it, and a vast amount of that enjoyment comes from looking at it. Engraving makes such looking much more satisfying and it's a particularly good feeling to look at such a rifle in the woods. Furthermore you have to put all things in perspective and realize that life is pretty short, so smell all the roses you can. Leaving a handsome, engraved gun behind for someone else to admire or sell is not my idea of getting full enjoyment out of it.

Incidentally, I think any hunting rifle should have a sling, even though it can be a mixed blessing at times. More than once I've spooked a deer and missed getting a shot because I had my rifle slung out of the way. But when you're carrying binoculars and a light day pack it often feels good to sling the rifle. I use a pair of lightweight Bushnell binoculars and a very light pack from L. L. Bean's that holds lunch, foul-weather gear, knife, extra ammo, etc. Even though this load carries easily, it does make sense to use a sling a great deal of the time. I've never been much of a sling shooter—that is, I don't ordinarily use a sling in shooting. I restrict my use of the sling to carrying to keep both hands free.

When you're making up your mind about a rifle for deer hunting you can keep in mind that there is no reason to restrict your rifle ownership to a single item. You may very well want to make the first purchase something of a universal choice—one that is good most anywhere, like the .30/30 carbine. It's as good a choice as you can make for the woods, and it can't be beat for a close deer shot anywhere.

That would leave the second rifle choice to be a combination deer and varmint rifle like the .243, which is a dandy long-range varminter and equally excellent on deer, black bear, and antelope. Or perhaps your next choice might be one of the bigger magnums. There are many ways to go, and the choice and selection is part of the fun.

FINDING A GUNSMITH
"Ask a gunsmith" is the answer you get when you ask a question—most any question—about a gun or its suitability for various purposes, especially when such a question is submitted to one of the gun magazines, because the person responding cannot personally examine the gun in question. The answer is correct. It is also a cop-out.

The "expert" responding knows how hard it is to locate a competent gunsmith. And the hitch lies in that word "competent." There are a lot of guys with shingles hung out, and a lot in the Yellow Pages, who are either incompetent or simply unskilled in the particular field in which you may be interested. Finding the right gunsmith to answer your question is a very difficult thing to do, and that's why the writers tell you simply to consult a gunsmith. They may as well say, "Lots of luck, Charley."

If you are tender, I suggest you visit a local gun club. This should be a club which specializes in one of the four major kinds of target shooting (trap, skeet, pistol, or rifle) and which holds registered shoots of one sort or another. Try to visit when some of the club's better shooters are attending, say on a Saturday afternoon. Ask some of these hot shooters for advice on finding a competent gunsmith; you'll find they are usually acquainted with such sources. Generally speaking, old guns often require the critical gaze of the oracle before you can consider them OK to shoot. Others may require some fiddling to tame them into becoming decent deer rifles.

It also must be said that there are now a new crop of writers giving advice in the nations's gun press. Some of these young guys are fine, offering good advice. But I see a lot of them making the same kind of mistakes I made when I was younger—that of thinking you know everything. It took a lot of learning on my part to know I didn't know it all, and I'm still learning. Don't necessarily believe everything you read just because it's in print. There are even mistakes in that sage Bible of gundom, *The American Rifleman!*

But it also must be said that black and white are not always a simple black and white. When your question is analogous to "How high is up?" the answer is going to be some shade of gray.

16

Shotgun Slugs and Slug Guns

The shotgun slug—sometimes called a punkin ball, pumpkin ball, Johnson ball, or some other hangover name from days when a round ball was used—is required equipment in many states. The reason is that lawmakers in those states reckon the areas are flat and sometimes relatively populated. It is not considered prudent to loosen a rifle bullet in such country. A case in point is my own state of Rhode Island, which isn't much above sea level, is pretty flat, and was recently nosed out by New Jersey as the nation's most densely populated. Rhode Island is a slug state. (New Jersey is a buckshot state, and I'll tell you something. I'd rather have a nut loose in the woods with a rifle than with a shotgun and buckshot. With the latter, he's spewing forth nine buckshot as opposed to a single rifle bullet or rifled slug.)

Western New York State is also slug country, and there are many other areas of rolling farmland where it's slugs, or buck and slug, but no rifles. This book will not cover buckshot, but the rifled slug is so commonly used that it must be part of the covered. It's a single slug like a rifle bullet and properly belongs in any discussion of "deer rifles."

The average hunter just sticks a shotgun cartridge loaded with a slug in his gun and figures he's ready to shoot a deer. Maybe yes, maybe no. That depends on a lot of factors which are not ordinarily considered.

First, slugs are made in 12, 16, and 20 gauge and .410 bore.

Remington's autoloading Model 1100, shown with slug barrel. It is available in 12 and 20 gauge.

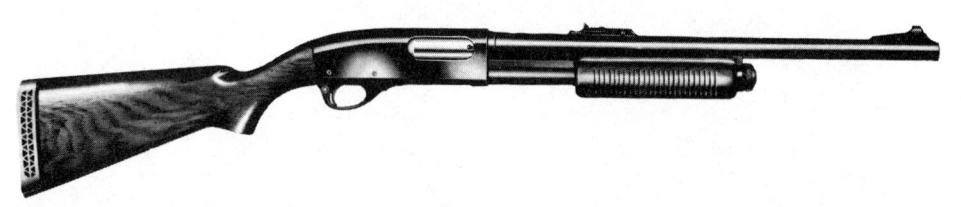

A Remington Model 870 pump shotgun with slug barrel. Guns with slug barrels have special "rifle-type" sights and are often bored specially for slugs.

But most of those used are in 12 gauge, with a few in 20 gauge. The 16-gauge gun is unfortunately becoming extinct, and the .410 slug is fit only for sparrows, not deer. You are well advised to stick to a 12-gauge slug gun if it's a slug gun you must use at all. I frankly do not like to hunt deer with a shotgun, but for those who must because of legal restrictions, there are proper ways to do it.

I will confine my discussion to the 12-gauge slug. And I would strongly advise any shotgun deer hunter to buy a special gun for this purpose, or a special barrel for his bird gun (provided it's a single-barrel gun of pump or auto style and for which such a barrel is available). This is really a rather small investment, and you should be able to stand it. The reasons for this suggestion will become apparent as we go along with this discussion. It's more than a mere suggestion—it's as strong a recommendation as I can make.

One of the main reasons you should choose a special slug barrel is that they are usually cylinder-bored from chamber to muzzle. There is no choke. As you know, choke in the muzzle of a shotgun barrel is to constrict the shot charge and produce tighter patterns. Ammunition makers manufacture shotgun slugs so they will pass through the tightest choke without getting hung up or delayed and raising pressures.

Shotgun barrels have been made by so many firms over so many years in so many countries that there are substantial varia-

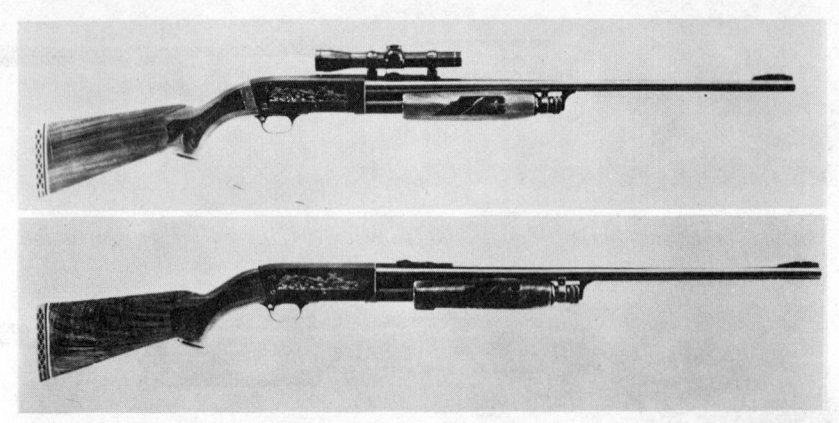

The Ithaca Model 37 Deerslayer comes in standard and deluxe grades. Ithaca bores these barrels just for slugs to a straight .715-inch diameter.

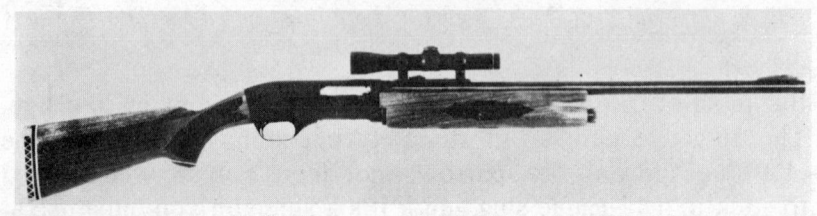

An Ithaca Model 51 autoloading gun with special slug barrel. Other makes are also available with special slug barrels, as are certain special "slug guns" like the Marlin Model 55 bolt-action.

tions in bore and choke. A 12-gauge gun has a bore size of .729 inch. At least that's what it should be according to standardization. But as authoritative a source as the current British Rules of Proof (1954) give the bore diameter of a 12-gauge gun as from .710 to .751 inch. Anything within those dimensions qualifies as a 12-gauge. You may accept the British figures as gospel, since the finest guns are made in Britain and their rules of proof are as stringent as anyone's.

If most shotgun bores measure about .729 inch, which they do, then what about chokes? I measured a Perazzi trap gun and a Winchester Model 12 trap gun, both of which are "super pucker" full choke. Both these guns measure .690 inch at the muzzle. It's obvious that anyone manufacturing slugs must make them so they will pass the tightest muzzle constriction with safety.

So slugs are made to smaller-than-bore-size diameter. A Federal slug measures .703 inch, a Remington .695 inch, and a Winchester .692 inch at their widest points—the flared rear end. Up ahead, at what might be called their major diameter, these slugs measure .688 inch Federal, .690 inch Remington, and .684 inch Winchester. Factory-loaded slugs are basically hollow for two reasons: the construction keeps the weight well forward so the slugs tend to fly point-on, and the thin walls at the widest part of the slugs can be easily squeezed down to slip through the tightest choke. The 12-gauge slug is supposed to weigh about 400 grains. The samples I weighed went 402 grains for the Federal, 404 grains for Remington, and 413 grains for the Winchester.

All things considered, I do not think the ammunition companies have paid much attention to the rifled slug for deer hunting. The combination generally produces lousy accuracy. The Ithaca 1976 catalog states, "With consistent loads, a good shooter can put five shots into a 3-inch circle at 40 yards, and into a 6-inch circle at 75 yards. That's all the accuracy anyone needs." Ithaca has qualified this statement by using the words "with consistent loads" and "a good shooter." That's what we call weasel wording, because who's to define what constitutes consistent loads or a good shooter? But I don't happen to think a 3-inch group at 40 yards or a 6-inch at 75 is "all the accuracy anyone needs." I'd think those who shoot shotguns with slugs at deer ought to expect better accuracy than that.

Look at the sort of performance you get from a rifled slug shown in comparison with a .44 Magnum, which rates as a pretty darned good deer rifle. I wouldn't suggest the slug at more than 50 or 75 yards, but this is well within the ranges at which most deer are shot. Why not have the kind of accuracy that will properly place your bullet (slug) to ensure a clean kill?

	Muzzle velocity	*Muzzle energy*	*Velocity* 50 yds	*Velocity* 100 yds	*Energy* 50 yds	*Energy* 100 yds
.44 Magnum rifle	1760	1650	1585*	1362	1375*	988
12-gauge slug	1600	2175	1175**	—	1175**	—

*Estimated.
**According to Remington, these figures are the same.

Decent slug accuracy is prohibited by the constraints placed on ammunition manufacturers from all the variations in gun barrels still in service. Most barrels being manufactured today run approximately .725-.730 inch, which means that a cylinder (*not* improved-cylinder) barrel will have no choke at all and will measure the same at the muzzle as it does in the bore. (An improved-cylinder has a slight choke, and a 12-gauge IC muzzle *usually* runs around .720 inch, though there is often variation among the many brands).

Were slugs to be manufactured to any larger dimension than they are, they might cause problems with certain barrels. Still, I'm not at all certain this is reason enough not to try to make a more accurate shotgun slug. There is a precedent in loading ammunition that can be unsafe with older guns and guns with less wall thickness in the barrels as well as some of the widely varying dimensions. I refer now to the present use of steel shot, which should not be used in nearly all double-barrel guns. And, for that matter, smokeless loads of any kind may not be fired in older damascus shotgun barrels. So there are precedents.

I think it would be possible for the ammunition producers to offer two kinds of slugs—and a premium line of more accurate slugs, usable only in certain guns, would be an interesting idea. A man named George Vitt did quite a lot of experimenting on this subject some years ago and developed a slug that outperforms the factory slugs by a country mile in certain guns. Where the average factory slug groups into 6 inches, more or less, with a good slug gun at 50 yards, it will perform a lot less accurately with *average* choked barrels. The Vitt slug can shoot groups as small as around 1 inch at 50 yards! That's some improvement.

To understand why, you first have to understand why the factory slugs do not perform. They are undersize. When you drive a too-small slug through a standard gun bore, you have no idea whether it's centered or running along one side. And since it's tapered or flared slightly at the base it may well be riding the bore in a squeehawed attitude. When this slug runs into the choke it will hit the tapered choke different than the last slug. No two will strike the choke alike and hence they will be shot at varying angles, more or less sprayed in the target's general direction.

Indeed, most shotguns do well to shoot slugs within a foot at 50 yards. And a foot at that short distance is no gun to hunt deer with. You can appreciate that the guy who takes an ordinary gun (with full or modified choke) with ordinary shotgun bead sights is at a serious disadvantage. He may well be a skilled artist on birds with the gun, but he won't be able to hit a barrel of apples with slugs.

The solution reached by George Vitt was a specially designed

A sample of the special Vitt slug, which is only available for reloaders. It is made to a full .730-inch diameter and greatly resembles the German Brenneke.

slug of soft lead, with a rounded nose, about $^{11}/_{16}$th inch long with thin fins to provide rotation and with wads screwed to its base. The wad column provides a "tail," like that on a kite, to keep the slug point-on in flight. The whole assembly is about an inch and a half long and weighs 575 grains (the wads fly with the slug, unlike wads in commercial loads). This slug is driven at good velocity according to the Lyman handbook, and I'll come to loads in a few moments.

The Vitt solution to bore-diameter irregularities was to make his slug to a .728-inch diameter. The wads are approximately the same size, and an Alcan air wedge (included in the wad column screwed to the slug) seals the bore against the gas. This serves to keep the slug centered in the bore of most guns. It is a little smaller than some bores, but there are very few 12-gauge guns with bores larger than .730 inch. When the slug runs into the choke it merely is squeezed down by the constriction, since its fins are quite thin and of soft lead. (The solid part of the slug is only about .600 inch, which will clear any 12-gauge choke.) Vitt slugs have been fired through tight chokes with no damage to gun barrels.

How do they shoot? Well, Vitt has shot a lot of targets that measure only slightly more than an inch—five shots at 50 yards.

The only problem with Vitt's slugs is that they are only available to reloaders. But loading is very simple. If you plan to use the gun as a repeater (which I should imagine most hunters will want to do) the shells should be roll-crimped. But I made my tests without crimping at all. I simply reprimed the cases, charged them with powder, and slipped the slugs in at the recommended pressure. I used two loads: 24 grains Hercules Unique and 41 grains DuPont SR 4756, which gives a muzzle velocity of 1450 fps according to Lyman. All my loads were in Federal plastic cases. The slugs are available at $7 per box of twenty-five (in 1977), which I consider a bargain price, from Vitt & Boos, 11 Sugarloaf Drive, Wilton, Conn. 06897. You can get specific loading information for this slug from Lyman.

Long before George Vitt developed his slug there was a precedent for him to follow: the German Brenneke slug, renowned for its deadly effect on major game species around the world. Brenneke slugs have been used since about 1900 (the present model dates from 1935) and have slain buffalo, lion, tiger, etc. Suitable for any shotgun with proof marks for nitro (smokeless) powder, the Brenneke is vastly different from any American commercially loaded slug.

Very similar to the Vitt slug, the Brenneke is roughly the same diameter as the Vitt (about .730 inch), has thin fins, and has its wad column screwed to the base. Where the Vitt slug weighs 575 grains, the Brenneke is lighter at 457 grains. In case you wonder about the diameter of these special slugs being so much larger than a choke bore, let me explain that they are made of soft lead and have very thin fins. It is very easy for the slugs to be crushed in a full-choke bore with no damage because of the soft, thin fins of pure lead. With the wad column screwed to the slug's base the whole unit is longer, which gives it better balance.

Brenneke slugs are imported by Interarms, which sent me some samples to use for this book. Loaded ammunition is available in Rottweil brand; you should be able to order from your dealer, and if he doesn't have it in stock, tell him to order directly from Eastern Sports International in Milford, New Hampshire. The 12-gauge loads are suitable for any 2¾-inch chamber.

You can also handload Brenneke slugs, and there are quite a number of loads worked up by DuPont in the DuPont reloading manual for Federal, Remington, and Winchester empty cartridges. These slugs are not at all difficult to reload and, according to DuPont, you can use a folded crimp whereas the Vitt procedure calls for a roll crimp. The latter is more difficult—only Lyman makes a crimper for roll crimp today.

I have heard, although I have no firsthand knowledge, of choke barrels that have been bulged with Brenneke slugs. Brenneke claims it won't happen. The late Sir Gerald Burrard in *The Modern Shotgun* gave very little space to shotgun slugs, but he did comment that they should not be used with more than half-choke barrels (about "modified" in American language). I would go one better than that. I would suggest that only special slug barrels be used for slugs, and one major reason for this is that the accuracy will be so much better. It is perfectly all right to employ a shotgun with Brenneke slugs for big game, as in a followup situation where the gun can be handled faster than a rifle. This applies only to thin-skinned game, and I would use nothing tighter than a modified or half-choke barrel. I think it also follows logically that if you're in such a situation, you've spent so much to get there that it would be stupid not to spend a little more and equip yourself with the correct shooting gear.

The shotgun slug is a relatively recent development. Prior to its conception the commonly used single projectiles for a shotgun were round balls. Now, it is *not* safe to drive a round ball through a choke unless that ball is small enough to fall through. As a matter of fact, many European guns were marked "not for ball," a requirement for a gun with any degree of choke at all. A round ball is also a miserable shape, because you can only drive it just so fast, as explained in Chapter 13.

It has always been a source of wonder if these rifled slugs actually spin. The intent is for the helical grooves alongside the lead slug to spin from air resistance. I have little doubt that some spinning occurs, but I'll bet you the price of a decent shotgun that they don't spin at 50 yards. The way they come out of most barrels, spewed at a squeehawed attitude, it would be a remarkable thing indeed if they had regained stability at that distance, let alone begun to turn. Slugs stay point-on because they are nose-heavy, not because they have fins.

The "accuracy" of slugs from so-called slug barrels is a severe disappointment to any experienced rifle shooter or hunter. In order to have an updated idea of what the situation really is, I obtained several guns to test for this chapter. One was a slug barrel for my Remington 1100; this is a 22-inch cylinder-bored barrel with rifle-type sights. And I got an Ithaca Deerslayer slug gun, which also is cylinder-bored except that Ithaca bores their barrels to .715 inch for slug use. The last gun I tried was a Marlin bolt-action Model 55 "slug gun." All these have open sights similar to those normally found on rifles, and all were fired from bench rest at 50 yards with these open sights. In running the tests I used factory-loaded slugs from Remington, Federal, and

This was my best group at 50 yards, shot with a Remington Model 1100 with slug barrel and open sights. The target shows three shots with Brenneke slugs; The group measures 1 5/8 inch. This barrel shot much better with Brenneke than with American slugs.

Winchester as well as the imported Brenneke slugs in the Rottweil brand. I have previously outlined the specifications of these various slugs.

The very best shooting I got was with the Remington Model 1100 with Brenneke slugs; groups of 1 5/8 and 2½ inches. But this barrel would not perform at all satisfactorily with any of the American-loaded slugs.

The Ithaca shot groups averaged 3 7/8 inches with Remington slugs, but the groups spread out to 7 and 10 inches with Winchester and Federal slugs and 6½ inches with the Brenneke. I'd conclude the accuracy with Remington slugs was "borderline acceptable," but none of the others are worth consideration.

Marlin's bolt-action shot similarly; 3½ inches for the Remington, about 9 inches with Federal, and way out to 13 inches with both Winchester and Brenneke.

This sort of "accuracy" was astounding. I'd have to call it very poor. About the only suggestion I can make to the deer hunter who must use slugs is that he try his gun using several brands of slugs before he thinks about hunting with it. And it certainly reinforces the earlier point about insisting on a special slug gun or slug barrel.

In addition to the fact that there are shotgun bores of so many varying sizes in existence, there is also the fact that manufacturers have some different ideas. For example, just consider the three guns I shot. The Remington 1100 is cylinder-bored, a straight .728 inch. The Ithaca is also cylinder-bored but it's a straight .715 inch while the Marlin has a bit of choke—about modified—and it actually measures .715 inch at the muzzle. That means that it's bored like a shotgun in that the bore is .730 inch, choked to .715 at the muzzle. But there's more to this story.

Like most manufacturers, Marlin swages chokes. This means that the company bores a straight barrel to .730-inch diameter all the way through. Then the outside of the muzzle is swaged (or squeezed) to constrict the inside. But there is no further operation to bore out the choke after swaging in order to assure it is concentric with the bore! Given a tube of different wall thickness, or varying wall thickness, it is reasonable to suspect that most swaged choked barrels have a choke which isn't parallel with the bore. This isn't so much of a problem with the ordinary shotgun because it won't much matter when you're throwing a cluster of shot (trap shooters will argue the point, but I'm talking about average guns and average hunters). But when it comes to a rifled slug, it's a different ball game.

Given what amounts to a bent barrel, an undersized slug, poor sights at best, and the immense variations among the ammunition brands, the average deer hunter toting a slug gun will be lucky to hit a washtub at 50 yards, let alone a deer.

The picture isn't very pretty. I did not test all the guns available, and it's possible others might perform better. But I have my doubts. In my opinion the handloader who wants to experiment could work up a very good load using the Vitt slug. This, in my estimation at this time, would be the best possible solution. Otherwise there is little one can do but try the different slugs and see what works best in your gun.

Given my druthers I'd prefer to use the Brenneke among available factory ammunition, as long as I had a gun that would shoot it with accuracy. It is heavier and it will do an outstanding job of killing once your deer is hit. Still, any slug will perform creditably as long as you can hit with it. But given the evidence at hand, one can see why buckshot is a good bet where you must

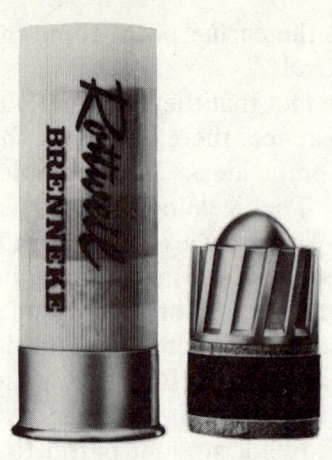

The present 2¾-inch shotgun cartridge featuring Brenneke slugs loaded by Dynamit/Nobel in Rottweil brand is imported by Eastern Sports International in Milford, New Hampshire. This ammunition will perform best among all shotgun slugs, provided you have a gun that will deliver decent accuracy.

use a shotgun for deer. And you can certainly see why most hunters are deluded, since they most likely will use their standard bird gun with standard shotgun sights. They will need all the luck one can offer them.

While I have not made any tests to support this theory, I believe both the Brenneke and Vitt slugs will perform best with a cylinder-bore barrel of .730 inch diameter. This hypothesis is that it seems logical, since these slugs must be squeezed to pass through either a choke (like the Marlin) or a tighter bore (like the Ithaca). In this event they are not squeezed uniformly and so their flights are unpredictable. At least we have proved that theory in rifle shooting, where bullets must not be larger than groove diameter and where, in bullet manufacture, you must not reduce the size of a bullet but always make it a trifle larger with each operation. This may well be part of the problem. I cannot, however, suggest any theory for the Remington slug's superior performance in the Marlin and Ithaca guns.

A long time ago a gunsmith friend of mine from upstate New York, the late M.S. Risley, rifled a few 20-gauge barrels with a very slight trace of rifling. Shirley Risley was a very competent shotgun gunsmith in addition to being a fine all-around craftsman, and these barrels shot slugs to beat the band. They were very accurate. But since he had rifled the barrels, they were now "rifles" and the law-enforcement boys would burn you if you got caught. Western New York state was then and is now shotgun territory. Similarly, the Williams boys of gunsight fame up in Michigan developed a muzzle attachment with rifling that was designed to help slug accuracy. It did just that, but, like the Risley-rifled bores, it too was illegal.

Legal interpretations of this sort have always seemed to me to be asinine. A rifled slug shot out of a rifled shotgun barrel, which otherwise was the same as any other shotgun, only increases the accuracy. It helps make the shot surer and more humane. Put another way, it aids the *intent* of the law even though it is contrary to the *letter* of the law.

But these situations will not improve until you, the hunter, make your voice heard. It wouldn't be hard to change such a legal interpretation if enough of you made your views known to lawmakers. You might even have to vote a few of them out or in. And if you want better-shooting slugs, you will have to write letters to the manufacturers of slug ammo. As long as you keep buying what they make, the situation isn't likely to change. There are a lot of shotgun deer hunters—it's time they woke up to the fact that they can have it better.

Some clarification of Brenneke slugs has been received just before this book went to press. It is important to note that Brenneke slugs themselves—the projectiles only—are manufactured in West Germany by a firm named Wilhelm Brenneke. The slugs, in turn, are sold to Dynamit/Nobel to load into finished ammunition. Dynamit/Nobel is one of the largest industrial firms in the world with sales of more than a billion dollars; it loads Brenneke slugs in the D/N Rottweil brand, which is distributed worldwide. (Rottweil ammunition with Brenneke slugs is distributed in the U.S. by Eastern Sports International).

The Brenneke firm also sells slugs to Interarms in Alexandria, Virginia, which Interarms in turn loads in the U.S. in its own brand of ammunition, which incorporates an Italian cartridge case, American powder, and the Brenneke slug.

Confusion exists because both firms (quite validly) use the words "original Brenneke slug." But it is important to realize that the slug is only the projectile. To further muddy this water, Rottweil ammunition using Brenneke slugs was formerly imported by Stoeger. And for a short period the same brand of ammunition was imported by Interarms.

If all that confuses you, there is still more! Rottweil has now lengthened the cartridge case used in this slug ammunition from

2½ to 2¾ inches. They claim better accuracy for the longer case because it produces less jump from the case's mouth to the gun's forcing cone. The shooting I reported above was with the older Rottweil ammunition which I received from Interarms. I have not had the opportunity to try the new, longer cartridges as presently loaded. Nevertheless the advice I've already given, to try all the available brands in your gun, still applies.

17

Whitetail Deer and Mule Deer

The principal deer of America are the whitetail and mule deer species. To vastly oversimplify things, the whitetail is the deer of the East and the mule deer is the deer of the West. But that's not really true at all, since the whitetail's range extends nearly to the Pacific in both northern and southern areas. On the other hand, the mule deer's range extends east nearly to the Great Lakes, including the Dakotas, through Nebraska, Kansas, and Oklahoma and into Texas. In many areas the species overlap and you have the happy occasion of hunting both at the same time.

There is a sort of subspecies known as the blacktail, often considered part of the mule-deer family, which primarily calls the far Northwest his home. However, some years ago, I hunted blacktail deer in southern California, where they were plentiful at that time. There are other subspecies of deer in North America, but they are in small numbers and of less importance. Among these are the Keys deer found in the Florida Keys and now listed as an endangered species, primarily because of loss of habitat.

The whitetail deer, also called Virginia deer, is the most widely distributed big-game animal in the United States, and some claim it is the smartest. Whitetails vary enormously in size and in development of antlers. One normally associates Maine with whitetail deer, for example, but perhaps the association has more to do with the fact that L. L. Bean is located in Maine. The big deer do not come from the Pine Tree State at all. You have to go to the 162nd place in the Boone & Crockett *Records of North American Big Game* to find a deer from Maine. There are also a lot of ties, so the biggest Maine deer in the listings is a lot farther from number one than that. First place, if you're interested, was taken in 1918 in Minnesota. Big deer are taken in some places that may astound you. When visiting a taxidermist in Montville, Conn. a few years ago, I spotted an enormous whitetail head he was mounting. When I asked the obvious question he told me it had been shot in Manchester, Conn. That's only a few miles from Hartford!

Just a few weeks ago while driving from Rhode Island to New York City on the Connecticut Turnpike, I spotted a dead doe lying on the median strip. She had obviously been killed by a car. The place was just south of Southport (where Sturm, Ruger is located). That's in the congested area between Bridgeport and Stamford! You don't have to go too deep into the puckerbrush to find a whitetail deer. This is one of the reasons there are many more deer in the United States today than there were when the pilgrims first landed—they can adapt to changing conditions.

I have always believed the best place to shoot any game animal is through the shoulders. The reason is simple. If you have chosen the right rifle and have properly placed your shot, you will hit the heart/lung area and destroy one or maybe both of these organs. Either will produce a quick kill. You may also (particularly important with any dangerous animal) break both shoulders, and no animal is going far with both shoulders destroyed. The neck or head shot is neat if you're using a small rifle and are close enough to pinpoint your shot. The heart shot on a deer is a very low shot, and I question whether it's the best shot. Deer shot in the heart/lung area without breaking shoulder bones will often run off as though unhit. The means you must always follow up. You may think you've missed entirely. I always make it a rule to carefully mark the spot from which I fired the shot (hang something in a tree, like your hat), then also mark the spot where the deer stood when I fired. These references prove very important if you don't find the animal quickly and have to reconstruct the shot.

Follow up your deer very carefully; if you've made a good shot you'll find it within a few yards and you'll certainly find it within 100 yards.

I would advise against a rear-end shot because it will ruin too much meat. Some like to make a spine shot, but this too is a risky shot even though it can drop a deer like a stone. The best shot, again, is to hold in the middle of the body up and down, and just behind the shoulder. If you hit a bit high, you'll hit the spine, a bit low and you'll hit the heart. A little bit forward will break the shoulders and a bit to the rear will either still be in the lungs or will hit the liver. This is your best shot.

Aside from the fact that a mule deer is larger, there is little difference in these animals and no difference in where you

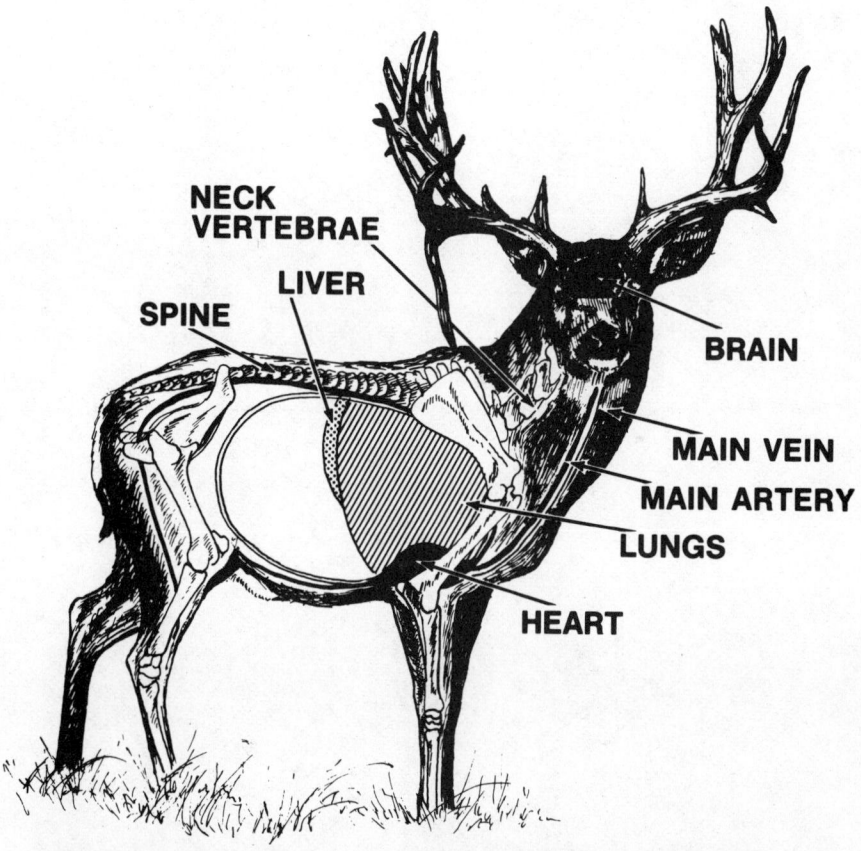

A study of a deer's anatomy is most important before you take to the woods. Whether whitetail or mule deer, you aim for the same spots; there is no practical difference. Best shot is the lung area, because it will strike either heart or lung and possibly the shoulder bones as well. Note that the lung area is very large, which is another reason to make that your target. Other good areas are brain, neck vertebrae, and spine. Sketches courtesy and by permission of **Pertersen's Hunting** *magazine.*

should aim. Mule deer are less spooky than whitetails and will not hide and sneak like wily old whitetails. One thing I have noticed about mule deer when you're trying to evaluate the size of a trophy head at some distance is that the huge ears with their fringe of hair blend into the antlers and make evaluation difficult. I often use my rifle scope for spotting and often wish I had lugged the big Bushnell spotter so I had a better advantage. It's too easy to think a relatively small head is a whopper when the ears and horns get mixed up in a scope with insufficient power.

Now I've told you what rifle to use, or at least I've given you the information on which to base your own buying decision, and I've told you where the bullet should be placed. The rest is up to you.

18

Favorite Deer Rifles

It becomes necessary to define the word "favorite" before you can begin to list certain rifles under that classification. It is obvious that a favorite deer rifle is going to be one with which you have killed a number of deer. Or perhaps, one with which you have made some good shots. Or, perhaps you have witnessed someone else make a great shot with this rifle. On the other hand, some superb deer rifles have often been taken from the rack and into the woods but have never been blooded. After all, you can shoot only so many deer legally, and you are not always successful. I have rifles in all those categories and I'm going to describe five rifles, not in any particular order, and will tell you why they are favorites.

The first is a .30/30 carbine. I got this little rifle when I first became associated with Marlin as its advertising agent. It's their straight-grip model, and the one I have was made in 1960. It has a Marlin scope in Marlin mounts and it shoots very close to 1-inch 100-yard groups. I have lifted the heads from a number of partridges on hunting trips in Maine. And I have shot several Maine whitetails with it. This rifle, and the Winchester 94, is what I call a "traditional deer rifle," and the term means, to me, a lever-action straight-grip carbine.

When you arrange your camping and hunting gear, whether at home or in camp, no other rifle looks as much at home as one of these carbines. This is sheer smoke, of course, but there's a lot of that when fellows get to talking hunting. All you have to

Two views of the prototype .30/06 bolt action rifle sired by a major company, gunsmithed by Al Biesen. It shoots into ½ inch at 100 yards with 180-grain Nosler Partition bullets and 51 grains Hercules Re21 powder. The rifle, with Redfield 4× scope, has taken several deer, caribou, Arctic wolves, and other North American game.

do is look at a Winchester 94 and your mind instantly says "deer rifle." It needs no added words, no headline, no body copy. The little gun says it all. The deer I have shot with this .30/30 all died instantly, and all were taken within 30 to 40 yards—pretty ordinary ranges for the bushy country around Maine's Allagash country. Truth is, that's the only times this carbine gets taken out of my rack—a deer-hunting trip in the northeast.

My next in the list of favorites is a .30/06 bolt-action that is a "prototype" rifle, meaning that it is a brand-new action that may or may not ever be produced. I can't tell you the maker except that it's a major American producer of sporting firearms. This rifle is unusual in that its bolt locking lugs are an interrupted thread which is reputed to be stronger than most others on the market. It was designed to be much stronger and, as far as I know, it is stronger. It is a fine rifle. It shoots into ½ to ⅝ inch at 100 yards with a handload with the 180-grain Nosler bullet and 51 grains of Hercules Re21 powder. I have shot several deer with it, plus several caribou in Quebec and two arctic wolves. The wolves were running; one was at 200 yards and the other at 285 paced yards. This is a great deer rifle; it has done everything that it could be asked to do. On one mule-deer hunt in New Mexico, I had the rifle sighted precisely 2 inches high at 100

Close-up of the grip section of my .240 Weatherby Magnum. This rifle is on a Mexican Mauser action, barreled by Weatherby; bolt-handle alteration is by Al Biesen and the stock by me. Scope is a Leopole 2.5-8× variable.

yards and knew its trajectory intimately. I was ready to take any reasonable shot offered, even out to 500 yards. So I got a shot at a fine buck at a distance of about 7 yards when I surprised him in the brush. But that's deer hunting. I have a Redfield 4× Widefield scope on this rifle in Redfield mounts.

Another favorite rifle is one that's been in the woods but has never been blooded. This is a .240 Weatherby Magnum built on a Mexican Mauser action. The barrel is a custom barrel that I had left over from my gunsmithing days when I had experimentally chambered it for the 6mm Holland & Holland Magnum, a whopping cartridge made by necking the .375 H&H to 6mm. This big cartridge was a complete flop. So I sent the barrel and action out to Roy Weatherby with a request to fit it to the action and chamber to .240. When it came back I made the French-walnut stock and mounted a Leupold 2.5-8× variable scope in Red-

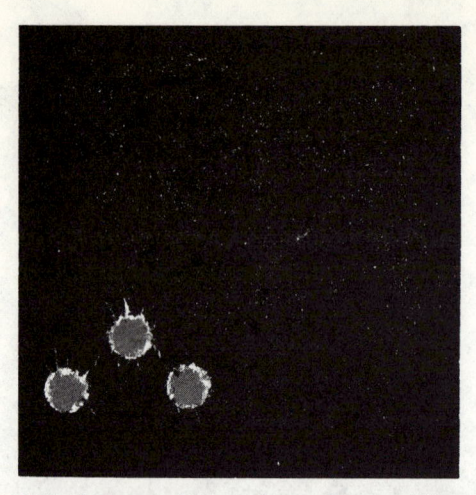

Here's how the .240 Magnum shoots: three shots at 100 yards. (I never fire more than three-shot groups from a hunting rifle. That's enough to prove a rifle won't shoot well, and it's as many shots as any hunter is apt to get at the same animal.) Load was 100-grain Nosler partition bullet with 54 grains Norma 205 powder, CCI magnum primer.

field mounts. The combination is excellent even though the rifle has never downed anything, only because I've never seen anything to shoot at when in the woods with it.

It shoots best with 100-grain Nosler bullets, putting them into ½ inch. With this load, using Norma MRP powder, I would not hesitate to take a very long shot at a deer. It would probably be acceptable to do so up to 400 or 500 yards provided conditions were right. The 100-grain Nosler roars out of this rifle at nearly 3400 fps according to Weatherby and Norma sources, and this is an awesome load that can't be approached with either the .243 Winchester or 6mm Remington rifles, great though they are. I use 54 grains of Norma MRP and the CCI Magnum primer to achieve this velocity.

Here's another favorite deer rifle that I've never had in the woods! It rates that distinction because it just feels, acts, and performs like a perfect deer rifle to me. It's a Remington Model 700 in .25/06 with a Lyman 3-9× variable scope in Redfield mounts.

I've shown targets shot with factory ammunition in three brands—Federal, Remington and Winchester. They are all around ¾ inch. This would seem to be plenty good enough accuracy to bag a deer, but handloading will tighten these up slightly.

A   B

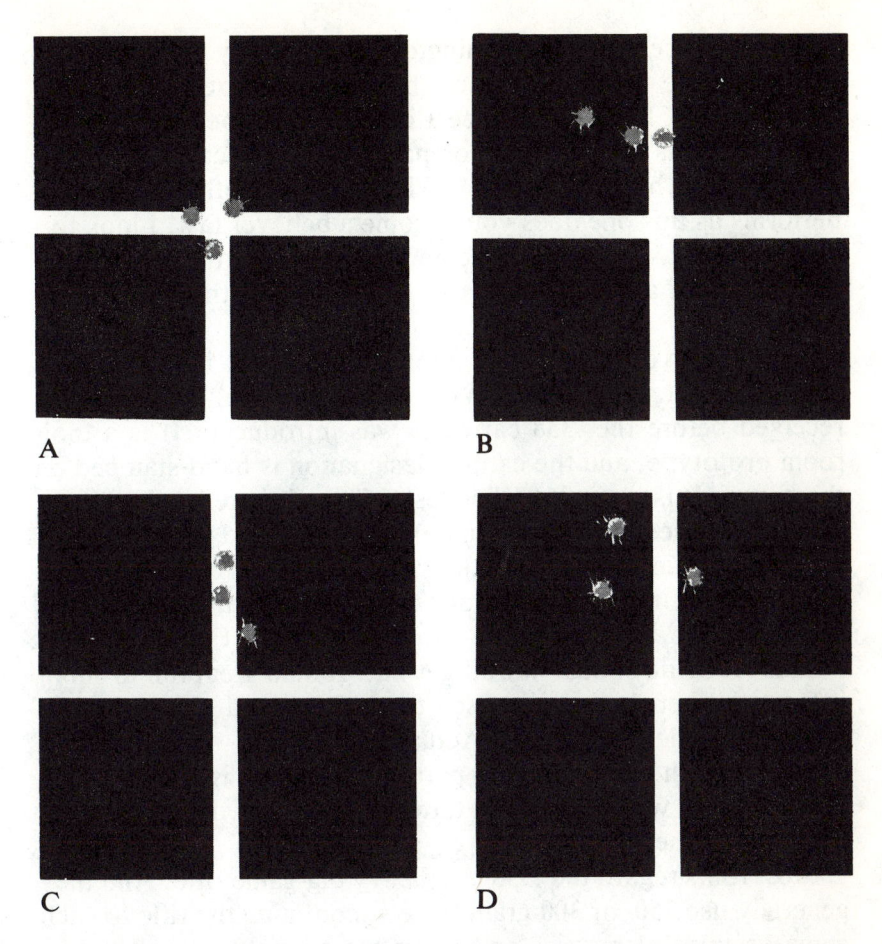

C   D

Four targets shot with the Model 70 .30/06 Winchester described in the text. I used three different brands of ammunition. All were fired the same day with Redfield 3-9× scope set at 9×. Group A was with Speer DWM ammunition, now off the market; groups B and C with Federal 165-grain boattail; and group D with Winchester 180-grain Silvertip. This kind of accuracy with factory ammunition was unheard-of a few short years ago. There is no reason why anyone can't duplicate this performance. The rifle must be "accurized" first, however.

While I have not yet settled on a firm deer load, it will be with a 100-grain bullet which can be driven at about 3300 to 3400 fps with DuPont 4831 or Norma MRP powders. You need a very slow-burning powder for maximum velocity with heavy bullets out of a small-bore rifle. The powders most commonly used for top speeds are DuPont 4350 and 4831, Norma MRP (Magnum Rifle Powder), Hodgdon's H4831 and H870, and Winchester-Western's #785 Ball Powder.

When I received this Remington 700 the only thing I did to it was to give it the cardboard-shim-at-forend treatment that I described in Chapter 15. Since I did not fire it before the treatment, there is no way to compare. But you can see that it couldn't have hurt its shooting. When you get a rifle like this that performs as this one does you become a believer fast. I look forward to the day when this rifle and I will take to the woods and, I hope, shoot a deer. There's no question that the rifle will do the job.

The last favorite rifle I'm going to talk about is my favorite long-range deer rifle, a .338 Winchester Magnum. This rifle was received before the .338 cartridge was introduced. It is a toolroom prototype, and the caliber designation is hand-stamped on the barrel. It is a pre-'64 Winchester 70 and therefore highly favored by collectors. I have mounted a Redfield 2-7× variable scope in Redfield mounts on this rifle. Until very recently I have used the rifle in its factory stock, but following a moose hunt a few years ago, I restocked it in a nice piece of French walnut.

This .338 rifle shoots like all-get-out. It's no great fun to shoot it from the bench except to see the bullets land one on top of the other time after time. Actually, this rifle shoots groups around ⅝ inch when I do my part, and my load is the 210-grain Nosler bullet with 68 grains Hercules Re21 powder and a CCI Magnum primer.

Most folks regard the .338 as a heavy big-game rifle. And they generally use 250- or 300-grain bullets, confining the rifle to such game as grizzly, moose, and other big animals as well as the plains game of Africa. But I see the .338 as much more than that because it possesses enormous accuracy, great speed with its lighter-weight bullets, and a trajectory that approximately parallels such hotshots as the .300 Winchester Magnum. That's sparkling performance, and it holds that out to a solid 500 yards.

Let me tell you about one shot I witnessed that was made with this rifle. Bob Behn and Brud Oberst were with me hunting mule deer in New Mexico. We were traveling up a deep, wide canyon toward a hunting area when we spotted a pair of mule deer feeding way off on the far canyon side. The guide stopped the truck, turned off the engine, and sat looking at the deer.

We looked with every sort of glass we had but none was powerful enough, and I regretted leaving the big Bushnell spotting scope home on this trip; its weight had decided me against it. I had already shot my deer and it was Bob Behn's turn, and it was up to him to decide whether or not to try for this buck. We were all trying mightily to see how big his rack was—at times it looked huge, at other times we had our doubts. It depended on how the deer stood, how the light glistened off his antlers, and how he twitched his ears, since the ears of a muley are large and fringed and they sometimes blur with the horns.

We glassed that buck for at least twenty minutes when finally Bob decided to have a try. The range was estimated at 500 yards by all of us—no argument there. I persuaded Bob to use my .338, since I knew exactly where it was shooting and how well it shot. Bob took a careful rest, held exactly where I told him to, and the big rifle finally boomed.

The deer went down as though struck by a bus. He didn't move—not even a twitch. The bullet had landed a bit to the left of where I had it figured, but the elevation was for a perfect heart shot. Since the buck was facing our left, the bullet tore out the throat. It was one of the most fabulous shots I've ever seen made and I was proud to have been in the party.

Let me relate my experiences with a brand-new Model 70 Winchester .30/06 right out of the factory box. Before I fired it at all I gave it the accurizing treatments I've mentioned in this book.

First, I adjusted the trigger properly. You need two very small ¼-inch open-end wrenches for this, because there are a pair of nuts that jam against teach other. There is a third nut in front of the trigger unit which must be loosened, then you need a very tiny screwdriver to turn the screw in until the trigger won't move perceptibly but will allow the gun to fire. A little moving back and forth will soon indicate where the screw should be. Once the screw adjustment is achieved, you hold the screw in place with the driver and tighten the nut. Now you loosen the two jam nuts behind the trigger and back them off until you have the weight of pull desired. The rifle I'm talking about has been set very light—yours should be from 3 to 4 pounds. You either use a scale (a special trigger scale) or you can use weights. The latter is simpler, just use a 3-pound weight with wire attached so you can hang it on the trigger with rifle held vertically. It should not fire with the 3-pound weight. Add a pound and it should fire. This adjustment really isn't much harder to accomplish than it sounds.

The next thing I did to this rifle was add the business card in front of the forend channel, under the barrel but behind the forearm tip. That gave me considerable upward pressure—enough for the guard screw to "draw" the metal into the wood close to $1/32$ inch. This also has been described more fully below.

Mounting a Redfield 3-9× scope in Redfield mounts and adjusting it to zero with a Bushnell Tru-Scope completed the job, and I went off to the range. The first shot was only about 2 inches from the aiming point, so only minor correction was needed.

From this point I shot 3-shot groups, all at 100 yards and all with factory ammunition. The results:

Norma 180-grain—1⅞ inch (one group)
Winchester Silvertip 180-grain—1³/₁₆, 1¼ inch (2 groups)
Federal 165-grain boattail—1 inch, 1¹/₁₆ inch (2 groups)
Speer DWM 165-grain—⁹/₁₆ inch, ¾ inch (2 groups)

The box of Speer ammunition was an old one that I had taken along just in case I needed to fire a number of shots to get sighted. The brand is no longer available, a pity considering how it shoots in this rifle. Made for Speer by DWM in Germany, the ammo was loaded with Speer bullets. In analyzing these groups it is interesting to note that both Federal and Winchester brands deliver excellent accuracy, with a slight edge going to the Federal. The fact that the rifle shoots so well with Speer is also an indication that handloading will help significantly. I have no hesitation in hunting with a rifle that shoots 1-inch groups, but I prefer to work with it and get everything out of it that I can. This rifle, with the perfect load, will shoot into ½ inch. No question about it.

The Norma load did not do as well as the rest, which is no criticism because this brand may work best in the next rifle to come along. To substantiate this, I've never had such accuracy with that Speer ammo as I did out of this rifle.

I have heard many shooters say they can't get a hunting rifle to shoot with good accuracy. This is usually false. And the little example I've just given ought to convince you that there is indeed an easy way to get this accuracy. The late Townsend Whelen used to say that only accurate rifles were interesting. He had a point and stated it well. It is no fun to shoot a rifle that won't keep its shots where it ought to, but it is most interesting to put several shots into a very small cluster at 100 yards. This Winchester Model 70, using the Speer DWM ammunition, will hit a dime at 100 yards with each shot fired. That's an interesting rifle!

Appendix

Equivalent Cartridges

There is an organization based in New York City known as the Sporting Arms and Ammunition Manufacturers Institute (SAAMI). It is always called "Sammy." The group exists primarily to standardize and to distribute technical information so that the cartridges loaded by Federal, for example, will always fit a rifle or gun made by Remington, Marlin, or any other maker, including foreign makers.

It is well known that there always exists the possibility of someone doing something stupid like stuffing a .35 Remington cartridge into a .30/06 rifle and pulling the trigger. While there are many cartridges that can be stuffed into the wrong chambers, the practice usually results in a dangerous situation. The .35 Remington has a .35 caliber bullet that is much larger than the .30/06's hole, through which it can't go without raising pressures way beyond the danger point. There are many other examples.

The safest rule is to use only ammunition specifically named for the rifle—as the caliber is stamped on the barrel. In this way you can never go wrong. The other way you stand a good chance of ruining a rifle and, very possibly, yourself along with it. SAAMI has recently issued a bulletin which the organization hopes will get the widest possible circulation in order to help keep the misguided and the fool out of trouble. I have listed part of their list, that part dealing with centerfire rifle cartridges. It is also important to note that only the more common examples are listed, not all of them. And it also should be borne in mind that a too-small cartridge might safely fire in a larger chamber without causing noticeable damage to rifle or shooter, but it may leave a bore obstruction which will cause the rifle to burst with the next shot. The only safe way is to follow the rule of using ammunition which matches the caliber marking on the barrel. If you're in doubt, leave it alone. Another good rule to follow would be never to buy any rifle for which ammunition is no longer available—or don't buy it without getting a supply of cartridges along with the rifle or the handloading gear necessary with which to reload it.

The list from SAAMI:

In rifle chambered for	Do not use these cartridges
6mm Remington (.244 Rem.)	.250 Savage
6.5mm Remington Magnum	.300 Savage
7mm Mauser (7×57)	.300 Savage
7mm Remington Magnum	7mm Weatherby Magnum .270 Winchester .280 Remington .35 Remington .350 Remington Magnum
8mm Mauser (8×57)	.35 Remington .7mm Mauser (7×57)
8mm Remington Magnum	.350 Remington Magnum .338 Winchester Magnum .358 Norma Magnum
.17 Remington	.221 Remington Fireball .30 Carbine
.17/.223 Remington	.17 Remington .221 Remington Fireball .30 Carbine
.223 Remington	.222 Remington
.243 Winchester	.250 Savage .225 Winchester
.257 Roberts	.250 Savage
.264 Winchester Magnum	.270 Winchester .284 Winchester .308 Winchester .303 British .350 Remington Magnum

In rifle chambered for	*Do not use these cartridges*
.270 Winchester	.30 Remington .30/30 Winchester .300 Savage .32 Remington .308 Winchester 7mm Mauser (7×57)
.280 Remington	.270 Winchester .30 Remington .30/30 Winchester .300 Savage .32 Remington .308 Winchester 7mm Mauser (7×57)
.284 Winchester	.300 Savage 7mm Mauser (7×57)
.30/40 Krag	.303 Savage .303 British .32 Winchester Special
.30/06 Springfield	8mm Mauser (8×57) .32 Remington .35 Remington
.300 Holland & Holland Magnum	.30/06 Springfield 8mm Mauser (8×57) .30/40 Krag
.300 Weatherby Magnum	.338 Winchester Magnum
.300 Winchester Magnum	8mm Mauser round-nose bullet .303 British .350 Remington Magnum .38/55 Winchester
.303 British	.32 Winchester Special
.303 Savage	.32 Winchester Special .32/40 Winchester
.308 Winchester	.300 Savage
.348 Winchester	.35 Remington

Index

Accuracy, and barrel length, 13; determining, 2–4; in shooting, 151–152, 172; with lever-actions, 32–34; with single-shots, 32–34
Accurizing, 202; bolt-actions, 202–205
Ammunition, 4–6; armor-piercing (AP), 138; ball, 137–138; brands, 162–163; incendiary, 138; reloading, 206; selecting, 205–206; trace, 138; *see also* Bullets
Arisaka rifle, 92
Autoloading rifles, 57–62; Browning BAR, 61, 118; disadvantages, 62; gas-operated, 57, 58; Harrington & Richardson, 60–61; recoil-operated, 57–58; Remington: Model 8, 58–59, 121, Model 81, 58, 121, Model 740, 59, Model 742, 59, 99; Ruger Model 44, 60–61; Winchester Model 100, 61, 98
Autoloading shotgun, Browning Auto-5, 58, 62
"Automatics," 57

Balickie, Joe, 66
Ballard rifle, vii, 21
"Ballistic coefficient," 159
Ballistics chart, 164, 165–166
Barrel length and accuracy, 13
Bassett, Doc, 13

Behn, Bob, 232–233
Bell, Karamojo, 97
Bench Rest Shooter's Association, 152
Bench shooting, 3
Biesen, Al, 50, 69, 110, 193, 228
Black-powder, vii, 13, 31–32
"Blowback," 58
Bolt-action rifles, 6, 11, 35–52; accurizing, 202–205; advantages, 51–52; camming power, 38–39; cartridges for, 39; Colt Sauer, 49; disadvantages, 52; Enfield Model 720, 37; first successful, 50; Krag, 36, 37; locking system, 37–38; Mauser: Model 98, 35–36, 155, Model 1898, 35; prototype of new rifle, 49–50, 228–229; Remington: Model 30, 37, 89, 110, Model 600, 43, 92, 122–123, Model 700, 90, 117–118, 201, 206, 230–232, Model 721, 40–41, Model 722, 40–41, 78, Model 788, 42–43, 47, 152, 204, Mohawk 600, 43; rifle stock styling, 50–51; Ruger Model 77, 10, 43–44, 99, 194; Sako, 48–49, 194; Savage: Model 20, 37, Model 40, 37, Model 45, 37, Model 110, 44–45, Model 340, 45; Springfield Model 1903, 36, 109–110, 152, 173, 176; surplus military rifles, 36;

239

Weatherby: Mark V, 46–47, 96, Vanguard, 47–48; Winchester: Model 54, 37, 95, 110, 176, Model 70, 37, 39–40, 76, 78, 94, 111, 118, 121, 124, 190, 191, 204, 205, 232–234

Brenneke slug, 216, 219–221

British gunmaking, 70–72

Browning, Ed, 21

Browning, John M., 21, 22, 53, 58, 62

Browning guns, Auto-5 shotgun, 58, 62; BAR, 61, 118; BLR, 26–27, 29, High Power, 99; machine gun, 58; single-shot shotgun, 30

"Brush-busting," 4–5

Bullets, 132–169; ballistics, 159, 164, 165–166; construction of, 139–143; flight outside the barrel—external ballistics, 157–162; flight inside the barrel—internal ballistics, 151–157; small bore high velocity vs. heavy slow-moving slug, 132–136; trajectory, 135–136, 158–159, 164, 167–169; types of, 136–143 *See also* Ammunition

Burgess, Andrew, 22

Burgess, Tom, 68

Burrard, Sir Gerald, 216–217

Bushnell scope, 10

Calibers, up to .25, 75–83; from .25 to .30, 84–102; .30 and over, 103–131; and efficiency, 137

Carbines, 103–104, 227–228

Carcano rifle, 101–102

Cartridges, .22 Hornet, 153; .22 Remington Jet, 85; .22 Savage High Power, 76; .22/250 Remington, 83, 91; .25 Krag, 91–92; .25 Remington, 87; .25/06 Remington, 90–91; .25/20 single-shot, 86; .25/20 WCF, 85–86; .25/35, WCF, 86–87; .220 Swift, 76; .222 Remington, 83; .223 Remington, 82–83, 156; .240 H&H Apex, 79, 80; .240 Wallack, 82; .240 Weatherby Magnum, 80–81, 82; .243, Winchester, 77–79; .250 Donaldson, 89; .250 Donaldson Ace, 90; .250 "Helldiver," 89; .250/3000 Savage, 87–88; .256 Winchester Magnum, 84–85; .257 Roberts, 88–90, 91; .257 Weatherby Magnum, 91; .264 Winchester Magnum, 94, 153; .270 Weatherby Magnum, 96; .270 Winchester, 95–96, 99; .275 H&H Magnum, 101; .280 Remington, 99; .284 Winchester 98–99; .30 M1 carbine, 103–104; .30 Remington, 106; .30/06 Winchester ("Super Thirty"), ix, 109–111, 156; .30/.30 Winchester, vii–ix, 21, 104–106, 157; .30/40 Krag, 108–109; .32 Remington, 116; .32 Winchester self-loading, 130; .32 Winchester Special, 115; .32/20, 129; .32/40, vii, 129; .33 Winchester, 118; .35 Remington, 120–121; .35 Whelen, 122; .38/40, 129; .38/55, vii, 129; .300 H&H Magnum, 111; .300 Savage, 107; .300 Weatherby Magnum, 112–114, 157; .300 Winchester Magnum, 112; .303 British, 114; .303 Savage, 128–129; .308 Norma Magnum, 111–112; .308 Winchester, 108; .338 Winchester Magnum, 118–119; .340 Weatherby Magnum, 119–120; .348 Winchester, 120; .350 Remington Magnum, 122; .351 Winchester, 129; .357 Magnum, 120; .358 Norma Magnum, 122–123; .358 Winchester, 121–122; .375 H&H Magnum, 80, 124; .375 Winchester, 123; .378 **Weatherby Magnum**, 124; .44 Remington Magnum, 124–126; .44/40, 130; .45/70, 127–128; .401 Winchester, 129; .444 Marlin, 126; .458 Winchester Magnum, 128; .460 Weatherby Magnum, 128; 6mm Remington, 77–79, 82; 6mm/222 Wildcat, 81–82; 6.5mm Carcano, 93; 6.5mm 4C55 Swedish Mauser, 94; 6.5mm Japanese, 92–93; 6.5mm Mannlicher-Schoenauer, 93–94; 6.5mm Remington Magnum, 92; 7mm Mashburn Magnum, 100; 7mm Remington Magnum, 96–97, 99–100; 7mm Weatherby Magnum, 100; 7.35mm Carcano, 101–102;

7.5mm Swiss, 107; 7x57mm or 7mm Mauser, 97–98; 7x61 Sharpe & Hart, 100–101; 7.62mm NATO, 108; 7.62mm Russian, 109; 7x64 Brenneke, 101; 7.65 Belgian Mauser, 114; 7.7mm Japanese, 115; 8mm Remington Magnum, 117–118; 8mm/06, 117; 8×57mm Mauser, 116–117

Cartridges, black powder, vii; cases "rebated," 98–99; equivalent, 235–237; for bolt-action rifles, 39, 41; for deep-woods hunting, 6–7; for lever-action rifles, 27; for long-range hunting, vii, 12–13; for plains hunting, 15–16; for pump-action rifles, 54; interchangeability of, 130–131; old and obsolete, 129–130; smokeless powder, vii; trajectory, 135–136, 164, 167–169

Checkered rifle stocks, 72–73
Colt guns, 21, 49, 58
Combination guns, 73–74, 207
Comfort, Ben, 111
"Cooked-off" round, 154
Crossman, Captain E.C., 174
Curtis, Paul, 174
Custom deer rifles, 63–74; artisans, 68–69; British, 70–72; checkering rifle stock, 72–73; combination guns, 73–74; engraving, 73; German Mauser military, 64; "magazine rifles," 70–72; women and hunting, 67–68, 69

Deep-woods hunting, 1–7; ammunition for, 4–6; cartridges for, 6–7; rifle accuracy, 2–4; rifles for, 1–2, 6–7; sighting rifle, 3–4, 6
Deer, blacktail, 223; mule, 223, 225–226; whitetail, 223–224
Dietz, Dick, 43
Donaldson, Harvey, 89–90
Double-barrel gun, 70
"Drillings," 74

Enfield rifles, Model 720, 37; Model 1917, 110; SMLE (Short Magazine Lee Enfield), 114

English Farquharson, 92, 201

Engraving, 73
Eskimo hunters, 75

Fecker, J. W., 174–175

Garand M1, 173
Gas operated rifles, 58, 59–60
Grip checkering, 64
Gun Digest, 66–67
"Gun that won the West, The," ix
Gunn, Bill, 125
Gunsmiths, 68–69, 209

Hageman, Wray, 174–175
"Hammer actions," 25
"Hammerless," 25
Harrington & Richardson, 30, 61–62
Hart, Richard, 100–101
Hatcher, General Julian S., 78
Hawken brothers, 32
Helldiver rifles, 89
Henry, B. Tyler, 20
Henry rifle, 20
Hepburn, Lewis, 22
Hodgdon, Bruce, 90–91
Holland & Holland, 79–80
Hoppe's, 4
Howe, James, 122
Hunting, accuracy, 2–3; African game, 124, 128; caribou, 75, 128; deep-woods, 1–7; mountain, 8–13; mule deer, 2, 223–226; still-hunting, 1; whitetail deer, 9, 223–226
Huntington, Fred, 77
"Hydraulic shock," 132

Italian service rifles, 93

Japanese rifles, 92–93, 115
Johnson ball, 210

Keith, Elmer, 132, 134
Kenna, Frank, 128
"Kentucky Windage," 10, 183
"Keyholed," 151
Krag rifles, 36, 37, 94, 108, 109

Lampert, Ron, 65
Lee, James Paris, 76

241

Lee, T. K. "Tackhole Dot," 186
Lee Navy, 76–77
Lever-action rifles, 20–29; accuracy of, 32–34; advantages, 27; Browning BLR, 26–27, 29; cartridges for, 27; Marlin Model 336, 22–26, 27, 29, 104, 105, 125, 207; Savage Model 99, 22, 24–26, 27, 29, 87, 99, 107, 122; Winchester: Model 94, 21, 22, 24–25, 27, 29, 86, 116, 120, 121, 173, 189, 207, 208, 227–228, Model 1886, 21, 118, 127
Long-range hunting, 8–13; barrel length and accuracy, 13; cartridges for, 12–13; range estimation, 9–10; rifles for, 10–13; scopes, 10
Lyman, scopes, 176; sights, 173, 174

"Magazine rifles," 70–72
"Magnum," 85
Mann, Dr. Franklin W., 152
Marlin, John 21–22, 86
Marlin rifles, Model 36, 22; Model 39, 208; Model 56, 85; Model 62, 104; Model 93, 86; Model 336, 22–26, 27, 29, 104, 105, 125, 207; Model 444, 22, 127; Model 1893, 22; Model 1894, 22, 105–106, 120; Model 1895, 22, 127, 128; Model 1889, 22; .30/30 carbine, 227–228
Mauser, Peter Paul, 35, 50
Mauser rifles, 35–36, 155
Maxim, Sir Hiram, 58
"Medium bore," 124
"Metering" system, 61
Milliron, Earl, 69
Monte Carlo, 44
Mountain hunting, 8–13
"Mountain rifle," 9, 12–13
Mule deer hunting, 223, 225–226
"Muzzle velocity," 162

New Haven Arms Company, 20
Newton, Chalres, 49, 87
Niedner, A. O., 90, 91
Noske, R., 175

Oberst, Brud, 232–233
O'Connor, Jack, 95
Ottmar, Maurice, 69

Page, Warren, 77–78, 99
"Parallax," 185–186
Pedersen, J. D., 53–54
Pilkington, Phil, 64, 65, 69
Plains hunting, 14–16
"Plains rifle," 31–32
Poachers, 75–76
"Primitive weapons," 31–32
Pump-action rifles, 11, 53–56; advantages, 56; cartridges for, 54; disadvantages, 56; Remington: Model 10, 54, Model 14, 53, 54, 55, 121, Model 141, 53, 55, 121, Model 760, 53, 55–56; Savage Model 170, 56; Winchester, 53
Pump-action shotguns, 53
Pumpkin ball, 210
Punkin ball, 210

Rabbeth, J. Francis, 86
Rangefinders, 182–185; Bushnell bullet drop compensator, 183–184; "Kentucky windage," 183–184; Ranging 1000, 184–185; Redfield, 182, 184–185
"Rebated" cartridge case, 98–99
Recoil, 57–58, 198–199
Redfield, rangefinder, 182, 184–185; scope, 184–185
Remington rifles, Model 8, 58–59, 121; Model 10, 54; Model 14, 53, 54, 55, 121; Model 30, 37, 89, 110; Model 81, 58, 121; Model 141, 53, 55, 121; Model 600, 43, 92, 122–123; Model 700, 90, 117–118, 201, 206, 230–232; Model 721, 40–41; Model 722, 40–41, 78; Model 725, 99; Model 740, 59; Model 742, 59, 99; Model 760, 53, 55–56; Model 788, 42–43, 47, 152, 204; Model 1100, 218, 219; Mohawk 600, 43
Repeaters, 20
Rifle stock checkering, 72–73
Rifled slugs, see Slugs, shotgun
Rifles, see individual types
Risley, M. S., 220–221
Roberts, Ned H., 88–89
Roosevelt, Theodore, 36
Rowe, C. Edward "Ted," Jr., 128
Ruger, Bill, 43–44, 128

Ruger Hawkeye pistol, 84
Ruger rifles, Model 44, 60–61; Model 77, 10, 43–44, 99, 194; Number One, 29; Number Three, 29–30, 72, 109, 201

Sako, 48–49, 194
Savage rifles, Model 20, 37; Model 23A Sporter, 176; Model 24, 73–74; Model 40, 37; Model 45, 37; Model 99, 22, 24–26, 27, 29, 87, 99, 107, 122; Model 110, 44–45; Model 170, 56; Model 340, 45; Model 2400, 73, 207
Scheutzen shooters, 174
Scope mounts, 177–179, 189–194; as integral unit, 193; bases, 194; Bausch & Lomb, 192; "claw-mounts," 190; Noske (side), 190–191; offset, 189; Pachmayr (swing), 193; recommended, 194; Redfield (top), 194; Stith (top), 191; Weaver, 192, 194
Scopes, 172, 174–182; Bushnell, 10; coated lenses, 176; development of, 174–177; eye relief, 187; field of view, 185; finish, 178; fogging of, 176–177; for deep-woods hunting, 6; for long-range hunting, 10; mounts, 177–179, 189–194; parallax, 185–186; powers, 180–182; rangefinders, 182–185; recommended, 187–188; Redfield, 179, 184–185; reticles, 179, 186–187; sighting with, 195–196; target, 174–175
Sears, Bob, 178
Selecting deer rifles, 197–209; accurizing, 202–205; ammunition, 205–206; "combination," 207; gunsmiths, 209; "myth of the magnum," 199–200; number of rifles, 207–208; recoil, 198–199; rifle weight, 197–198, 199; shooting from bench, 199; sling, 208; testing new rifle, 200–201
"Self-loading," 57
"Semiautomatic," 57
Sharpe, Phil, 100–101
Shooting, 3, 224–226
Shotgun slugs, 210–221
Sighting, 3–4, 195–196

Sights, 170–174; open, 170–173; peep, 173; scopes, 172–174; "tang," 173
Single-shot rifles, 20–21, 29–31; accuracy of, 32–34; advantages, 30–31; Browning, 30; disadvantages, 31; Harrington & Richardson, 30; Ruger, 29–30; Wickliffe, 30; Winchester, 21
Single-shots, black powder, 31–32
Slugs, shotgun, 210–221; accuracy of, 213–214, 217–219; Barrel, 211–212; Brenneke, 216, 219–220; size of, 211–213; Vitt slug, 214–216, 219, 220
Smart, Jack, 4
Smith & Wesson .22 Jet, 85
Smokeless powder, vii, 13
Spencer repeater, 20
Sporting Arms & Ammunition Manufacturers Institute (SAAMI), 155, 235
Springfield rifles, Model 1903, 36, 109–110, 152, 173, 176; "trapdoor," 97, 127, 128
Still-hunting, 1

Thompson/Center single-shot pistol, 84, 85, 86
Trajectory, 135–136, 158, 164, 167–169
Trombone actions, 53

Unertl, John, 175

Velocity chart, 165–166
Vitt, George, 214
Vitt slug, 214–216, 219–220
Von Dreyse, Johann Nikolaus, 35

Waldron, Herman, 68
Walker, Mike, 40, 77, 99
Warren, John, 68
Weatherby, Roy, 44–46, 85, 91, 113, 132, 134, 135
Weatherby rifles, Mark V, 46–47, 96; Vanguard, 47–48
Weaver, Bill, 175–176
Westley Richards, 92
Whelen, Colonel Townsend, 18, 122, 174, 239
White, Alvin, 68

White, Stewart Edward, 36
Whitetail deer, 9, 223-224
Wickliffe rifle, 30
Widner, Joe, 123
Wild-cat cartridge, 81-82, 89, 91-92
Winchester Repeating Arms Company, 20
Winchester rifles, Model 12, 212; Model 54, 37, 95, 110, 176; Model 61, 53; Model 62, 53; Model 70, 37, 39-40, 76, 78, 94, 111, 118, 121, 124, 190, 191, 204, 205, 232-234; Model 71, 118, 120; Model 88, 98, 122; Model 94, vii-ix, 21, 22, 24-25, 27, 29, 86, 116, 120, 121, 173, 189, 207, 208, 227-228; Model 100, 61, 98; Model 101, 46; Model 243, 13; Model 1885, 21; Model 1886, 21, 118, 120; Model 1890, 53; Model 1894, 21; Model 1895, 109, 115; Model 1906, 53; Model 1907, 130; Model 1910, 130; Model 9422, 207, 208
Women, and hunting, 67-68, 69; cartridges for, 88; rifles for, 200
Wotkyns, Grove, 91
Wundhammer, Louis, 36